History of Analytic Philosophy

Series Editor
Michael Beaney
King's College London
Humboldt University, Berlin
Berlin, Germany

The main aim of this series is to create a venue for work on the history of analytic philosophy, and to consolidate the area as a major branch of philosophy. The 'history of analytic philosophy' is to be understood broadly, as covering the period from the last three decades of the nineteenth century to the end of the twentieth century, beginning with the work of Frege, Russell, Moore and Wittgenstein (who are generally regarded as its main founders) and the influences upon them, and going right up to the recent history of the analytic tradition. In allowing the 'history' to extend to the present, the aim is to encourage engagement with contemporary debates in philosophy, for example, in showing how the concerns of early analytic philosophy relate to current concerns. In focusing on analytic philosophy, the aim is not to exclude comparisons with other earlier or contemporary traditions, or consideration of figures or themes that some might regard as marginal to the analytic tradition but which also throw light on analytic philosophy. Indeed, a further aim of the series is to deepen our understanding of the broader context in which analytic philosophy developed, by looking, for example, at the roots of analytic philosophy in neo-Kantianism or British idealism, or the connections between analytic philosophy and phenomenology, or discussing the work of philosophers who were important in the development of analytic philosophy but who are now often forgotten.

Editorial board members:
Claudio de Almeida, Pontifical Catholic University at Porto Alegre, Brazil · Maria Baghramian, University College Dublin, Ireland · Thomas Baldwin, University of York, England · Stewart Candlish, University of Western Australia · Chen Bo, Peking University, China · Jonathan Dancy, University of Reading, England · José Ferreirós, University of Seville, Spain · Michael Friedman, Stanford University, USA · Gottfried Gabriel, University of Jena, Germany · Juliet Floyd, Boston University, USA · Hanjo Glock, University of Zurich, Switzerland · Nicholas Griffin, McMaster University, Canada · Leila Haaparanta, University of Tampere, Finland · Peter Hylton, University of Illinois, USA · Jiang Yi, Beijing Normal University, China · Javier Legris, National Academy of Sciences of Buenos Aires, Argentina · Cheryl Misak, University of Toronto, Canada · Nenad Miscevic, University of Maribor, Slovenia, and Central European University, Budapest · Volker Peckhaus, University of Paderborn, Germany · Eva Picardi, University of Bologna, Italy · Erich Reck, University of California at Riverside, USA · Peter Simons, Trinity College, Dublin · Thomas Uebel, University of Manchester, England.

More information about this series at
http://www.springer.com/series/14867

Anna Boncompagni

Wittgenstein and Pragmatism

On Certainty in the Light of Peirce and James

Anna Boncompagni
University of Florence, Italy

History of Analytic Philosophy
ISBN 978-1-349-92799-9   ISBN 978-1-137-58847-0 (eBook)
DOI 10.1057/978-1-137-58847-0

Library of Congress Control Number: 2016948824

© The Editor(s) (if applicable) and The Author(s) 2016
Softcover reprint of the hardcover 1st edition 2016 978-1-137-58846-3
The author(s) has/have asserted their right(s) to be identified as the author(s) of this work in accordance with the Copyright, Designs and Patents Act 1988.
This work is subject to copyright. All rights are solely and exclusively licensed by the Publisher, whether the whole or part of the material is concerned, specifically the rights of translation, reprinting, reuse of illustrations, recitation, broadcasting, reproduction on microfilms or in any other physical way, and transmission or information storage and retrieval, electronic adaptation, computer software, or by similar or dissimilar methodology now known or hereafter developed.
The use of general descriptive names, registered names, trademarks, service marks, etc. in this publication does not imply, even in the absence of a specific statement, that such names are exempt from the relevant protective laws and regulations and therefore free for general use.
The publisher, the authors and the editors are safe to assume that the advice and information in this book are believed to be true and accurate at the date of publication. Neither the publisher nor the authors or the editors give a warranty, express or implied, with respect to the material contained herein or for any errors or omissions that may have been made. The publisher remains neutral with regard to jurisdictional claims in published maps and institutional affiliations.

Cover image © Heritage Image Partnership Ltd / Alamy Stock Photo

Printed on acid-free paper

This Palgrave Macmillan imprint is published by Springer Nature
The registered company is Macmillan Publishers Ltd.
The registered company address is: The Campus, 4 Crinan Street, London, N1 9XW, United Kingdom

The affiliation of the author was corrected: University of Florence

Series Editor's Foreword

During the first half of the twentieth century analytic philosophy gradually established itself as the dominant tradition in the English-speaking world, and over the last few decades it has taken firm root in many other parts of the world. There has been increasing debate over just what 'analytic philosophy' means, as the movement has ramified into the complex tradition that we know today, but the influence of the concerns, ideas and methods of early analytic philosophy on contemporary thought is indisputable. All this has led to greater self-consciousness among analytic philosophers about the nature and origins of their tradition, and scholarly interest in its historical development and philosophical foundations has blossomed in recent years, with the result that history of analytic philosophy is now recognized as a major field of philosophy in its own right.

The main aim of the series in which the present book appears, the first series of its kind, is to create a venue for work on the history of analytic philosophy, consolidating the area as a major field of philosophy and promoting further research and debate. The 'history of analytic philosophy' is understood broadly, as covering the period from the last three decades of the nineteenth century to the start of the twenty-first century, beginning with the work of Frege, Russell, Moore and Wittgenstein, who are generally regarded as its main founders, and the influences upon them, and going right up to the most recent developments. In allowing the 'history' to extend to the present, the aim is to encourage engagement with contemporary debates in philosophy, for example, in showing how the concerns of early analytic philosophy relate to current concerns. In focusing on analytic philosophy, the aim is not to exclude comparisons with other—earlier or contemporary—traditions, or consideration of figures or themes that some might regard as marginal to the analytic tradition but which also throw light on analytic philosophy. Indeed, a further aim of the series is to deepen our understanding of the broader context in which analytic philosophy developed, by looking, for example, at the roots of analytic philosophy in neo-Kantianism or British idealism, or the connections between analytic philosophy and phenomenology, or discussing the work of philosophers who were important in the development of analytic philosophy but who are now often forgotten.

Ludwig Wittgenstein (1889–1951) is not only one of the main founders of the analytic tradition but also one of the greatest and most influential philosophers of the twentieth century. While his *Tractatus Logico-Philosophicus*, published in 1921, is indisputably one of the canonical texts of analytic philosophy, however, his later work has had a more controversial status. According to some, in seeking to correct his earlier views, Wittgenstein offers a powerful critique of analytic philosophy; while according to others, his later work is better seen as inaugurating a further phase – or phases – in analytic philosophy, such as the 'ordinary language philosophy' that came to dominate Oxford in the two decades after the Second World War. The key text here is *Philosophical Investigations*, mainly based on remarks written in the 1930s (although the text was not translated and published until 1953, after his death). More recently, some scholars have suggested that a 'third Wittgenstein' be identified, marking the development of his views in the last years of his life, as reflected most notably in *On Certainty*, written in the 16 months before he died. Whatever the phases that might be identified in Wittgenstein's thought, however, an understanding of that thought in all its phases clearly belongs to (the discipline of) history of analytic philosophy, not least in making sense of its complex relations to the work of many other thinkers, both within and outside the analytic tradition.

One important set of relations concerns the connection between Wittgenstein's work and pragmatism, understood as originating in the writings of Charles S. Peirce (1839–1914), William James (1842–1910) and John Dewey (1859–1952), in particular. Whether or not one counts pragmatism as a form of 'analytic' philosophy (in its broadest sense), there is no doubt that it influenced such early analytic philosophers as Bertrand Russell (1872–1970), G. E. Moore (1873–1958) and Frank P. Ramsey (1903–30), and it was certainly influential on later American analytic philosophers such as C. I. Lewis (1883–1964) and W. V. O. Quine (1908–2000). As far as Wittgenstein is concerned, he seems first to have become interested in pragmatism as a form of philosophy – probably under the influence of Ramsey – in 1930, but it is in his later writings, and especially in *On Certainty*, that serious engagement with pragmatism can be found. It is this engagement that Anna Boncompagni explores in the present volume.

Boncompagni focuses on the connections between Wittgenstein's later philosophy and the ideas of Peirce and James. That Wittgenstein was familiar with some of James' writings is well known: he read *Varieties of Religious Experience*, for example, in 1912, and James' psychological works in the 1930s. His knowledge of Peirce, on the other hand, seems to have mainly been indirect, through the writings of others, such as Ramsey. Boncompagni examines and assesses, carefully and helpfully, the evidence concerning what Wittgenstein knew, either directly or indirectly. Her main concern, however, is not with what causal influences there may have been, but with the systematic relationships between their respective philosophies, and she explains the similarities and differences here with great clarity and insight, rooted in a thorough knowledge of the relevant texts. Important similarities concern, for example, their emphasis on practice – embedded in habits and forms of life – in understanding concepts and meaning, and their approach to scepticism. Important differences concern, perhaps most centrally, their views on the relationship between philosophy and science, where Peirce and James saw more of a continuity than did Wittgenstein, who stressed the distinction between empirical and grammatical propositions, even if it varies across contexts, as his famous image of the riverbed of thoughts suggests: even though the riverbed can move, there remains a distinction between the riverbed itself and the water that flows along it. In elucidating these similarities and differences, Boncompagni sheds a great deal of light on some of the deepest themes of Wittgenstein's philosophy, such as his conception of the relationship between philosophy and common sense, the role that *background* – rather than *ground* – comes to play in his thinking, and the connection between his methodology and his critique of *Weltanschauung* in philosophy.

July 2016　　　　　　　　　　　　　　　　　　　Mike Beaney

Acknowledgements

This work would not have been possible without the presence, support, and advice of many, to whom I owe its most creative and insightful moments. To mention just a few, I greatly benefitted from the guidance of Rosa Calcaterra, my PhD supervisor at the University of Roma Tre, and from the generous encouragement of Cheryl Misak: the dialogue with both is a precious and enduring stimulus. Suggestions, clarifications, and new hints on this work or parts of it, in different stages of their development, came from Luigi Perissinotto, Joachim Schulte, David Stern, Anne-Marie Christensen, Alois Pichler, Danièle Moyal-Sharrock, Joseph Rothhaupt, Cecilie Eriksen, as well as from friends and members of the Pragma cultural association, among them were Francesco Panaro, Sarin Marchetti, Michela Bella, Guido Baggio, Roberta Dreon, Matteo Santarelli, Giovanni Maddalena, and Stefano Oliva. Finally, let me thank an anonymous reviewer for very helpful comments, and the Palgrave Macmillan team.

Portions of Chapters 3, 5 and 6 ('Common Sense and *Weltbild*', 'From Ground to Background', 'Between Method and *Weltanschauung*') are revisions of arguments previously published, respectively, as '"The Mother-Tongue of Thought". James and Wittgenstein on Common Sense', *Cognitio—Revista de Filosofia*, 13 (1) 2012, 'Elucidating Forms of Life. The Evolution of a Philosophical Tool', *Nordic Wittgenstein Review*

Special Issue 2015, and 'Streams and River-Beds. James' Stream of Thought in Wittgenstein's Manuscripts 165 and 129', *The European Journal of Pragmatism and American Philosophy*, 4 (1) 2012; many thanks to the publishers for permission to make use of these works here.

Contents

Introduction: 'A kind of *Weltanschauung*'   1

Part I   Before *On Certainty*

Chapter 1: Pragmatism in Wittgenstein Before *On Certainty*   15

Part II   *On Certainty*

Chapter 2: Reasonable Doubts and Unshakable Certainties   59

Chapter 3: Common Sense and *Weltbild*   99

Chapter 4: Action and the Pragmatic Maxim   139

Part III   Broadening the Perspective

Chapter 5: From Ground to Background   181

Chapter 6: Between Method and *Weltanschauung*   221

Conclusion: 'I'll teach you differences' 263

Bibliography 271

Author Index 295

Subject Index 301

List of Abbreviations

Wittgenstein's Writings

BBB	*The Blue and Brown Books*
BEE	*Wittgenstein's* Nachlass. *The Bergen Electronic Edition*
BT	*The Big Typescript*
CE	Cause and Effect: Intuitive Awareness
CV	*Culture and Value*
LC	*Lectures and Conversations on Aesthetics, Psychology and Religious Belief*
LCA	*Wittgenstein's Lectures. Cambridge, 1932–1935 (A. Ambrose)*
LCL	*Wittgenstein's Lectures. Cambridge, 1930–1932 (D. Lee)*
LCM	Wittgenstein's Lectures in 1930–1933 (G.E. Moore)
LE	A Lecture on Ethics
LFM	*Lectures on the Foundations of Mathematics*
LPP	*Wittgenstein's Lectures on Philosophical Psychology 1946–47*
LW	*Last Writings on the Philosophy of Psychology*, 2 voll.
MTD	Movements of Thought: Diaries 1930–1932, 1936–1937
NB	*Notebooks 1914–1916*
OC	*On Certainty*
PE	Notes for Lectures on 'Private Experience' and 'Sense-Data'
PI	*Philosophical Investigations (part I)*
PO	*Philosophical Occasions 1912–1951*
PPF	*Philosophy of Psychology—A Fragment (PI part II)*
PPO	*Public and Private Occasions*

PR   *Philosophical Remarks*
RC   *Remarks on Colour*
RF   Remarks on Frazer's *Golden Bough*
RFM *Remarks on the Foundations of Mathematics*
RPP *Remarks on the Philosophy of Psychology*
TLP *Tractatus Logico-Philosophicus*
WA   *Wiener Ausgabe (Band II)*
Z   *Zettel*

Peirce's Writings

CLL *Chance, Love and Logic*
CP   *The Collected Papers of Charles Sanders Peirce*, 8 voll.
EP   *The Essential Peirce*, 2 voll.
RLT *Reasoning and the Logic of Things. The Cambridge Conference Lectures of 1898*
SW   *The Philosophy of Peirce: Selected Writings*
W   *Writings of Charles S. Peirce: A Chronological Edition*, voll. I–VI and VIII

James' Writings

EPH *Essays in Philosophy*
ERE *Essays in Radical Empiricism*
MEN *Manuscripts, Essays, and Notes*
MT   *The Meaning of Truth*
P   *Pragmatism*
PBC *Psychology. Briefer Course*
PP   *The Principles of Psychology*, 2 voll.
PU   *A Pluralistic Universe*
TT   *Talks to Teachers on Psychology and to Students on Some of Life's Ideals*
VRE *The Varieties of Religious Experience*
WB   *The Will to Believe and Other Essays in Popular Philosophy*

Note

Full details of the references are in the bibliography. For Wittgenstein's manuscripts and typescripts (MS and TS), numbers refer to the von Wright (1993) catalogue and quotes are from BEE (I have preferred to use the normalized transcriptions, but I also use the diplomatic transcriptions when necessary, and occasionally refer to the *facsimile*). For Peirce's texts from CP, W, and EP, I have followed the ordinary convention: volume number followed by paragraph number for CP and volume number followed by page number for W and EP.

Introduction: 'A kind of *Weltanschauung*'

To approach the work of a philosopher drawing from the work of another philosopher or of another school of thought, one bears the risk of being guided by the desire to show the analogies between the two, losing sight of what is specific and, therefore, genuine and authentic in both of them. On the other hand, the search for the 'genuine' is itself, perhaps, a myth, and does not allow one to catch the significance of the belonging of a thinker to her proper epoch (or why not to an epoch to which she does *not* belong). It also omits the relevance of social and cultural factors as well as the strong or weak influences which other thinkers or other ways of seeing can exercise precisely in the genesis and development of that 'genuine'. In the specific case of Ludwig Wittgenstein, the methodological caution, which would suggest avoiding analyses based on the comparison with other thinkers, is also bracketed by his own awareness of being a *soil*, more than a *seed*[1]: of

---

[1] 'I believe that my originality (if that is the right word) is an originality belonging to the soil rather than to the seed. (Perhaps I have no seed of my own.) Sow a seed in my soil and it will grow differently than it would in any other soil', CV, p. 36, remark dated 1939–1940, original formulation in MS 162b, p. 60r. See Goldstein (2004).

© The Author(s) 2016
A. Boncompagni, *Wittgenstein and Pragmatism*, History of Analytic Philosophy, DOI 10.1057/978-1-137-58847-0_1

being able to receive, to gather, and to grow ideas and stimuli of others, more than producing new ideas *ex novo*. That Wittgenstein's image of himself be faithful or not to reality, it is a matter of fact that he, on the one hand, never considered the systematic study of other thinkers relevant, and on the other hand, often took other philosophers' ideas as a starting point without necessarily feeling the need to cite them nor to make his sources of inspiration explicit.

Given this situation, what remains to be said in respect of the attempt to parallel Wittgenstein and other thinkers, in our case the classical pragmatists, does not consist in the risk of losing sight of the authenticity of the one or others, but rather in the opportunity to pay equal attention to similarities and differences, keeping in mind that the usefulness of a comparative approach emerges precisely in its capacity to highlight, both through similarities and differences, aspects of the movement of thought of the authors considered, which would otherwise remain unseen. It is with this spirit that we are going to work, without having as an end that of deciding whether Wittgenstein was or was not, in any specific sense, a pragmatist, but trying to let some aspects of his thought emerge, as well as of the thought of the pragmatists', and be seen in a particular light.

We will not, of course, examine the parallel with the pragmatists in its generality: it would be a desperate enterprise, as there is more than one single type of 'pragmatism', as there are several interpretations of them, and the work of Wittgenstein itself undergoes relevant changes in the course of time, especially in relation to the themes which are more connected to pragmatism. The aim of this inquiry is, therefore, limited both on the Wittgensteinian and on the pragmatist sides. As for the former, it focuses on the notes of OC.[2] As for the latter, it is circumscribed to the thought of the two 'founding fathers' of classical pragmatism, Charles S. Peirce and William James. Clearly, there will also be references to other writings by Wittgenstein and to other philosophers of the pragmatist tradition, but the attention will centre on OC as a text

---

[2] Although when quoting from Wittgenstein's writings I will often refer to the original manuscripts of the *Nachlass*, with respect to OC the examination of the original formulations will normally not be necessary, OC being, as is well-known, a collection of a part of the last manuscripts.

which, in literature, has often been identified as the expression of a pragmatic turn in Wittgenstein's later thought, and on Peirce and James as the repositories of the original formulations which gave birth to pragmatism.

OC, together—according to some interpreters—with other writings belonging to the last years of Wittgenstein's life, embodies a partly new way of seeing, though stemming from former reflections: a way of seeing centred on the relevance of action and praxes, which assume a key role, to the detriment of the relevance of language which was formerly highlighted by Wittgenstein. It is this kind of turn that critics refer to when they speak of a 'Third Wittgenstein' (Moyal-Sharrock 2004; Moyal-Sharrock and Brenner 2005). It is not my intention to go into this debate more deeply. I will use it only as a starting point. I think it is significant that the question has arisen, but nevertheless it seems to me that the characterization of the 'Third Wittgenstein' as a pragmatic or even a pragmatist philosopher remains sometimes generic, making reference mostly to standard concepts of action, practices, praxis, instinct, and so on. In particular, and what is relevant for this study, it seems to me that there is a gap in literature. The later Wittgenstein, especially in the last years of his work, is often described as bearer of a pragmatic turn; Wittgenstein himself affirms in OC, §422: 'So I am trying to say something that sounds like pragmatism. Here I am being thwarted by a kind of *Weltanschauung*'. Yet there are no detailed analyses regarding what, specifically, in the notes of OC, resonates with pragmatism intended as a historical current of thought, nor regarding the reasons why Wittgenstein acknowledges this, at the same time feeling the need to distance himself from it. Also, there are not many studies about the writings by the pragmatists which Wittgenstein might have read, or might have heard of. Here, then, is the aim of the present work: to offer some elements which may contribute to filling at least a part of the gap.

The comparison with the pragmatists will run along two parallel tracks: a textual analysis, aimed at individuating direct and indirect suggestions which the pragmatists' writings might have left in Wittgenstein's work (sowed in his soil, to use the metaphor already mentioned), and a thematic examination, aimed at showing not only the objective convergences but also divergences between the two approaches beyond the possible 'debts'.

I hope to further clarify the scope of this investigation by highlighting from the outset what it does *not* take into account. Following this, I will present the argumentative strategy and the main contents of the different chapters.

On the pragmatist side, the choice to privilege Peirce and James means excluding other philosophers who could be used and have indeed been used in relation to the later Wittgenstein; first of all, John Dewey, who, although he does not belong to the very first generation of the pragmatists, is in fact often linked to Peirce and James and began to work when they were both still alive and active in philosophy. Wittgenstein did know something by Dewey (maybe he even attended to one of his lectures[3]), although the testimonies which he offers in this respect are not very positive.[4] It is possible, even probable, that the Viennese philosopher came into contact with the pedagogical ideas of Dewey as early as 1920, when he trained as an elementary school teacher: he attended courses in a school which followed the reform movement of the Austrian education system promoted by Otto Glöckel, a movement which was deeply influenced by Dewey's approach (Gullvåg 1981, p. 72; Monk 1991, p. 188). But also other, more strictly philosophical, aspects of Dewey's work show some resemblance to some typical Wittgensteinian themes: the insistence on the contextuality of meaning, the intertwining of the natural and the cultural, the characterization of the mind, the ascribing of many seemingly philosophical problems to language; not to mention the therapeutic and edifying nature of the two philosophical approaches, widely emphasized, though with controversial outcomes, by Richard Rorty.[5]

---

[3] Bouwsma (1986, pp. xxiv, 39) records a conversation in which Wittgenstein affirmed of having heard John Dewey talk about education, it seems, during a lecture.

[4] He cites Dewey during his lectures on philosophical psychology (1946–1947), asserting that according to Dewey belief consists in an adjustment of the organism to its environment, an idea which in Wittgenstein's opinion is valid only in limited cases (LPP, p. 90); during the aforementioned conversation with Bouwsma; and during another conversation, again with Bouwsma, in which, being surprised at the fact that Dewey was still alive, he commented: 'Ought not to be' (Bouwsma 1986, p. 29).

[5] On the cited themes see Medina (2006, Chap. 1), Chauviré (2012), Rorty (1979).

Introduction: 'A kind of *Weltanschauung*'

Yet, the need to set limits to this work for simple reasons of space, together with the fact that regarding OC the affinities with Dewey appear to be less relevant[6] than those with James and Peirce, require to focus the attention on the 'first generation'. Moreover, this implies the exclusion of George H. Mead, although an analysis of the convergences between the two would surely prove interesting and would bring new content to the debate. The same can be said of George Santayana, who in particular presents strong analogies with the way in which Wittgenstein characterizes certainty in OC,[7] and of F.C.S. Schiller, who, working in Oxford, had a certain relevance for the way in which pragmatism was perceived in the UK.[8] Finally, I will not consider in general more recent exponents of the pragmatist, neo-pragmatist, or new-pragmatist tradition, although some of their interpretations will come into play in so far as they contribute to the clarification of the connections between Wittgenstein's thought and James' and Peirce's philosophy.[9]

I *will* take into account, instead, especially in the first chapter, Frank P. Ramsey, a quite certain link between Wittgenstein and Peirce. Ramsey had a crucial role in the way in which Wittgenstein perceived pragmatism after his return to Cambridge in 1929, besides in his rethinking of some aspects of the *Tractatus Logico-Philosophicus* (TLP).

Regarding Wittgenstein's writings, the choice to privilege OC does not imply a drastic exclusion of all the other texts and manuscripts: these will be considered when they contribute to a more complete understanding of the genesis and of the 'surroundings' of the dominant themes of OC, and, of course, when they are of help in the characterization of Wittgenstein's

---

[6] The theme on which the comparison between Wittgenstein and Dewey is probably more feasible is that of the connection between truth and consequences, but it would require a further inquiry, which it is impossible to undertake here.

[7] See Santayana (1923) and Bennett-Hunter (2012) for a comparison.

[8] Wittgenstein speaks in a quite disparaging tone about him, using a work of his on logic as an example of evident nonsense: see Britton (1967, p. 58).

[9] For an up to date reading of the fertility of the comparison between Wittgenstein and pragmatism, in connection with thinkers such as not only Richard Rorty and Hilary Putnam but also Robert Brandom and Huw Price, see Margolis (2012a). On recent and contemporary pragmatism more generally see Misak (2007).

attitude towards pragmatism. But the focus on OC will sacrifice many other issues on which the comparison with pragmatism is possible and has sometimes been proposed. First of all, there are analyses which highlight pragmatic elements in the *early* Wittgenstein, beyond affinities with James' religious thought and with some aspects of Peirce's semiotics[10] (the following words, for instance, are not Wittgenstein's but Peirce's: 'A fact is so much of the reality as is represented in a single *proposition*. If a proposition is true, that which it represents is a *fact*', CP 6.67). Moreover, regarding the 'PI Wittgenstein', the latter and Peirce share the opposition to the ideas of the alleged privacy of the internal world and of the alleged possibility of immediate introspective intuitions, an opposition which leads both to put the role of the *external* in the knowledge of the internal in the foreground.[11] In this sense, Peirce's externalism can be read as an anticipation of Wittgenstein's private language argument, but James has also been indicated as a precursor of the same issue, especially in the moral field (Putnam 1992a). With respect to James, despite the fact that many Wittgensteinian commentators are often rather dismissive and portray him simply as a target of Wittgenstein's criticism,[12] there are also scholars who highlight the richness of the suggestions which Wittgenstein found in James' psychological descriptions.[13]

Other affinities with the pragmatists have to do, for example, with the Wittgensteinian themes of family resemblance, grammar, and aspect seeing (Bambrough 1981). Peirce, by the way, had worked with Joseph Jastrow, the author of the duck-rabbit image, later famously revived in a stylized version by Wittgenstein.

All these issues and fields, therefore, will only be touched on in the following pages, with the aim of restricting the analysis to those

---

[10] See Bernstein (1961); Moser (2012); Goodman (2002, Chap. 2); Fabbrichesi (2002, pp. 77, 106–107).

[11] By Peirce, see in particular the essays 'Questions Concerning Certain Faculties Claimed for Man' and 'Some Consequences of Four Incapacities' (W 2, pp. 193 ff. CP 5.213 ff.). On this topic see also Calcaterra (2003a, Chap. 2).

[12] A paradigmatic example is P.M.S. Hacker: see Hacker (1990, Chap. 2), Hacker (1996a, Chaps. 4, 5, 6); see also Hilmy (1987, Chaps. 4, 6).

[13] Besides Goodman (2002), see Schulte (1993) and Nubiola (2000).

pragmatic aspects which are more relevant in OC and which, probably, Wittgenstein himself felt were too akin to the pragmatist perspective. Yet, in order to understand what the later Wittgenstein meant with pragmatism, why he felt the proximity with pragmatism with worry, and why he identified it with a *Weltanschauung*, it will be necessary to examine the way in which the philosopher wrote and spoke about pragmatism through the years, starting from his return to Cambridge.

After these brief notes about what this book is not, a few words about what it (hopefully) is. The work is structured in six chapters. Chapter 1, 'Pragmatism in Wittgenstein Before *On Certainty*' (constituting Part I), reconstructs Wittgenstein's initial perception of pragmatism in the early 1930s. The three following chapters (Part II) concern the most relevant 'pragmatist' themes in OC, proposing a close comparison with the American thinkers; the two final chapters (Part III) widen the horizon, tackling more general subjects, and finally taking the discussion back to where it began: Wittgenstein's remark about pragmatism as thwarting *Weltanschauung*. The Conclusion summarizes the results of the inquiry, also highlighting the most relevant differences between the two approaches.

I would now like to use the last pages of this Introduction to offer a more detailed guide to what follows.

The first chapter stems from Wittgenstein's first remark about pragmatism, dated January 1930. It is not well known in literature, probably partly because of a little mistake in the transcription of the manuscript (MS 107), which transformed the quite specific adjective *pragmatistischen* into a generic and less compromising *pragmatischen*. This remark is not contained in PR, which collects other parts of the manuscript, and this also has contributed to the scarce attention it has received. I will, therefore, propose a detailed examination of it, which will call into question the pragmatist conception of truth, the object of Wittgenstein's reflection, but also of the debate that was going on in Cambridge when Wittgenstein moved there, in January 1929. The young Frank Ramsey, with whom Wittgenstein had continuous exchanges that year, was working on a book on truth, and we will see how much the two thinkers' reflections bear signs of their conversations. Ramsey was well acquainted with Peirce's and James' writings. This will lead us to examine the texts of the classical pragmatists with which Wittgenstein came into contact. It has already been ascertained that Wittgenstein read and knew very well some of James' texts; I will also sustain the hypothesis—it will not be mere conjecture, as we shall see—that Wittgenstein knew some articles by Peirce as well. Bearing this in mind and in anticipation of the focalization of OC, we shall finally examine all the other (few) occasions, before OC, in which Wittgenstein mentions pragmatism, in order to see if and how his opinion about it undergoes any changes.

Part II of the volumes is its core and it deals specifically with OC. The second chapter will lead us *in medias res*, to the heart of these late notes, with the themes of doubt and certainty. It is indeed precisely on these issues that the proximity between Wittgenstein and the pragmatists is more evident and, I would add, more surprising. The anti-Cartesianism characterizing particularly Wittgenstein and Peirce takes the form of a refusal of the strategy of doubt as the *beginning* of philosophy, and in the parallel acknowledgment that any doubt originates from a set of shared certainties which are unproblematic because they are not turned into a problem, not put in question. This set of certainties is the substratum and the environment of any activity of thought, and not only of thought. Thus the derivative nature of doubt leaves room for the emergence of the 'hinges' around which human life and cognitive practices rotate. Some commentators have put beside the Wittgensteinian concept of hinge, extensively debated in literature, two Peircean notions, the 'indubitables' and the 'regulative assumptions' of inquiry, which we shall therefore examine.

This analysis will require the comparison to be widened, including in it the theme of common sense, which is the subject of the third chapter. It is, indeed, in the perspective of what he calls *critical common-sensism* that Peirce offers his characterization of certainties, paying homage to, but also going beyond, the Scottish tradition of common sense. The issue of common sense will bring back William James into the discussion; he talks of it in terms of the 'mother-tongue of thought' in one of the lectures of his *Pragmatism* (1907). Hence, we will be able to compare both pragmatists to the approach of OC, in which Wittgenstein prefers not to use the expression 'common sense', but introduces instead the term *Weltbild*, picture of the world, a conceptual tool through which he contrasts the more traditional notion of common sense also used and defended, in his peculiar way, by George E. Moore. The focalization of the theme of common sense will also help to clarify some significant differences between the pragmatist and the Wittgensteinian approaches, differences which rotate around the connection between certainty and action and the distinction between the grammatical and the empirical.

In the next chapter, the key issue of action will lead to analyse the core of the pragmatist method: the so-called pragmatic maxim, which, very roughly stated, identifies the meaning of a concept with its practical bearings and behavioural consequences. Considering the remarks Wittgenstein expresses in a brief but very fertile period during the last months of his life, I will argue that it is precisely the proximity with the pragmatic maxim that he perceives when noting the disturbing presence of pragmatism on his path. In these remarks, indeed, what is at stake is the connection between knowing something (or asserting to know something) and being able to predict its consequences in the world of facts and in one's behaviour. Behaviour and action represent the notions with which we will close the chapter, with a specific inquiry into the importance of the Jamesian psychological reflections on the will and action in the development of Wittgenstein's thought.

In the last two chapters, constituting Part III of the volume, the work done about pragmatism in OC will be distilled and more general issues will take form. Therefore, these two chapters are more tentative in their interpretations and proposals, offering hints and suggestions rather than complete analyses. As we shall see, in Wittgenstein as well as in the pragmatists what is going on, maybe in an undercover way, is a conceptual shift with vast consequences. It is a shift which moves the traditional notion of foundation or *ground* towards a more nuanced, but at the same time stronger, notion of *background*, by nature immune from any sceptical danger. We will approach this change of perspective through the concept of form of life, a concept which Wittgenstein, for intrinsic reasons, does not describe precisely, but which he uses as a methodological tool, with the aim of directing the attention to that 'whole hurly-burly' (RPP II, §629; Z, §567) of human actions which both permits and limits the meaningfulness of practices and words. Of the concept of form of life, we will examine both the contexts of use in Wittgenstein's writings, and the main interpretations in the secondary literature, also tackling some of the usual ways of depicting Wittgenstein as a relativist and/or as a conservative: two descriptions that the instrumental nature of the notion of form of life helps to contextualize and partly to contest. As for the comparison with pragmatism, what emerges is a new way of conceiving the idea of the beginning of philosophical activity, no longer in need of an absolute *primum*, but wholly at ease in the framework of a *human* objectivity, feasible, solid but (and because of its being) to a certain extent changeable.

At this point, it is time to return to the question as to why Wittgenstein perceived pragmatism as a *Weltanschauung* which one should (probably) distrust. In the sixth and last chapter, I will try to distinguish and thoroughly analyse the two sides of pragmatism: the methodological side, with respect to which Wittgenstein himself expressed unequivocally positive words, and the *weltanschauliche* side, its systematic aspect, which Wittgenstein opposed, especially with regard to the extent to which it could undermine his own way of doing philosophy. Yet this very distinction, though useful for grasping Wittgenstein's attitude towards pragmatism in its general terms, will have to be softened in order to offer a faithful account of the complexity of the relationship between method and *Weltanschauung*. Wittgenstein himself, in fact, particularly with respect to James, did not appreciate only the method but also, to a certain extent, the *attitude*, a way of approaching philosophical activity and more generally life itself. And, on the other hand, with respect to his own method, or rather to one of his techniques, namely synoptic presentation, he asked himself if it did not imply a whole *Weltanschauung*. As for Peirce and James, it must be said that they both were well aware of the connection between method, philosophy, and *Weltanschauung*: there are remarks making this explicit in the writings of both. In conclusion, we will try to understand what, specifically, of the pragmatist *Weltanschauung* Wittgenstein could not share. And the answer will have to do with one of the best-known images of OC and perhaps of the whole of Wittgenstein's philosophy, the image of the river which flows in its riverbed, and which partly, but only partly, can modify the riverbed. It is a metaphor that we will put beside James' even more famous image of the stream of thought. According to the interpretation I will propose, James' stream was a possible source of inspiration for Wittgenstein's image. Basically, through the distinction between the water

Introduction: 'A kind of *Weltanschauung*'

of the river and the riverbed, Wittgenstein highlights what he takes as a defect in James' use of the image of the stream of thought: the lack of distinction between empirical and grammatical. This theme calls into question the relationship between *science* and *philosophy*, and it is on this terrain, eventually, that is placed, at least in Wittgenstein's perception, one of the clearest differences between his perspective and pragmatism.

Part I

Before *On Certainty*

Chapter 1: Pragmatism in Wittgenstein Before *On Certainty*

Preliminary Remarks

Although this work focuses on Wittgenstein's later writings, it is also worth examining the earlier occasions in which the Viennese philosopher referred directly to pragmatism. Indeed, in order to fully understand Wittgenstein's worried acknowledgement, in OC, §422, that he was saying something that 'sounded like pragmatism' and that this kind of *Weltanschauung* was 'thwarting' him, we need a clarification of what Wittgenstein *meant* by 'pragmatism'. Such a clarification will benefit from a survey of what he said about it in earlier years, which will also help to shed light on the reasons why he seemed to identify it with a disturbing *Weltanschauung*. It is the aim of this chapter, by analysing all the occurrences (to my knowledge) of the term 'pragmatism' in Wittgenstein's writings, in his lectures, and in the testimonies of his students and friends, both to verify the way in which he talked and wrote about it and to see if his attitude towards it changed through time.

As we shall see, the first hint at pragmatism in Wittgenstein's writings dates back to the beginning of 1930, one year after his return to Cambridge and to philosophy. The cultural atmosphere that characterized the debate around this philosophical approach was quite critical, in particular towards the Jamesian conception of truth. This very conception is what Wittgenstein refers to in the remark that I shall go through in depth. The theme of truth and the issues connected to it would also appear in Wittgenstein's *later* comments on pragmatism; yet, as I hope the following pages will help clarify, these references to the pragmatist conception of truth would not suffice to give a satisfactorily explanation of what Wittgenstein meant by pragmatism in OC. In his later manuscripts, indeed, Wittgenstein deals with other crucial issues—doubt and certainty, common sense, the bond between knowledge, belief, action, and consequences—belonging, so to speak, to the 'core business' of the pragmatists. Hence, in my view, although he would often refer to (and oppose) the Jamesian conception of truth, Wittgenstein's attitude towards pragmatism in general would develop through time, and he would soften his criticism, eventually accepting and partly sharing some methodological cues stemming from it.

The analysis of the textual contexts in which Wittgenstein mentions pragmatism will suggest examination of the pragmatists' writings and his contemporaries' commentaries on pragmatism as the possible sources of his reflections. In this way, as anticipated in the introduction, the inquiry will proceed in parallel on two levels, exegesis and content, with the aim of using the former to clarify the latter, and vice versa.

'Die pragmatistiche Auffassung von Wahr und Falsch'

The first time Wittgenstein mentions pragmatism in his writings is on 20 January 1930. At the time, he was writing MS 107, third of the four notebooks, from which a few months later he extracted TS 208, a 'synopsis' (as he called it) of the work he sent to Bertrand Russell, via George E. Moore. Russell, on that basis, would write a letter to ask Trinity College, in Cambridge, to renew Wittgenstein's research grant. Rush Rhees later published a version of this 'synopsis',

TS 209, as PR.[1] Hence, some parts of the manuscript also appear in PR, but not the note we are going to examine.

The first lines annotated on 20 January are encoded. As is well known, Wittgenstein used this system for personal thoughts. On that very day, he began to teach in Cambridge, and these were his impressions: 'Today given my first regular lesson: so so. I think next time it will go better—if nothing unexpected happens' (MS 107, p. 247).[2] What follows contains the remark we are interested in. Since there is no literature (to my knowledge) regarding these passages,[3] I will add the original text of the most relevant remarks in the notes.

> Sentences [*Sätze*][4]—that is, what we ordinarily call so: the sentences of our everyday use—seem to me to work differently from what in logic is meant by propositions [*Sätze*], if there are such things at all.
> And this is due to their hypothetical character.
> Events do not seem to verify or falsify them in the sense I originally intended—rather a door, as it were, is still left open. Verification and its opposite are not definitive (MS 107, pp. 247–248).

Many themes already emerge in these lines. Wittgenstein clearly distances himself from a certain vision of logic and shows an interest in the ordinary use of language. He then introduces the idea that a sentence, in the ordinary sense, consists of a hypothesis and that this implies the

---

[1] I must thank David Stern for the reconstruction of these passages, on which the literature is not always clear.

[2] The translations from the *Nachlass* are mine (except where specified differently), but I am indebted to Joachim Schulte for his precious suggestions. When the text also appears in published works, I usually adopt the existing translation, unless specified otherwise.

[3] In Boncompagni (forthcoming*a*), I work on this note by contextualizing it within the relationships between pragmatism, analytic philosophy and phenomenology. See also Misak (2016, Chap. 7).

[4] As is well known, there is a debate in the Wittgensteinian literature concerning the translation of the term 'Satz' as 'proposition' or as 'sentence'. Here I will generally use 'sentence' when Wittgenstein seems to refer to ordinary language, and 'proposition' when he seems to refer to logic and phenomenological language. Yet one should bear in mind that Wittgenstein uses the same word, and not two words, for both aspects.

abandonment of his previous conception of verification and falsification. Indeed, a couple of days before, he had written: 'It is likely that *my entire (previous) conception of the proposition* should be rotated by a small angle, in order to really work' (MS 107, p. 247). What Wittgenstein had in mind is the *Tractatus* conception, which in 1929 he saw through phenomenological lenses.[5] Roughly, according to this conception, a proposition is confronted with the flux of experience, which verifies or falsifies it, depending on whether or not there is a correspondence between the atomic facts constituting experience and the atomic propositions composing the sentence. The 'rotation' Wittgenstein seems to augur passes through a concept of hypothesis such that the comparison with reality always remains open and the act of verification/falsification is never definitive. This will shortly become clearer.

In the lines that follow (MS 107, p. 248), while apparently skipping to another theme, Wittgenstein wonders—in a surprising anticipation of issues which would be at the centre of OC—whether it would be possible that everything he believes to know for sure (for example, his having parents and siblings or his being in England) turned out to be false. The problem in this case would be what kind of evidence could prove that these basic certainties are false. What if the grounds of a person's life get suddenly swept away—he seems to ask himself—and on what basis could such a radical change be ascertained? And conversely, what kind of evidence could prove that *that* was just a deceptive impression, and that it is in effect true—to keep to the given examples—that he has parents and siblings and lives in England? Are there *proofs* which can guarantee such basic and obvious platitudes against any possible doubt?

It is not easy to see the connection with the preceding considerations. I would like to suggest that Wittgenstein is working in the region of the idea that this kind of certainty, knowledge, or belief, has a mostly practical or pragmatic character and that its solidity, its steadfastness, derives from this character, much more than from any evidence given in the flux of experience. In other words, he is questioning the capacity of

---

[5] See Marion (1998, pp. 129–131), Stern (1995, Chap. 5), Engelmann (2013a, Chap. 1).

his previous conception of the proposition to catch and account for the ordinary certainty governing everyday life. To be sure, these remarks by Wittgenstein are very preliminary and sketchy observations. Yet, the clear affinity that they show with the key themes of his later thought (we will have the chance to come back to this) suggests that already in 1930 Wittgenstein was interested in this sort of instinctive, practical, and not mediated sureness constituting a hinge or an axis around which any subsequent piece of knowledge rotates. By putting reflections concerning immediate experience, linguistic understanding, the hypothetical character of sentences, verification, certainty, and sureness side by side, Wittgenstein anticipates his later views, and explores the pragmatic character of what constitutes the background of these notions.

It is not by chance, then, that the pragmatist approach is explicitly evoked in the following passage.

> When I say 'There is a chair over there', this sentence refers to a series of expectations. I believe I could go there, perceive the chair and sit on it, I believe it is made of wood and I expect it to have a certain hardness, inflammability, etc. If some of these expectations are mistaken, I will see it as proof for retaining that there was no chair there.
> Here one sees the access [*Zugang*] to the pragmatist [*pragmatistichen*] conception of true and false. A sentence is true as long as it proves to be useful. (MS 107, p. 248)[6]

The theme of the hypothesis is discussed here in connection with the concept of expectation: a sentence generates a series of expectations, it opens a door, as Wittgenstein exemplified, in such a way that, if these expectations are disappointed, the sentence will be deemed mistaken. The conception which is envisaged is that of verificationism, or perhaps better, of falsificationism: Wittgenstein is not affirming that if the

---

[6] Wenn ich sage 'dort steht ein Sessel', so hat dieser Satz Bezug auf eine Reihe von Erwartungen. Ich glaube ich werde dorthin gehen können, den Sessel befühlen und mich auf ihn setzen können, ich glaube er ist aus Holz und ich erwarte von ihm eine gewisse Härte, Brennbarkeit etc. Wenn gewisse dieser Erwartungen getäuscht werden so werde ich dies als Beweis dafür ansehen daßdort kein Sessel gestanden ist./Hier sieht man den Zugang zu der pragmatistischen Auffassung von Wahr und Falsch. Der Satz ist solange wahr solang er sich als nützlich erweist.

expectation is satisfied, then the proposition is true, but that if the expectation is disappointed, the proposition is false, and indeed, he had specified that verification always remains open. Hence, as long as the expectations are not frustrated by an experience which contradicts them, the sentence *works*. And it is here that Wittgenstein mentions pragmatism: if the sentence is true as long as expectations are not frustrated, if— Wittgenstein seems to sum up—it is true as long as it is useful, we are dealing with a pragmatist conception of truth.[7] Let me correct both the *Wiener Ausgabe* (Band II, p. 175) and the BEE *Nachlass* transcriptions (MS 107, p. 248) here. As is clear from the manuscript, the adjective Wittgenstein uses is not *pragmatischen*, as transcribed in WA and BEE, but *pragmatistischen*, with an unequivocal reference to *pragmatism*, and not to a generic pragmatic idea of truth.[8] The oversight is unfortunately perpetuated in the only texts which, as far as I know, consider this passage, Bogen (1972, pp. 137–138) and Rosso (1999, p. lxxvii).[9]

In this remark, there are no value judgments regarding pragmatism: Wittgenstein simply mentions it. It is nevertheless significant that he did not select this remark for his 'synopsis' and that in later years, he is unequivocally critical towards this approach (which, as we shall see, is more precisely William James' conception of truth). On the other hand, this remark does not concern the *content* of the pragmatist conception: it limits itself to showing the 'entrance', the way through which one can be led to this kind of view. To put it differently: the pragmatist conception can be right or wrong, but the exigency to which it aimed to give an answer was genuine, and it stemmed from a reflection on the connection between expectation and action.

---

[7] The relevance of this early remark in the development of Wittgenstein's thought towards a pragmatic viewpoint is even clearer if one considers PI, §80 as a middle step: here, again, Wittgenstein makes the example of the chair and applies it to the theme of the rules for the use of words. In the following remark, PI, §81, Ramsey's idea of logic as a normative science (an idea Ramsey probably derived from Peirce) is also evoked. Both passages are already in MS 142 (1936).
[8] The editors of BEE will include the correct transcription in the next edition of the *Nachlass*. The facsimile of MS 107 was recently added to the Wittgenstein Source website and can be freely accessed on line by browsing www.wittgensteinsource.org.
[9] The passage is also mentioned in Scharfstein (1980, pp. 20, 400n4) and Upper (1998), both of whom cite Bogen (1972), and in Fabbrichesi (2002, p. 20), who cites Upper (1998).

Chapter 1: Pragmatism in Wittgenstein Before *On Certainty*

In the reflections that follow the quoted passage and that have partly found their way into PR, §226, Wittgenstein states that the sentences we utter in everyday life appear more similar to hypotheses than to propositions because they do not seem to refer to sense data or immediate experience but to the future: to something that *could* or *would* happen, to an expectation, and not to what is immediate. The rules governing hypotheses and those governing propositions are different. Only if one looks for a non-hypothetical representation, does immediate experience have a role. 'But now—he then observes—it seems that the representation loses all its value if the hypothetical element is dropped, because then the proposition does not point to the future any more, but it is, as it were, self-satisfied and hence without any value' (MS 107, p. 249). Here Wittgenstein is explaining the reason why his previous conception should be 'rotated by a small angle'. Only if the proposition is intended as a non-hypothetical representation, does it make sense to speak of sense data or atomic facts; yet, why should we look for a non-hypothetical representation? What is it for? If the hypothetical—that is, pragmatic[10]—element is dropped, the representation ceases to be directed towards the future; one could add: it ceases to be directed *tout court* because it does not bear an intentional character any more.

In the following lines, Wittgenstein is even more explicit.

> The expectation says something like 'It's nice elsewhere too and I'm here anyway'. And with the perspective of the expectation, we look into the future.
> It makes no sense to speak of sentences [*Sätzen*], if they have no value as instruments.
> The sense of a sentence is its purpose (MS 107, p. 249).[11]

---

[10] It is interesting to see the manuscript on this point: before the expression 'hypothetische Element' there is a 'p', or perhaps 'pr', crossed out; one could speculate that Wittgenstein was about to write 'pragmatische Element' and changed his mind.

[11] Die Erwartung sagt gleichsam 'schön ist es auch anderswo und hier bin ich sowieso'. Und mit dem Perspektiv der Erwartung schauen wir in die Zukunft./Es hat keinen Sinn von Sätzen zu reden die als Instrumente keinen Wert haben./Der Sinn eines Satzes ist sein Zweck.

Upon citing a curious sentence from a short story for children by Wilhelm Busch,[12] Wittgenstein affirms that the expectation generated by a sentence with a hypothetical character is what permits us to look towards the future and to have a direction. It is precisely in its instrumental aspect then that the sense (the direction) of a proposition or of a sentence lies. Wittgenstein is exploring the pragmatist approach: he identifies its source in the need to account for the open and hypothetical aspect of sentences, and he sums it up in a rather crude version of instrumentalism—'the sense of a sentence is its purpose'—yet does not distance himself from this result. Wittgenstein made a similar point a few days before too, in a remark later part of PR, within a reasoning concerning the use of words: 'You might say: The sense of a sentence is its purpose. (Or of a word, "Its meaning is its purpose")' (MS 107, p. 234).[13]

Proceeding in his reasoning, Wittgenstein observes that by telling someone 'There is a chair over there' the speaker wants to produce in him or her certain expectations and certain ways of acting. But then he abruptly stops this line of thought, probably disturbed by some aspects or consequences of it, and writes: 'It is terribly hard here not to get lost in questions which do not concern logic' (MS 107, p. 250).

It seems now that the remarks regarding the pragmatic sense and the purpose of sentences fall outside logic, the sphere in which Wittgenstein intends to remain. Considering that a few lines before Wittgenstein was asking himself whether logic itself, or at least a certain conception of logic existed, now there is a change of mind. Before the (still Tractarian) aspiration to see logic 'as a whole from the outside', an expression that he repeats here, certain muddles of questions appear complicated and, all in all, irrelevant.

What is clear, as I take it, is that Wittgenstein is in the middle of a deep change in his thought and struggles between different perspectives, trying to remain faithful to some of his previous views and at the same time

---

[12] *Plisch und Plum*, published in 1882; see Busch (1974).

[13] Cf. PR, §15c, modified translation. The sentence 'Its meaning is its purpose' is in English in the original text.

Chapter 1: Pragmatism in Wittgenstein Before *On Certainty* 23

searching for satisfactory ways of dealing with new themes. In particular, he is now interested in issues connected to the everyday and practical use of language. The risk that he seems to envisage is that if the explanation of the meaning of a sentence is given by appealing to what the speaker wants to produce in the listener, this explanation does not concern the *logic* of the sentence, but something else—perhaps something having to do with the speaker's will, or even worse, with causes and effects.

In the last remarks written on the same day, Wittgenstein reflects on verification and confirmation, with a couple of examples regarding the experiential verification of sensible occurrences, like a pointer moving and, after a given threshold, producing pain in the head of the observer, and a circle gradually turning into a square (MS 107, p. 250). Without lingering over a theme that would require much more attention, for our purposes suffice it to say that there is an oscillation between the idea that confirmation or verification concerns propositions and the idea that it concerns hypotheses. This is evident in the manuscript, where both terms appear and neither of them is deleted. A distinction is beginning to emerge, but Wittgenstein would only clearly differentiate between propositions and hypotheses a few weeks later.

This theme calls to mind some discussions of the Vienna Circle, and it might be useful to point out that the notes we are considering were written after a short break in MS 107, corresponding to the winter vacation that Wittgenstein spent in Vienna. In those weeks, Wittgenstein began to write another notebook, MS 108, because he did not take MS 107 with him; when he returned to Cambridge he got back to MS 107, and, once finished, he filled the rest of MS 108.[14] During the vacation, Wittgenstein met Friedrich Waismann and Moritz Schlick six times, as documented in Waismann (1979). One could think, therefore, that it was these conversations which gave rise to Wittgenstein's reasoning on hypotheses. It is not so. Neither the first part of MS 108 nor the conversations annotated by Waismann in this period bear signs of this reflection. On the contrary, the theme emerges with most clarity precisely after the notes we have seen concerning the

---

[14] Wittgenstein himself explains this in MS 107, p. 227; see also von Wright (1993, pp. 492–493).

pragmatic nature of expectations. It is an apparently autonomous reflection by Wittgenstein which would lead him to the conclusion that 'a hypothesis is a law for forming propositions' or 'a law for forming expectations' (MS 107, p. 283).[15] The same attitude can be found in Wittgenstein's lectures at the beginning of the 1930s:

> A proposition can be verified; a hypothesis cannot, but it is a law or a rule for constructing propositions and it looks to the future—i.e. enables us to construct propositions which can be verified or falsified (LCL, p. 16).[16]

As Egidi (1983, pp. 106–107) efficaciously sums up, hypotheses: (1) do not have the nature of propositions but work as laws for the construction of propositions; (2) have a different relationship with reality to verification; (3) do not have a descriptive but a prescriptive and normative function; (4) do not have a historical character; and (5) are connected to the concepts of probability and expectation.

Wittgenstein and Ramsey

I wrote that Wittgenstein's reflection on hypotheses is 'apparently' autonomous because there is actually a strong affinity between his words and some remarks by Frank Ramsey concerning what the latter called 'variable hypotheticals'. Therefore, it is likely that Ramsey's work had a role in his friend's parallel, albeit slightly later, reflection. Before looking at this in more detail, a few biographical facts.

On 19 January 1930—the day before Wittgenstein's note on the pragmatist conception of truth—Ramsey, not yet 27, died after an illness and a surgical operation. The two thinkers had already known each other for a few years. Ramsey wrote one of the first (and most insightful) reviews of TLP (Ramsey 1931, pp. 270 ff.) and edited the

---

[15] Note written on 4 February 1930; then in PR, §228d and in BT, p. 94.
[16] See also LCL, pp. 53, 66, 82, 110, and LCM, pp. 55, 59. The theme is also in BT: see in particular section 32.

first English translation, together with C.K. Ogden. In 1923, when the review was already written but not yet published, Ramsey visited Wittgenstein in Puchberg, where the latter had a job as an elementary school teacher, and for two weeks, the two worked intensively on the *Tractatus*, examining and discussing each section (Monk 1991, p. 216). From then on, they remained in contact, meeting occasionally, sometimes quarrelling, until Wittgenstein decided to move to Cambridge, where Ramsey was based, at the beginning of 1929. There, at Trinity College, Wittgenstein presented TLP as his doctoral dissertation, under the supervision of the young Ramsey himself.

During 1929, Ramsey and Wittgenstein met on a very regular basis, so much so that, according to some testimonies, Wittgenstein, who was perpetually afraid of dying, prepared a copy of his own work each day to give it to his friend for safekeeping (Leavis 1981, p. 74). An example of this strong relationship is a document written in German and found among Ramsey's papers, which, according to reliable reconstructions (McGuinness 2006, p. 24), was probably the draft of Wittgenstein's presentation held by the Aristotelian Society in 1929. Indeed, although the official text of the presentation, later published in the *Proceedings of the Aristotelian Society*, was 'Some Remarks on Logical Form', on that occasion Wittgenstein talked about the infinite in mathematics, which is the subject of the notes found among Ramsey's things.[17]

The reciprocal influence between Ramsey and Wittgenstein is patent in the writings of both.[18] In this context, I will limit my analysis to the influence that Ramsey might have had on facilitating and orienting Wittgenstein's encounter with the pragmatist tradition.[19]

In that year, Ramsey wrote a lot, although none of the articles and notes achieved a definite formulation. In particular, Ramsey's concept of the

---

[17] Wittgenstein told Russell about this in a letter (see McGuinness 2012, p. 172). This text is published in English in Venturinha (2010). The theme of the infinite in mathematics was a central topic in the discussions between Ramsey and Wittgenstein: see Wrigley (1995), Marion (1998).

[18] See Thayerm (1981, Chap. 2), Sahlin (1995); for a more critical approach see Glock (2005), McGuinness (2006).

[19] Among the rich literature on Ramsey and pragmatism, two recent contributions (both focused on Peirce's influence) are Tiercelin (2015) and Misak (2016).

'variable hypothetical' appears in 'General Propositions and Causality', 'Knowledge' and 'Causal Qualities' (a postscript to 'Theories').[20] There are two kinds of general propositions, says Ramsey: real conjunctions, like 'everyone in Cambridge voted', and variable hypotheticals, like 'all men are mortal', which are of the form $x \cdot \varphi(x)$. The latter look like conjunctions, but they are not because infinity, which characterizes them, cannot be the object of a judgement grounded in truth conditions: we would never be able to list each and every x in order to assert that $x \cdot \varphi(x)$. While explaining this point, Ramsey adds an interesting parenthetical note, often cited in literature independently from its context.[21] Here are Ramsey's words:

> When we ask what would make [the variable hypothetical] true, we inevitably answer that it is true if and only if every x has φ; i.e. when we regard it as a proposition capable of the two cases truth and falsity, we are forced to make it a conjunction, and to have a theory of conjunctions which we cannot express for lack of symbolic power.
>
> (But what we can't say we can't say, and we cannot whistle it either) (Ramsey 1990, p. 146).

Ramsey continues noticing that if the variable hypothetical is not a conjunction, then it is not a proposition in the proper sense, and wonders how one can say that it is 'right or wrong' (interestingly, he does not use the words 'true or false'). The stinging joke Ramsey dedicates to his friend and to his distinction between saying and showing, alluding to the paradoxicality of TLP, which speaks about what should be passed over in silence, and to Wittgenstein's habit of whistling, is instructive for two reasons. First, it shows that one of the origins of the idea of the variable hypothetical resided in the necessity to overcome a problem in Wittgenstein's approach. Second, given the 'innumerable conversations'[22] the two had in 1929, it demonstrates

---

[20] See Ramsey (1990).

[21] Glock (2005, p. 48) is an exception.

[22] As stated in Wittgenstein's preface to PI.

that Wittgenstein most likely discussed these themes with Ramsey. Indeed, the problems connected with conjunctions and general propositions are one of the motives that prompted Wittgenstein to distance himself from the perspective of TLP in those years. As he once told von Wright, the 'biggest mistake' of his early work was the identification of general propositions with infinite conjunctions and disjunctions of elementary propositions (von Wright 1982, p. 151n28).[23]

How did Ramsey deal with these problems? He defined variable hypotheticals as causal laws which 'form the system with which the speaker meets the future', and as 'not judgments but rules for judging' (Ramsey 1990, p. 149). Wittgenstein, as we saw, defined a hypothesis as 'a law or a rule for constructing propositions'. It is quite evident that their strategies are similar, as they both make use of the concept of law and rule to give account of the non-propositional nature of hypotheses. As has been noticed, it is likely that on this point both thinkers followed Herman Weyl, who had characterized universal quantifiers as '*Anweisung für Urteile*', instructions for judgements.[24] Bearing in mind that chronologically speaking Ramsey's notes precede Wittgenstein's, it seems correct to conclude that the Ramseyan concept of variable hypothetical (not a judgement but a rule for judging) was a source of inspiration for the Wittgensteinian concept of hypothesis (not a proposition but a law for forming propositions).[25]

Beyond hypotheses and variable hypotheticals, several other themes in Ramsey and Wittgenstein's writings confirm how much they worked side by side: the relation between the 'primary' and 'secondary' systems or languages, the problem of the regularity of nature, induction, and probability, are some examples. But the issue of hypotheses seems particularly interesting for us, owing to the connections it has with pragmatist issues. Two aspects are worthy of notice.

---

[23] See also LCL, p. 119, LCM, p. 90. On general propositions, see also James, PP, p. 963.
[24] In Weyl (1921). See Sahlin (1990, p. 240n6) and (1995, p. 153), Majer (1991, p. 169n15), Glock (2005, p. 50), Price (2011, p. 155), Marion (1998, pp. 86–87) and (2012, pp. 71 ff.).
[25] See also BT, p. 62 (sec. 18).

In the first place, Ramsey's discussion of variable hypotheticals makes explicit reference to pragmatist themes like the Peircean notion of habits. And it is precisely the pragmatic element that Ramsey identifies as *lacking* in TLP, when, in the final paragraph of 'Facts and Propositions' (1927), he acknowledges his debt to Wittgenstein for the latter's conception of logic, while nevertheless adding: 'Everything that I have said is due to him, except the parts which have a pragmatist tendency, which seem to me to be needed in order to fill up a gap in his system' (Ramsey 1990, p. 51). According to Ramsey, a pragmatic criterion can solve the problem of general propositions: belief in a variable hypothetical can be traced to a practical acting. Belief belongs to our conduct, and our conduct in turn reflects the fact that we normally think in general terms.

Second, the two thinkers' reflection on hypotheses is intertwined with the concept of truth, and, as we saw, it is with regard to truth that Wittgenstein draws attention to pragmatism.

Let us finally come to what Wittgenstein, in the quoted passage from MS 107, calls 'the pragmatist conception of true and false'. Wittgenstein identifies it with the idea that the sentence is true as long as it proves to be useful. What did Ramsey say about truth, and what did he say about pragmatism?

In 1929, he worked extensively on truth, as it was his intention to publish a book on the subject. His position is usually identified with a redundancy theory and with a form of deflationism. Yet, it is clear from his notes that he was after a more complex and 'dense' idea: what is normally associated with the name of Ramsey is only a part of the story. Indeed, in the notes collected in 'On Truth', he lists three kinds of theories of truth: correspondentist, coherentist, and pragmatist.[26] Ramsey places his own approach within the *first* type, but to simply assert that his position is correspondentist is reductive. According to him, roughly, the belief that *p* is true only and only if *p*, and there is no need to add 'and *p* is true'. Yet, Ramsey specifies, while underlining that

---

[26] Wittgenstein discusses the same three approaches, as we shall see, during a lecture in the early 1930s.

this is the important thing, what the connection between the belief that *p* and *p* consists of, that is, to use his terminology, what 'propositional reference' is, remains to be explained. With respect to this, he surprisingly cites William James, saying that the latter frequently insists in defining truth as agreement of ideas with reality and in stating that the problem is precisely to understand the meaning of this agreement (Ramsey 1991a, p. 23).

This is surprising because on other occasions Ramsey criticizes James, sometimes harshly, retaining him responsible for having 'ruined' the positive contribution of pragmatism on truth. It is chiefly of Charles S. Peirce that Ramsey was thinking when speaking of the positive contribution of pragmatism. Of Peirce, he particularly appreciated the analysis of belief, which he considered a relevant input for the analysis of propositional reference. In Ramsey's reconstruction, according to Peirce, the belief that A is B is analysable in terms of 'a belief leading to such actions as will be useful if A is B, but not otherwise' (Ramsey 1991a, p. 91). Although this does not suffice to give a complete account of propositional reference, it is not something to make fun of, says Ramsey. What is ludicrous is, instead, 'the way in which William James confused [this idea] especially in its application to religious belief' (we will see James' position in more detail shortly). According to *this* Ramsey, James overlooked the most obvious aspect a theory of truth should consider, that is, correspondence with reality (1991a, p. 91).

Hence, for Ramsey, the positive contribution of pragmatism to the analysis of truth is represented by Peirce's attempt to work on propositional reference in terms of actions. Ramsey adopts a similar point of view when he analyses judgement (a term under which he includes knowledge, belief, and opinion):

> To say a man has such and such knowledge, beliefs and opinions means then generally something hypothetical, something about what he would think, say or do in suitable circumstances.
> ...
> [It is impossible] to give any satisfactory account of belief or even of thought without making any reference to possible resulting actions (Ramsey 1991a, pp. 44–45).

The proximity to Wittgenstein's MS 107 note is clear, as is the debt Ramsey owed to pragmatism, an aspect on which one can find other evidence in other writings. In 'Truth and Probability' (1926) for instance, we read that judging mental habits by whether they work or by whether the opinions they lead to are generally true (as he does) is a kind of pragmatism (Ramsey 1990, pp. 93–94).

It is interesting to see that in 1927, Ramsey cites the person responsible for his own pragmatism as neither James nor Peirce but *Russell*. At the end of 'Facts and Propositions', in fact, after stating that pragmatism is the missing element in Wittgenstein's perspective, he adds: 'My pragmatism is derived from Mr. Russell', explaining that in his view, although this is still a rough sketch of the matter, the core of pragmatism is in the idea of defining the meaning of a sentence 'by reference to the actions to which asserting it would lead, or, more vaguely still, by its possible causes and effects' (Ramsey 1990, p. 51).

It is usually argued in literature that Ramsey was here referring to Russell's 1921 *The Analysis of Mind* and to its causalist perspective on meaning.[27] Picardi (1987), moreover, identifies in Russell (1921, p. 278) the criticism according to which the *Tractatus* is not able to explain the greater appropriateness of actions stemming out of *true* beliefs, rather than false beliefs, an aspect that is clearly connected to usefulness and purpose. As she takes it, this is the starting point of Ramsey's reasoning. In my view, besides Russell (1921), there is another important source that is usually overlooked. What Ramsey had in mind was probably Russell's 'Theory of Knowledge': not the famous unpublished 1913 manuscript (Russell 1984), but a lesser known 1926 entry for the *Encyclopaedia Britannica* (Russell 1926). In this text, Russell affirms that beliefs and inferences, as characteristics of behaviour, can be attributed both to humans and animals and that in this sense when a person or an animal succeeds in achieving a certain result it means that their relevant beliefs are true, and when they fail it means that at least one of their beliefs is false. So in Russell's words,

> a sentence may be taken as a law of behaviour in any environment containing certain characteristics; it will be 'true' if the behaviour leads

---

[27] On the impact of this work on Ramsey see Acero (2005).

Chapter 1: Pragmatism in Wittgenstein Before *On Certainty* 31

to results satisfactory to the person concerned, and otherwise it will be 'false'. Such, at least, is the pragmatist definition of truth and falsehood.

The impression that Ramsey was acquainted with this article is reinforced if we consider that a few years later, he too wrote an entry for the *Encyclopaedia*, and it was the entry on Bertrand Russell. In it, he mentioned the 'Theory of Knowledge' as testifying Russell's shift towards 'a pragmatist or behaviourist direction' (Ramsey 1991b, p. 137), words that seem to describe this text more than the 1913 manuscript.

Just like Russell, in 'Facts and Propositions' Ramsey refers to what we could call an 'animal belief'. He is concerned with this kind of belief in an oft-cited passage:

> [I]t is for instance possible to say that a chicken believes a certain sort of caterpillar to be poisonous, and mean by that merely that it abstains from eating such caterpillars on account of unpleasant experiences connected with them.... [I]t might well be held that in regard to this kind of belief the pragmatist view was correct, i.e. that the relation between the chicken's behaviour and the objective factors was that the actions were such as to be useful if, and only if, the caterpillars were actually poisonous (Ramsey 1990, p. 40).

As Methven (2015, p. 142) underlines, despite the fact that these lines have enjoyed considerable success in literature, Ramsey is clear in stating that he is *not* interested in animal belief, but in beliefs expressed in words or symbols, to which he turns immediately after the 'chicken' passage. Yet, I do not think that the interest of commentators is totally misplaced. Indeed, when Ramsey analyses the content of beliefs expressed in words, he is again ultimately referring to actions and behaviour. Hence, if it is true that beliefs expressed in words are not equated to animal belief, it is also true that Ramsey seems to envision a continuity between the two kinds. This continuity justifies the claim that in this paper Ramsey is making at least a partially pragmatist move, though in a vague and imprecise way, as he himself admits at the end of the paper.

Going back to the theme of truth, besides James' conception, Ramsey also knew Peirce's view. In 'General Propositions and Causality' (1929), he describes it as the idea of truth as 'what everyone will believe in the end', but he specifies that it applies to scientific systems and not to statements of facts (Ramsey 1990, p. 161).

In general terms, one could read Ramsey's criticism of James as moving roughly along Peircean lines, not by negating but by qualifying the notion of usefulness. Usefulness thus is not primarily referring to the subject of belief but rather to the durability of the belief itself, that is, to its capacity of resistance and to the efficacy of its predictive power, which go far beyond the subject's impulses and desires. So for Peirce, as well as for Ramsey and (as we shall see in a moment) for Wittgenstein, 'the true conclusion would remain true if we had no impulse to accept it; and the false one would remain false, though we could not resist the tendency to believe in it' (W 3, p. 244).[28]

To conclude on this, the themes which Ramsey and Wittgenstein discussed were variously intertwined with the subject of truth[29] and particularly with the pragmatist approach to truth. This not only permits us to imagine but also suggests that it was precisely through the lenses of these discussions that Wittgenstein came to think about pragmatism.

Wittgenstein Reader of James

Apart from Ramsey's influence, what did Wittgenstein know of the classical pragmatists? And were there other personalities who could have had a role in shaping his perception of this tradition?

Wittgenstein's familiarity with some texts by William James is certain and already documented in the literature.[30] Yet, there is no direct evidence proving that he read the books and essays in which James is more explicit on pragmatism and on truth (*Pragmatism* 1907, *The*

---

[28] From Peirce's 'The Fixation of Belief', also in CP 5.365.

[29] Other affinities between the two can be identified in the perspective of redundancy; see Koethe (1996, pp. 135 ff.).

[30] See Goodman (2002), Boncompagni (forthcoming*c*).

Meaning of Truth 1909).³¹ The books which it is certain he knew are *Varieties of Religious Experience* (VRE 1902), *Principles of Psychology* (PP 1890), the so-called *Jimmy*, that is, *Psychology. Briefer Course* (PBC 1892), and perhaps *Essays in Radical Empiricism* (ERE 1912). It is likely that he came into contact with the psychological texts around 1930. In the *Nachlass*, James' name appears for the first time on 14 February 1931, in a remark concerning the idea that 'a man doesn't cry because he is sad: he is sad because he cries' (MS 110, p. 73), which can be traced back to PP, pp. 1065–1066.³² As for VRE, he read it very early, in 1912, as he himself wrote to Russell in June that year: 'Whenever I have time I now read James's 'Varieties of religious exp[erience]'. This book does me *a lot* of good' (McGuinness 2012, p. 30). Russell was a bit worried about what his young pupil was reading, and he continued to be worried for quite a long time. In a letter to Lady Ottoline, in 1919, he affirmed that Wittgenstein was becoming 'a complete mystic' and that he was contemplating the hypothesis of becoming a monk, and that it all started when he read VRE (McGuinness 2012, p. 112).

For his part, Wittgenstein remained deeply fond of this book, and indeed in 1930 he recommended it to his friend Maurice Drury, telling him: 'A book you should read is William James' *Varieties of Religious Experience*; that was a book that helped me a lot at one time'. On the same occasion, he said that what made James a good philosopher was that he was 'a real human being' (Rhees 1984, p. 106).

It seems clear that what attracted Wittgenstein was not the pragmatist aspects of VRE, although in it, it is possible to read a general tone and some passages directly connected to pragmatism. For instance, here James cites Peirce's pragmatism as stated in 'How to Make Our Ideas Clear', offering his own version of the so-called pragmatic maxim: 'To attain perfect clearness in our thoughts of an object—he affirms—we

---

[31] Except for an indirect testimony according to which he referred to an example from P during a conversation, in 1941; see PPO, pp. 388–389.

[32] It is possible that Wittgenstein had read PP even earlier: Ramsey already knew James' psychological work at least by 1929. See Ramsey (1991b, p. 76). See Biesenbach (2014, pp. 265 ff., 564, 682 ff.) for a systematic presentation of Wittgenstein's citations and allusions to James.

need then only consider what sensations, immediate or remote, we are conceivably to expect from it, and what conduct we must prepare in case the object should be true' (VRE, p. 351). More generally, in VRE the religious life itself is interpreted through broadly pragmatist lenses. Says James:

> [T]he uses of religion, its uses to the individual who has it, and the uses of the individual himself to the world, are the best arguments that truth is in it. We return to the empirical philosophy: the true is what works well, even though the qualification 'on the whole' may always have to be added (VRE, p. 361).

To embrace a religious life, then, is to give an overall *meaning* to one's life, a meaning in which the 'useful', intended in the widest possible sense, plays a primary role. Given that religious truths cannot be accounted for in terms of correspondence to matters of fact, the individual realizes that the value and the justification of religious beliefs lie in their general pragmatic aspect, in the way they stimulate a particular approach to life and to the world and a consequent line of conduct.

Yet, as mentioned, it is in other works that James is more explicit and articulated on the pragmatist conception of truth, and it is with reference to these other works that his theses were criticized. His conception of truth was deeper and more complex than it appears in his critics' descriptions. It is impossible here to deal with it in a complete way. Suffice it to say that in order to comprehend James' approach to truth in its subtleties and ramifications, it would be necessary to see it against the background of his entire philosophy, without limiting the analysis to the epistemological level but expanding it to his personal and existential reflection on the one hand, and to his peculiar way of combining pluralism and empiricism on the other. Nevertheless, to be sure, there were reasons for harsh criticism: some formulations by James, especially in P, were an easy target for denigration. He talked there of ideas that '*become true just in so far as they help us to get into satisfactory relation with other parts of our experience*', and said that 'any idea upon which we can ride, so to speak . . . is true *instrumentally*' (P, p. 34), thus emphasising

Chapter 1: Pragmatism in Wittgenstein Before *On Certainty* 35

that truth in his view was something changeable and not fixed once and for all. He was very explicit on this:

> The truth of an idea is not a stagnant property inherent in it. Truth *happens* to an idea. It *becomes* true, is *made* true by events. Its verity *is* in fact an event, a process: the process namely of its verifying itself, its veri-*fication*. Its validity is the process of its valid-*ation*. ... This function of agreeable leading is what we mean by an idea's verification. (P, p. 97)

James also candidly equated truth to our ideas' 'power to work' (P, p. 34), to 'the expedient in the way of our thinking' (P, p. 106) and to '*whatever proves itself to be good in the way of belief*' though adding '*good, too, for definite, assignable reasons*' (P, p. 42). Finally, he spoke of *truths*, in the plural, explaining that truth is not a univocal notion and that, therefore, different ideas can be considered true just in so far as they, simply, *pay* (P, p. 104).

Yet, on closer examination, as mentioned James' conception does not simply establish an equation between truth and usefulness, in that it depends on a reconceptualization of the very ideas of reality and correspondence to reality in such a way that the idea of usefulness, too, is reshaped. And this reconceptualization is not devoid of metaphysical elements, despite James' declaration that his radical empiricism and his pragmatism were independent from one another (P, p. 6).[33] In other words, if—according to his often cited image—the trail of the human serpent is over everything (P, p. 37), it is so not in virtue of a crude pragmatist idealism that wants to bend reality to human desires; rather in virtue of the acknowledgement of a reciprocal inevitable dependence that nevertheless does not undermine the unconditional nature of things with respect to the human will. Hence, the concept of usefulness, as intended by James, not only is not confined to the economic domain (in spite of the metaphor of truth as the 'cash value'[34]) but applies more

---

[33] As Hookway (2012, p. 194) notices, Peirce's view on the connection between pragmatism and metaphysical aspects is exactly the opposite.

[34] See, for instance, P, p. 32; MT, pp. 3, 112.

generally to what is *interesting* for the human being, to what is *relevant*, to what is *important*.[35] More generally, as Putnam (1997) has shown, there are multiple strains in James' view on truth, including a Peircean strain that appeals to the 'long run' and the ultimate consensus of the community of inquiries. In this sense, James is also committed to truth as an *ideal*—in fact, only by recognizing this can we appreciate the 'vital link between his melioristic vision of morality and his pragmatic theory of truth' (Colapietro 1986, p. 190). Therefore, when James talks of truth in terms of the 'satisfactory', this should be understood in a broad sense, as pointing to 'the end of orienting ourselves in the fullest possible way towards our world' (Colapietro 1986, p. 198).

Nevertheless, on reading the short passages quoted above it is not difficult to see that James' writings left themselves open to simplification and irony.

Instrumentalism, the connection with the issue of verification and the reference to future actions are all elements that we also find in the remark by Wittgenstein from which we started. Besides Ramsey, who cites James' works in his writings,[36] other thinkers who were quite close to Wittgenstein in those years had also surely read P, and they could have been the vehicle through which Wittgenstein came into contact with some parts of this book. I am thinking in particular of G.E. Moore and Bertrand Russell: both wrote reviews of P and both were particularly concerned with James' conception of truth.

Moore's article, 'William James' *Pragmatism*' (Moore 1970),[37] describes James' perspective as a view according to which 'our true ideas . . . are those that "work", in the sense that they are or can be "verified", or are "useful"', and 'true ideas "pay" and false ones don't'. Moore's detailed objection classifies all the possible cases resulting from these identifications and it confutes them one by one, only sparing the obvious remarks that we can

---

[35] See Putnam, A.R. and Putnam, H. (1992); Putnam (1997); Cormier (2002); Marchetti (2015a, Chap. 4).

[36] In particular, in *On Truth* he cites MT and P (Ramsey 1991a, pp. 15n12; 24n3; 94n15).

[37] Originally published with the title 'Professor James' Pragmatism' in *Proceedings of the Aristotelian Society*, 1907–1908.

Chapter 1: Pragmatism in Wittgenstein Before *On Certainty* 37

verify true ideas and that most true ideas 'pay' (Moore 1970, pp. 97, 123, 107, 124). It is an extremely analytical commentary, but it does not seem to capture the deepest contents of the criticized conception. Indeed, James did not consider Moore's objections worthy of reply: in the preface of MT he included Moore among the critics that show 'an inability almost pathetic, to understand the thesis which they seek to refute' (MT, p. 10), and in a 1908 letter to his pupil Horace M. Kallen, he hastily described Moore's article as 'a pretentious *fiasco*' (MT, p. 305).

As for Russell, who as is well known appreciated James for other aspects of his work,[38] he wrote negative commentaries of P in the article 'Transatlantic Truth' (1908) published in *Albany Review*, and then in his 'Pragmatism', written while James was working on a reply to the first article. In these two papers, which Wittgenstein certainly read because they are part of Russell's collection *Philosophical Essays*,[39] Russell offers very simplified and sometimes almost ironic descriptions of the Jamesian conception of truth. According to *his* James, in order for a belief to be true, it is enough to be relevant for a certain purpose and to further its achievement (Russell 1910, p. 89), or, even more straightforwardly, to have good practical consequences once adopted (Russell 1910, p. 116), or to tend to the satisfaction of desire (Russell 1910, p. 92). Russell's target is the idea that usefulness can give the *meaning* of truth because according to this idea, which is effectively central in the Jamesian conception though not exhaustive of his position, if a belief is useful then it *must* be true (Russell 1910, p. 100). Russell's crudest statements are probably the following:

[S]ince all beliefs are absurd, we may as well believe what is most convenient.
. . .

---

[38] James' influence is evident in particular in *The Analysis of Mind*, 1921. In this work Russell does not deal with the pragmatist conception of truth, except for a passage in which he states that pragmatists wish all truth to be 'practical' (1921, p. 165). Interestingly, referring more generally to pragmatism, he affirms (1921, p. 26) that the three founders of this philosophy were James, Dewey and Schiller, without mentioning Peirce at all. Yet, from Russell (1946) (cited in Nubiola 1996) we know that he read CLL. See also Misak (2016) for a description of Russell's partial 'conversion' to pragmatism.

[39] See Russell (1910). The first article appears here with a different title, 'William James' Conception of Truth'. That Wittgenstein read this book is documented in von Wright (1974, p. 10).

We may then sum up the philosophy in the following definition: 'A truth is anything which it pays to believe'.

...

If... we agree to accept the pragmatic definition of the word 'truth', we find that the belief that A exists may be 'true' even when A does not exist (Russell 1910, pp. 105, 118, 129).

The simplification of James' position is patent.

The very concept of usefulness does not *per se* necessarily lead to such a reductive reading. Even Peirce, who had a different view, emphasized similar aspects in his 'foundational' writings on pragmatism and underlined the practical value of establishing beliefs.[40] His neat separation between theory and practice notwithstanding,[41] he pointed out that in order to be sound a theory must be 'susceptible of applications'.[42] The classical pragmatists, on the whole, were pretty aware of the theoretical density and complexity of the concept of usefulness.[43]

To conclude on the possible sources for Wittgenstein's perception of the Jamesian conception of truth, one more text should be mentioned: *The Meaning of Meaning* by Ogden and Richards.[44] Wittgenstein did not appreciate it (in a letter he defines it 'a miserable book', McGuinness 2012, p. 137), but he certainly knew it. Besides citing the exponents of pragmatism on many occasions, this work offers a survey of the existent theories of meaning (not of truth, but of course the two concepts are connected), one of which is defined as its account in terms of 'practical consequences' (Ogden and Richards 1960, p. 186). This theory is linked to pragmatism

---

[40] See 'The Fixation of Belief' and 'How to Make our Ideas Clear', W 3, pp. 242 ff., CP 3.358 ff.

[41] See 'Philosophy and the Conduct of Life', CP 1.161 ff. More on this in Chap. 6, Section 'Beyond Method'.

[42] In 'Critical Analysis of Logical Theories', ca. 1902; CP 2.7. See also Bergman (2010), to whom I owe this quote.

[43] Besides Peirce, James himself agrees with utilitarianism on the relevance of practical aspects (P, p. 32), but he adopts a more cautious attitude when it comes to utilitarianism as a theory for moral life (WB, pp. 155 ff.). Dewey too both praises and criticizes utilitarianism in Chapter VII of *Reconstruction in Philosophy* (Dewey 1948); see also Chapter VI on the intertwinement between logic, practice, and usefulness.

[44] On this topic see Engelmann (2013a, pp. 67 ff.)

and explained through James' words on ideas being true when we can 'assimilate, validate, corroborate [and] verify' them. Again, this is the typical move which characterizes the reception of pragmatism: the pragmatic maxim, explained as an account of meaning in terms of practical consequences, is assimilated to the conception of truth as usefulness, in such a way that, as Misak (2008, p. 199) sums up, 'the story of the reception of classical pragmatism is mostly a story of the reception of James' application of the pragmatic maxim to the concept of truth'.

Hence pragmatism and, in particular, the pragmatist perspective on truth were core themes of the Cambridge philosophical debate of the time, and it was impossible not to be touched by these discussions, as they constantly appeared in volumes, articles, and public disputes. As Uebel (2015) and Ferrari (2015) have interestingly shown, moreover, the Jamesian conception of truth was often discussed also in Vienna, and pragmatism had a significant (though still under evaluated) role in shaping the views of some of the members of the Circle, especially in its early years.

To conclude, in a sense, even if Wittgenstein did not directly read James' P, he *did* read it indirectly—he read it in books and articles, heard of it in conversations and debates, dealt with it himself in his lectures and writings.

Wittgenstein Reader of Peirce?

It was thanks to *The Meaning of Meaning*, it seems, that Ramsey knew about Peirce's work (Marion 2012). Ogden was a friend both of Wittgenstein and (mostly) of Ramsey, with whom he translated the *Tractatus* into English. The bilingual edition appeared in 1922 through the publisher Kegan Paul, Trench, Trubner & Co in the series edited by Ogden himself, 'International Library of Psychology, Philosophy and Scientific Method'. A year before, in that same series, Russell's *Analysis of Mind* was published; a year later, Ogden and Richards' *The Meaning of Meaning* and Peirce's collection CLL. *The Meaning of Meaning* had an appendix dedicated to Peirce's semiotics, which Ramsey praised in the review of the book that he published in *Mind* (Ramsey 1924). It is likely, then, that Ramsey 'encountered' Peirce in *The Meaning of Meaning* and that he subsequently read CLL. In Ramsey's writings, references to Peirce abound; for instance, among his papers in the Pittsburgh Archives there is a seven-page note composed almost exclusively of citations from CLL.[45]

Given the attention Ramsey dedicated to Peirce's work and given the intellectual and personal friendship between Ramsey and Wittgenstein, it would be strange if the former did not talk about Peirce to the latter, although there are no explicit references to the American thinker in Wittgenstein's writings. Indeed, many affinities between PR and Peirce's CLL were already highlighted in 1981 (Gullvåg 1981). Common traits, often also present in Ramsey's work, are, for example, the themes of infinity, the continuity of space, the internal relation between sign and object, the nature of symbols, and the impossibility of going outside language or signs. While sustaining that many remarks in PR become easier to understand with a background of familiarity with CLL, Gullvåg thinks that Wittgenstein did *not* read Peirce's text but that its contents were 'filtered' to him by Ramsey. Yet, there is a document attesting that Wittgenstein *knew* something of Peirce's work—at least, that he was familiar with the paper 'The Probability of Induction' in 1943. Indeed, a few lines from this paper are quoted in a conversation between Wittgenstein and Rush Rhees in that year. The quote, according to Rhees (2002, p. 13), is the following:

> To the question 'How is it that a man can observe one fact and straightway pronounce judgment concerning another different fact not involved in the first?' (C.S. Peirce), we might ask instead 'How do we?' Otherwise the question seems queer, like 'How can I walk?'[46]

---

[45] Ramsey's manuscripts are available on-line on the University of Pittsburgh archive website, www.library.pitt.edu/frank-p-ramsey-papers. The paper I refer to is titled 'Peirce, Chance, Love and Logic' and is in Box 5, Folder 30. On Peirce and Ramsey, see Hookway (2005) and Misak (2016); on Ramsey as a channel between Peirce and Wittgenstein see also Nubiola (1996).

[46] The quote is from CLL: 102; the same article was also published in volume II of CP in 1931 and in SW in 1940 (W 3, p. 304, CP 2.690, SW, p. 187). Rhees would return to these themes in 1970, see Rhees (2003, p. 73 ff.).

Chapter 1: Pragmatism in Wittgenstein Before *On Certainty*

In the context of his paper, Peirce was reformulating the Kantian question on the conditions of possibility of synthetic *a priori* judgements. More precisely, he was saying that before asking this question, Kant should have asked the question on the conditions of possibility of synthetic judgements in general. Wittgenstein in turn (to very roughly sum up the reasoning that emerges from Rhees' notes) affirms that this very question should not be formulated within a transcendental framework but rather from a linguistic-anthropological point of view.

It is a conversation from 1943, and of course, it cannot prove that Wittgenstein had read Peirce in 1929. Moreover, the two could have talked about this passage simply because *Rhees* was interested in it. Yet, it is noteworthy that the way in which Wittgenstein discusses it in that conversation is not so different from the way in which he discussed induction in MS 107. Let us go back to that notebook and compare it with Rhees' notes.

Wittgenstein's notes from 21 January 1930—the day after the remark on pragmatism—are also part of PR (§§226c to 227d). The context is different from the 1943 conversation. In 1930, Wittgenstein deals with the method of choice between hypotheses, and (mathematical) induction is seen as a process which follows an economic principle of simplicity. In 1943, the point is anthropological: according to Wittgenstein, asking how induction is possible, just like asking how it is possible to be able to walk, stems from the wrong way of posing the question, in terms of *justification*. In other words, we should not ask ourselves what justifies induction (while answering, for example, that it is the uniformity of nature), but simply ascertain that we use it, that it is natural for us, and that to describe a world devoid of some sort of order would be simply impossible.

Although the context is different, both in 1930 and in 1943 Wittgenstein makes use of the same example, that of a curve (in the manuscript and in PR there is also a drawing illustrating it). In the 1930 note Wittgenstein explains:

> If our experiences yield points lying on a straight line, the proposition that these experiences are various views of a straight line is a hypothesis.

The hypothesis is a way of representing this reality, for a new experience may tally with it or not, or possibly make it necessary to modify the hypothesis (PR, §227g).

And in the 1943 conversation he observes:

'How can induction lead us to truth?' One answer is that it *doesn't* always. I may draw a curve through a series of dots, continuing it in the same way, and in fact the next dot may not fall in that curve at all (Rhees 2002, p. 14).

Since in the second quote Wittgenstein is referring to Peirce, it is possible that the former reflection was also stimulated by reading Peirce's article. The fact that Ramsey dedicated most of the aforementioned note on CCL to 'The Probability of Induction' (two and a half pages out of seven) is a further element going in the same direction.

It is, therefore, plausible to surmise that Wittgenstein, partly stimulated by Ramsey's interests, had read at least part of CLL by January 1930.

How is this relevant for our considerations about pragmatism? Regarding the pragmatist conception of truth, I do not think that Peirce might have been a source for Wittgenstein. As we shall see, it is on other issues that similarities emerge with more clarity. Peirce in fact had a different approach to truth than James, to whom Wittgenstein seems to refer more directly. Ramsey also underlined the distance, and not the vicinity, between the two pragmatists. Their approaches are not completely separate: James too appeals to the 'long run', as we saw, and Peirce too refers to usefulness and the satisfaction of desires. In CCL, p. 16, for instance, he affirms that 'it is certainly best for us that our beliefs should be such as may truly guide our actions so as to satisfy our desires'.[47] Yet, in his view, it is inquiry and the convergence of the researchers' opinions that occupy the centre of

---

[47] Also in W 3, p. 23 and CP 5.375.

the stage. Again, in CLL, p. 57, he offers this definition: 'The opinion which is fated to be ultimately agreed to by all who investigate, is what we mean by the truth...'.[48] Wittgenstein does not mention it.

Let us sum up on Wittgenstein's first remarks on pragmatism. The idea he had of the pragmatist conception of truth probably is derived from a direct or an indirect reading of James, a reading influenced by the criticism that Russell, Moore, Ramsey, and more generally the philosophical community in Cambridge had addressed to James' conception. Ramsey's figure was particularly relevant for Wittgenstein's initial contact with pragmatism. As we shall see, while on the one hand, Ramsey may have been a vehicle for Wittgenstein's approaching pragmatism, on the other hand, he was a vehicle of a rather *critical* approach, which would emerge more clearly in the remarks Wittgenstein issued on pragmatism in the following years.

Other References to Pragmatism Before OC

In LCL there is a section, probably dating back to the 1931–1932 academic year, concerning some comments expressed by Wittgenstein on the views put forth by another professor in Cambridge, Charlie Dunbar Broad. The lecture begins by stating that according to Broad, there are three theories of truth, the correspondence theory, the coherence theory, and the pragmatic theory (LCL, p. 75). Wittgenstein in first place replies that 'philosophy is not a choice between different "theories"', but then he briefly deals with the three approaches. Of pragmatism, he says:

> Pragmatism. The hypothesis that there are electrons is taken as being true because in practice you can work as if it were the case. So also Einstein's

---

[48] Also in W 3, p. 273 and CP 5.407. See also CLL, p. 105 (CP 2.693, W 3, p. 305). On Peirce's conception of truth see Misak (2004).

theory of relativity is accepted because it works in practice. Thus Euclidean space is used for everyday purposes, and relativity for immeasurable and astronomical distances. To decide between them would need a great deal of empirical evidence, and this is certainly the sense of truth we apply to them (LCL, p. 75).

He then goes on by highlighting that in different situations, we use the word 'true' with different meanings and that, therefore, it makes no sense to search for *one* theory of truth that is allegedly valid in every context. Like in the 1930 remark, Wittgenstein does not express any value judgement about the pragmatist conception of truth. He limits himself to observing, with specific attention to scientific theories,[49] that it is reasonable to adopt one theory as true when it is apt for the practical purposes for which it is used, regardless of the possibility of verifying its adherence to reality *in general*. This kind of verification is not relevant: the point is that, in any case, it would 'cost too much', it would need too much empirical evidence. If the theory works, and as long as it does, it is true, in the context in which it is used. Hence, in the case of the choice between different scientific views, we define 'truth' in a pragmatist way.

Yet, between the lines, one might also read a criticism of the pragmatists: they go wrong precisely when they try to define *one* theory of truth, valid for any context and for any purpose. In a sense, Wittgenstein is applying a pragmatist-linguistic criterion to the theoretical claims of pragmatism itself. By examining the linguistic uses of the word 'true', we can see that in some contexts, we use it like the pragmatists seem to do, by emphasizing the fact that what is true is what works; nevertheless, in other contexts, we do not use 'true' in this way. Not always can we let ourselves be guided by what works, what satisfies our desires, or what leads to the best consequences. Along these lines, a more articulated criticism was emerging.

A note written in 1932 makes this explicit.

> If I want to carve a block of wood into a particular shape any cut that gives it the right shape is a good one. But I don't call an argument a good

---

[49] Again, like Ramsey; cf. Ramsey (1991a, pp. 33–34).

Chapter 1: Pragmatism in Wittgenstein Before *On Certainty*

argument just because it has the consequences I want (Pragmatism). I may call a calculation wrong even if the actions based on its result have led to the desired end. (Compare the joke 'I've hit the jackpot and he wants to give me lessons!') (PG, p. 185).[50]

Wittgenstein would later copy this note in TS 213 (*The Big Typescript*), leaving out the parenthesis with the reference to pragmatism, but adding in handwriting the explanation of the joke:

A tells B that he won the jackpot in the lottery: he saw a crate lying in the street and on it the numbers 5 and 7. He calculated that 5 × 7 is 64 and filled in 64. B: But 5 × 7 isn't 64! A: I win the jackpot and he wants to give me lessons (BT, p. 185).

The remark is expressed within a reasoning concerning the issues of rules, grammar, arbitrariness, and games. Wittgenstein is distinguishing between two different kinds of justification (*Rechtfertigung*). In the case of the block of wood, the justification of action is the result that one desires to achieve. In the case of the calculation, actions must follow rules that are not justified by the desired result, but by other elements (the system of arithmetic). Therefore, Wittgenstein explains, while a calculation can be compared to a game like chess, the shaping of a block of wood is similar to the activity of cooking, as in these latter cases, actions are appropriate when they lead to the desired end. If there is a rule according to which soft-boiled eggs must be boiled for three minutes—the example is again Wittgenstein's—but one can obtain the same result by boiling them for five minutes, 'you don't say "that doesn't mean 'cooking soft-boiled eggs'"' (BT, p. 186) (although a smart alec chef could say precisely that). Conversely, in the case of multiplying 5 × 7 and obtaining 64, one *can* conclude that 'that doesn't mean calculating'. Although the result satisfies our desire, the multiplication is wrong: it is not, properly, a multiplication.

---

[50] Originally in MS 113, p. 33r - without '(Pragmatism)' -, then in MS 114, p. 158.

Wittgenstein now seems to consider pragmatism the position according to which the justification, motive, or reason for *every* action is the desired end. There is a drastic simplification and a clearly negative judgement here.

A similar attitude can be found in a remark from a 1935 lecture. In discussing meaning, logic, rules, and use, Wittgenstein states: 'The pragmatic criterion of the truth of a proposition is its usefulness in practice. But the person who says this has in mind one particular use of "useful"' (LCA, p. 142). So, typically, a scientific hypothesis may be called true if it is useful for predicting the future. Yet, there are other uses of 'usefulness': 'If a mad physicist were to offer a prize for a completely wrong hypothesis', Wittgenstein continues, then a person holding a most unlikely hypothesis 'would find it useful although it was useless for prediction' (*ibid.*). Again, Wittgenstein underlines that there cannot be a univocal criterion of truth, not even one based on the apparently flexible notion of usefulness, because this very notion depends on the contexts in which it is used. Is a hypothesis useful if it predicts the future correctly? It can be, within one context. But in the context of a prize like the one described in Wittgenstein's example, the usefulness of a hypothesis would be disconnected from the correct prediction of the future, and we would not call the mad hypothesis true, even though it were useful.

The criticism Wittgenstein addresses to pragmatism in these two remarks seems to trace, both in tone and in content, the criticism Ramsey had levelled at the Jamesian conception of truth.[51] Ramsey observed that, in examining truth, if we drop the element of correspondence to reality, the criterion of usefulness itself is empty. Wittgenstein's criticism does not necessarily entail anchorage in a form of realism, in the sense required by a correspondentist perspective. Rather, it entails anchorage in 'the kind of life we lead' (*ibid.*), or in our form of life. It is in this spirit that, in my view, Wittgenstein's notion of use is to be interpreted. The famous maxim 'for a *large* class of cases (. . .) the meaning of a word is its use in the

---

[51] See Boncompagni (forthcoming*b*).

language' (PI, §43) has the methodological sense of directing our attention to the way in which we use words, in order to understand the meaning we have attached to them. The notions of use and of usefulness are married together, but they do not overlap,[52] and the latter—which Wittgenstein does not link to *truth*, but to *meaning*— bears with it precisely the reference to 'the kind of life we lead' that the former risks overlooking. By considering this wider context, it is easy to see that *sometimes, but not always*, we do act and think because actions and thoughts have proved useful. This 'sometimes, but not always' is the point of Wittgenstein's critiques of the pragmatists.

There is an interesting section on this in BT, which partly found its way into PI.[53] Wittgenstein asks himself why human beings think, what for, and considers the example of why they calculate the dimensions of boilers. This way of proceeding has proved its worth. Does it mean that human beings, more generally, *think* because it has proved to pay? Wittgenstein reflects on this, adding some handwritten notes to the typescript. He acknowledges that '*sometimes* one does think because it has proved its worth' (BT, p. 179): in the example of the boilers, after people started calculating the dimensions according to a certain method, the number of explosions decreased. Therefore, in this case thinking has proved its worth. At the same time, Wittgenstein's open questions seem to cast doubt on the possibility of explaining the whole of human thinking by this appeal to what pays or is advantageous:

> Does one think because one thinks that it is advantageous to think?
> Do humans raise their children because that has proved its worth?
> How could one find out *why* humans think? (*ibid.*)

Cautiously, within a general reflection on the connection between usefulness, use, and way of life, Wittgenstein seems to recognize the relevance of usefulness, while also limiting it to certain circumstances.

---

[52] On use and usefulness, see Chap. 4, Section 'Meaning and Understanding'. On the difference between the two concepts in pragmatism and in Wittgenstein, see Schulte (1999) and Moyal-Sharrock (2007, p. 171).

[53] BT, section 55; PI, §§466–470. Note that something similar resurfaces in OC, §474.

In so doing, he also relativizes and contextualizes the pragmatist approach in general.

A few years later, while working on mathematics, Wittgenstein again acknowledges a particular link between usefulness and truth. In a 1937 note, now in RFM,[54] he emphasizes the centrality of the practice of counting in our life. It is because we count in a vast number of everyday activities that we learn this practice with accuracy, attention, and reiteration, he observes. To his imaginary sparring partner who asks him: 'But is this counting only a *use*, then; isn't there also some truth corresponding to this sequence?' Wittgenstein replies: 'The *truth* is that counting has proved to pay [*sich bewährt hat*]'. And to his counterpart, who urges: 'Then do you want to say that "being true" means: being usable (or useful) [*brauchbar (oder nütlich) sein*]?' he replies:

> No, not that; but that it can't be said of the series of natural numbers—any more than of our language—that it is true, but: that it is usable [*brauch bar*], and, above all, *it is used* [*sie werde verwendet*]. (RFM, p. 38)

What matters, then, is not whether or not there is a mathematical truth in the sense of the correspondentist conception of truth but rather whether or not counting is part of our practices. The same lack of sense which characterizes a correspondentist comparison between mathematics and reality, characterizes a correspondentist comparison between 'our language' and reality. The point is that numbers and words are used, and being used in the way they are is what gives them all the meaning there needs to be.[55]

Has Wittgenstein forgotten the joke about the calculus which leads to the desired end but is wrong? What I see here is the overcoming of that objection through a wider conception of usefulness. Usefulness is now connected to use and not simply equated to the satisfaction of desires. At the same time, the concept of rule, not equal but connected to the

---

[54] MS 117, p. 4; RFM, pp. 37–38.
[55] On 'useful', 'usable' and 'used' see Bouveresse (1987, p. 573).

concept of calculus, permits us to see the relationship between mathematics and language games in a new light.

In the development of Wittgenstein's thought, these are the years of the elaboration and re-elaboration of what would become Part I of PI. In the middle of the 1930s, new travel companions emerge—Piero Sraffa[56] among them—as well as new interests and methods. Yet, some background issues as well as some general attitudes about the activity of philosophy persist. In particular, William James remains a constant presence. His PP is for Wittgenstein at times a polemical target, at times a stimulus for the exploration of a psychological phenomenology rich in details, examples, and stories.

After World War II, Wittgenstein's attention towards these aspects becomes even greater. In the last series of lectures that he gave in Cambridge before deciding to stop teaching, explicit and implicit references to James abound, like in the manuscripts and typescripts of the same period.[57] In these texts, although Wittgenstein's desire to avoid any identification with pragmatism is constant, the tone is not totally negative, and the 'good' in pragmatism—to use his expression—is also highlighted.

In August 1946, Wittgenstein reflects on the function of spoken words and pictures in religion's teaching, pointing out that sometimes pictures can perform the same 'service' (*Dienst*) of words in helping us understand some issues, for instance, the idea of the soul that can exist after the body's disintegration. It is here that pragmatism is mentioned again. Indeed, he seems to suggest, in underlining the function or the service of words (and pictures), one may risk overemphasizing the importance of the usefulness of words, and therefore may risk been considered a pragmatist:

> But you aren't a pragmatist? No. For I am not saying that a proposition is true if it is useful.
> The usefulness, i.e. the use, gives the proposition its special sense [*seinen besondern Sinn*], the language-game gives it.

---

[56] On Sraffa and Wittgenstein, see Engelmann (2013b).

[57] See LPP. The 'psychological' manuscripts are those from MS 130 to MS 138, the typescripts are TS 229 and 232. Parts of these writings were later published in RPP, LS and PPF. For a wide-ranging analysis of the manuscripts, prior to their publication, see Schulte (1993).

And in so far as a rule is often given in such a way that it proves useful, and mathematical propositions are essentially akin to rules, usefulness is reflected in mathematical truths.[58]

Wittgenstein once again identifies pragmatism with the equation of useful = true, but what is interesting and new is the explanation he offers as to why he is not a pragmatist. Indeed, Wittgenstein *does not differentiate* the notions of use and usefulness: on the contrary, he seems to equate them. But what he spots is that use or usefulness do not give the sentence its *truth* but rather its *sense*; and that the use, usefulness, or sense is not decided by an external purpose, or by a desired result or end, but by the linguistic game. The priorities are reversed. As Perissinotto (1991, p. 228) puts it, 'it is not that people play this or that game because it has proved useful; rather, the games people play show, among other things, what they consider useful; which scopes they pursue; what is so important and essential for them that it pervades their life, and what instead has only a marginal role'.

As for mathematics, Wittgenstein uses it again to highlight the vicinity between rules and mathematical propositions, in virtue of the fact that rules are, normally, useful, and so usefulness is 'reflected' by—but does not consist of—mathematical truths. In fact, mathematics, one might argue, has developed historically because it served some purposes, and it offered a service.

The clarifications presented in this remark are, in my view, crucial for understanding the vicinity *and* the distance between Wittgenstein and pragmatism. He affirms in no uncertain terms that he is not a pragmatist, because, unlike the pragmatists, he retains: (1) that use or usefulness gives the sense, and not the truth, of a sentence; and (2) that use or usefulness corresponds to the language game; although it is clear that (3) in those contexts in which rules are defined in terms of usefulness, the truth of a sentence is reflected in its usefulness. The main point is that for Wittgenstein it is the language game, ultimately, that gives the sense of a sentence. In other words, sense (use, usefulness) is *internal* to the language

---

[58] MS 131, p. 70. The remark is then in TS 229, p. 252 and TS 245, p. 184 and finally published in RPP I, §266 (I quote from the published version).

game. It is not a purpose, a desire, an expected result *outside* this context, which justifies and gives sense to actions and words. But at the same time, the language game is not a logical-linguistic sphere separated from reality: on the contrary, reality is real, the world is a world, precisely because it is already inevitably within the language game, within the sphere of sense.

A pragmatist could object that in pragmatism too, or at least in some versions of it, there is the same kind of internal relation between the linguistic context and the sense of sentences. Yet I am not suggesting that in pragmatism it is not so. The point is that *in Wittgenstein's perception*, by making truth dependent on a notion of usefulness too abstract with respect to the ordinary contexts of 'the kind of life we lead', pragmatism fails to acknowledge the essential intertwinement between language games and forms of life.

As we have seen, Wittgenstein also recognizes a kinship with pragmatism, although, one might say, not of a very close degree. An undoubtedly *positive* remark on pragmatism—the only one, to my knowledge—was expressed in the same year (1946) during a lecture on philosophical psychology. While dealing with the theme of description and commenting the words of a student who said that 'One might ask what you want the description for', Wittgenstein affirmed: 'Yes; this is the good in pragmatism. What is the description for?' (LPP, p. 26–27).[59]

What is interesting here is that the 'good' in pragmatism, according to Wittgenstein, has to do with *method* and not with a theory of truth (although, of course, the two aspects are not disconnected). In order to understand whether a description is correct, he notices, it is important to ask ourselves how we *use* that description, in which circumstances, and for what purpose. This is a typical Wittgensteinian move, but it is also a typical pragmatist move. We shall return more extensively to this remark and to the issue of method in Chapter 5. Let me just add for the moment that what emerges in the later Wittgenstein's work, especially after World War II, is a re-evaluation of some aspects of the pragmatist approach in which the points of contact with his own approach are explicitly recognized.

---

[59] See also LPP, pp. 145, 266, and a similar point in RPP I, §§635–636.

Finally, let us look quickly at the last occasion in which Wittgenstein refers to pragmatism before OC. In MS 136 (January 1948), in the context of a discussion on seeing aspects, we can read rather problematic remarks concerning how a person can express or explain her experience of 'seeing-as'. Using the well-known example of the duck-rabbit, we can paraphrase the situation as follows; a person might say 'Now *I see it as* a rabbit', or alternatively, 'Now *for me it is* a rabbit'. What is the difference (if any) between these two descriptions? Is there any reason why we should prefer one over the other? 'If he says, "Now for me it is..."'—Wittgenstein observes—one wonders what the advantage may be [*was wir davon haben*]. After all, it could be sheer madness'. After a few lines, referring to the latter expression, he mentions pragmatism: 'The question "What's the advantage" sounds quite pragmatist [*pragmatistisch*]. Though of course it is not (MS 136, pp. 118b, 119b).[60]

This is clearly an unpolished note, and interpreting it is not easy. I will just try to offer one comment. Wittgenstein is reflecting on the possibility, for observers, of modifying the way they see a figure, with the aim of seeing one aspect or another. For instance, before the image of the duck-rabbit, especially if already familiar with the image, observers can alter their gaze and now see a duck, and then a rabbit. Wittgenstein considers the description a person can give of this situation, using expressions such as 'seeing' or 'conceiving', or alternatively describing the object as 'being' something for the observer. One might ask what the advantage is of describing the experience in one way or another. This question, he adds, may sound like a pragmatist question, but 'naturally' it is not.

Now: why does the question sound pragmatist, and why is it not? As I grasp it, Wittgenstein is making a comparison between his technique of asking what the advantage is in adopting a certain description and pragmatism, and he is specifying that he is *not* making a pragmatist move. This sounds a bit surprising as it seems to contradict the remark on the 'good' in pragmatism we have just

---

[60] The lines that follow are in RPP II, §390.

come across. The connotation now seems negative. Yet, in this new context, what Wittgenstein is warning against is a reductive view of pragmatist, its aiming for the mere 'cash value', so to speak. But if we look at both Wittgenstein and pragmatism in a more charitable light, Wittgenstein's move is *not* so distant from pragmatism. In the previous remark from LPP, we needed to grasp the context of an expression in order to understand its meaning. In this remark, we need to be able to manipulate a figure in our imagination, in order to see one or another aspect of it. Therefore, Wittgenstein's invitation, once read in its breadth, is a deeply pragmatist invitation, in the 'good' methodological direction hinted at above, but not in a reductive sense. To ask oneself what the benefits of a given description can be is to pay attention to the effective circumstances and use of our expressions and so, ultimately, to the way we live. Indeed, the whole of Wittgenstein's reflection on 'seeing-as' can be read very fruitfully from a pragmatist standpoint. Wittgenstein, just like the pragmatists to some extent, and particularly William James, works precisely on attitudes or ways of seeing things. I shall come back to this in Chapters 5 and 6.

Concluding Remarks

In the previous pages, I looked at all the occasions in which Wittgenstein refers directly to pragmatism, with the aim of getting a sense of what he meant by 'pragmatism' in OC. In particular, the focus was placed on the first time the term appears in his writings, with an examination of the circumstances in which he encountered this tradition. We saw that the intellectual atmosphere surrounding pragmatism in Cambridge in the first decades of the century was rather hostile and that this hostility was chiefly associated with the Jamesian conception of truth. Wittgenstein himself, in spite of his familiarity with James, in general terms shared this point of view. The work on the first remark on pragmatism also gave the opportunity to take a look at some intellectual friendships and influences and to point out the relevance of Ramsey in Wittgenstein's approaching pragmatism and in his development of a critical attitude towards it, especially in connection to the issue of truth. The conclusion was also drawn that Wittgenstein knew, at least indirectly, the contents of James' P and that it is likely that he read, at least in part, Peirce's CLL.

In the examination of the following remarks, it emerged that while in the first half of the 1930s Wittgenstein shows a critical attitude towards pragmatism, paralleling Ramsey's criticism of the Jamesian conception of truth, in later remarks and chiefly in the second half of the 1940s, he acknowledges some affinities with the pragmatist approach.

At this point, it might be useful to distinguish two aspects of pragmatism and two kinds of attitude in Wittgenstein. The first aspect, exemplified by the pragmatist conception of truth, is that of pragmatism as a *Weltanschauung*, a vision of the world, or a system of philosophy. The second aspect, exemplified by the pragmatic approach to the sense of sentences, is that of pragmatism as a method. It is not a novel distinction. Bertrand Russell already traced it in one of the articles in which he commented on James' P.[61] Russell agreed with the pragmatist method to the extent that it is a form of anti-dogmatism, which casts aside theoretical discussions in the name of pragmatic criteria. But for Russell, the pragmatist conception of truth had to be stigmatized, precisely because it is dogmatic in spite of its good methodological intentions. Yet, the distinction I would like to draw is wider, in both directions, than Russell's. On the one hand, I would like to consider pragmatism as a *Weltanschauung* without limiting it to the Jamesian (or the Peircean) conception of truth, but by extending it to the whole picture of the world that might be built starting from a pragmatist point of view. On the other hand, I would like to consider the pragmatist method as something broader than the anti-dogmatic push envisioned by Russell, and include in it a global attitude towards life and the relationship between life and philosophy, while privileging the concrete and the 'significant'. Let me remain vague on this here: it will become clearer as

---

[61] See the opening paragraphs of 'William James' Conception of Truth', in Russell (1910).

we go along. The general clue, which I think already emerges in what we have examined thus far, is that Wittgenstein expresses a basically negative attitude towards pragmatism as a *Weltanschauung*, but acknowledges affinities with pragmatism as a method. We will have the opportunity to go deeper into this after analysis of the pragmatist themes in OC.

Part II

On Certainty

Chapter 2: Reasonable Doubts and Unshakable Certainties

Preliminary Remarks

After examining the way in which Wittgenstein referred to pragmatism in earlier years, it is now time to enter into the merits of OC, the specific topic of this study.

First, a few words are in order to place OC in the framework of Wittgenstein's development. Part I of PI comprises a work commenced at the beginning of the 1930s and concluded in 1945, by and large prepared for publication by Wittgenstein. From the middle of the 1940s, Wittgenstein continued to fill manuscripts and typescripts, which later were published as Part II of PI (PPF in the 2009 edition), RPP and other volumes. OC belongs to these materials and—together with RC and a part of Volume II of LW—it comprises notes written roughly in the last year and a half of Wittgenstein's life, which never reached the stage of typescript. The editors of the volume affirm that Wittgenstein himself marked the notes as belonging to a single thematic corpus, but there are actually no precise indications as to this; indeed, alleged thematic unity notwithstanding, the interpretations in the literature diverge considerably.[1] What can be said is that the fourth and last part of OC, which contains the majority of the remarks (from §300 to §676), seems the most homogeneous: all of the remarks come from Wittgenstein's last three notebooks, MS 175, 176, and 177, and they are dated with precision from 10 March to 27 April 1951 (Wittgenstein died on 29 April). As we shall see in Chapter 4, it is in these last weeks that Wittgenstein's reflection shows clear affinities with the themes put forward by the classical pragmatists, and especially the so-called pragmatic maxim. The former remarks of OC (from §1 to §299) come from MS 172, 174, and 175; not everything is dated, but the beginning is likely to date back to the first months of 1950 (von Wright 1993, pp. 498, 509).

OC is usually described as particularly pragmatic, so much so that, according to some commentators, it is possible to identify a 'Third Wittgenstein' on the basis of these notes, after the early Wittgenstein of TLP and the later Wittgenstein of PI (Moyal-Sharrock 2004; Moyal-Sharrock and Brenner 2005). Passing over the dispute about whether it is opportune to make this kind of division, the question remains if and to what extent there are features in the last period of his work that allow us to speak of a pragmatic or even a pragmatist turn. In this and the following two chapters, the examination of OC will privilege some themes which, in my view, can lead to a fruitful comparison with pragmatism, in order not only to enrich the characterization of the 'Third' Wittgenstein, but more specifically to individuate positions, examples, arguments, and points of view which can be properly described as pragmatist. It will emerge that the vicinity Wittgenstein felt to pragmatism was real and that when, in OC, §422, he underlined this with some preoccupation, he well knew what he was talking about. By 1951, his familiarity with this tradition went far beyond what the remarks of the preceding years showed, and it certainly was not limited to the Jamesian conception of truth. Naturally, I will not leave out the differences, as they are

---

[1] See van Gennip (2008, pp. 52 ff.); Perissinotto (2011, pp. 151 ff.).

important in understanding the reasons why Wittgenstein would never have accepted an identification with pragmatism.

The following pages move from the clear consonance between Peirce and Wittgenstein on the issue of doubt. Both thinkers show an anti-Cartesian strategy manifest in their rejection of the privacy of the internal world, of the dualism stemming from it, and of doubt as the first move of philosophy. This analysis will lead us to touch on the themes of scepticism and fallibilism. Wittgenstein and Peirce's consonance on doubt is mirrored in their consonance on the issue of certainty. For both, if certainty features as a starting point, it does so not because it is a *foundation*, in a traditional sense, but because it is a *background*; and if it is indubitable, it is so not because it is infallible, but because 'in deed' it is not put in doubt.

Doubt

Doubt and certainty are central issues in OC. Yet, as Stern, van Gennip, and for certain aspects Moyal-Sharrock have highlighted, these themes are not exclusively present in *this* work.[2] There are remarks that show a close resemblance to those of OC in CE, that is, chiefly in MS 119 (1937).[3] MS 119 is indeed also interesting for the comparison with pragmatism. For instance, it contains the same example of the chair as MS 107 and the quote from Goethe's *Faust*, 'In the beginning was the deed', which would reappear in OC.

Here is a note from MS 119, p. 101, as published in CE, p. 379.

> So what does it mean to say: at first the game has to start without including doubt; doubt can only come into it subsequently? Why *shouldn't* doubting

---

[2] Stern (1996, p. 447); Moyal-Sharrock (2007, p. 123); van Gennip (2008) and (2011). See also Citron (2015b).

[3] Other affinities have been identified with respect to RFM (Hutto 2004, p. 29), PI (Perissinotto 2011, p. 169; Rhees 2003, p. 5) and RPP (Perissinotto 2011, pp. 163–164). See also in this light the fragment from MS 107 examined in Chap. 1, and the reflection on 'I know' in Rhees (1984, p. 132) and in section V of PPF.

be there right from the start? But wait a minute—what does doubting look like? The point is—whatever it feels like or however it is expressed, its *surroundings* are quite different from those we are familiar with. (For, since doubt is an exception, the rule is its environment.) . . .

As things are, the *reasons* for doubting are reasons for leaving a familiar track.

Wittgenstein's point, as he further explains in the manuscript, is that doubt cannot be the starting point of a linguistic game because it always occurs within certain surroundings which are *not* doubted. It is certainty, or the rule, and not uncertainty, or doubt, which constitutes the environment of actions and words: without this unquestioned background, doubt itself would not be a doubt, that is, we would not call it 'doubt' because, in a sense, the grammar of this word already includes certainty (CE, p. 383).[4]

These remarks offer a useful introduction to the issue of doubt in OC, as they approach it from a similar point of view, which is also Peirce's point of view. It is the critique of Cartesian doubt as the first step of philosophical reflection. As Wittgenstein puts it in OC, 'if you tried to doubt everything you would not get as far as doubting anything. The game of doubting itself presupposes certainty' (OC, §115).[5]

The philosophical use of doubt overlooks what is essential in its ordinary use: that doubt only occurs within 'surroundings' of certainty. In Wittgenstein's view, this is connected to the public and communitarian character of language. As human beings, we are already within a meaningful world, and a radical doubt operated by a metaphysically isolated subject would be an impossible attempt to escape the shared character of meaning. The Wittgensteinian theme of *Übereinstimmung*, agreement, not meant as a mere convention but as the consonance of voices, is the conceptual tool that unmasks the fancifulness of total doubt. Consequently, a linguistic analysis of the uses of the word 'doubt' sheds light on how certainty itself gives doubt its horizon of sense.

---

[4] See also CE, p. 399.
[5] See also OC, §354.

Similarly, according to what Coliva (2010a, pp. 103 ff.) calls 'the linguistic argument against Cartesian scepticism', for Wittgenstein scepticism proves to be devoid of sense because it violates the criteria of the meaningfulness of a sentence like 'I may be dreaming right now'. The sceptical strategy wants to demonstrate that, since it is not possible to ascertain that I am not dreaming, doubt cannot be defeated by an alleged sensorial awareness: this awareness itself could be part of the dream. Wittgenstein's measure for measure is to notice that, if I were dreaming, these very words—'I may be dreaming'—would be part of the dream, and would not refer to anything external to it; more radically, meaning itself would belong to the dream (OC, §383). The linguistic argument applied to the example of the dream shows the same point as the previous remarks: that doubt can only be the second move of the game, not the first.

Peirce's view is very close to that of Wittgenstein. As Meyers (1967) suggests, in order to understand Peirce's point on doubt, it is useful to start from two principles that shape his vision of knowledge: (1) belief is a habit of action, which can be there even if the individual is not aware of it; (2) human beings cannot go beyond their beliefs and reach the facts of reality. This implies that, although the meanings of 'I believe that *p*' and 'I know that *p*' are different, it is impossible to distinguish between them in the knowledge situation.[6] The starting point is very distant from that of Descartes, and indeed, Peirce's criticism of Cartesianism is radical (according to Meyers, because of this distance, it is also misplaced):

> We cannot begin with complete doubt. We must begin with all the prejudices which we actually have when we enter upon the study of philosophy. These prejudices are not to be dispelled by a maxim, for they are things which it does not occur to us can be questioned. . . . Let us not pretend to doubt in philosophy what we do not doubt in our hearts (W 2, p. 212).[7]

---

[6] Wittgenstein seems very close to this point of view in OC, §177.
[7] Also in CP 5.265, from 'Some Consequences of Four Incapacities', 1868.

Peirce mocks those philosophers—and clearly the main target is Descartes—who imagined that in order to start an inquiry it is sufficient to utter a question or to express a proposition in the interrogative form: this alone 'does not stimulate the mind to any struggle after belief' (W 3, p. 23),[8] and the very idea that a philosophical study could begin by putting everything in doubt is not consistent. If doubt is to have a role, it must be a 'real and living doubt', without which 'all discussion is idle' (*ibid.*).

What is, then, the starting point of philosophical inquiry, if not radical doubt? It is pointless, Peirce argues, to simply write down on a piece of paper that one doubts; rather, researchers must acknowledge that they are constantly 'laden with an immense mass of cognition already formed' (CP 5.416).[9] It is within this complex and multifarious body of knowledge or of beliefs that doubt itself can arise. Of course, it will not concern the *whole* of this system. The point is that the inquiry starts with some *beliefs* which are then put in doubt, and not with doubt itself. In Peirce's words: 'genuine doubt does not talk of *beginning* with doubting' (CP 6.498).[10]

Like Wittgenstein, Peirce opposes the Cartesian strategy by appealing to the background of certainty—that is, belief, in his approach—that makes doubt itself possible.[11] Neither for Wittgenstein nor for Peirce is certainty the result of a process of the purification of ideas led by means of methodical doubt. On the contrary, certainty is primary with respect to any conceptual refinement. As Broyles (1965, pp. 87–88) puts it, doubt is parasitical upon prior belief, and there is an asymmetry between them: while it is always possible to ask people why they doubt, it does not always make sense to ask them why they believe (or why they are sure of) something. Peirce's note on the 'idleness' of abstract discussions, moreover, sounds very akin to

---

[8] From 'The Fixation of Belief', 1878, also in CP 5.376.
[9] From 'What Pragmatism Means', 1905.
[10] From 'Answers to Questions Concerning my Belief in God', ca. 1906.
[11] In both cases, the opposition also concerns other aspects; see Bambrough (1981).

Wittgenstein's image of the 'idle wheels' of language when it 'goes on holiday' (PI, §§38, 132).

The parasitical nature of doubt upon certainty implies that doubt cannot be universal. If it were possible to cast doubt on everything, knowledge on the whole (says Peirce) or language on the whole (says Wittgenstein)—which constitute the *basis* of doubt itself—would be inconceivable. The project of radical doubt is, at bottom, self-undermining. 'A doubt that doubted everything' simply 'would not be a doubt' (OC, §450), because doubts, just like hallucinations, mistakes and false perceptions, are the exceptions, not the rule. In other words, doubt must originate in a particular context and from particular reasons or motives,[12] and this 'must', as Wittgenstein would put it, is logical: it derives from the grammar of the word 'doubt'. The *circumstances* surrounding doubt are an integral part of it, determining its specific features and the manner in which it can arise.[13]

Wittgenstein explains it in this way:

> One doubts on specific grounds. The question is this: how is doubt introduced into the language-game? (OC, §458)

And Peirce, very similarly:

> A person may, it is true, in the course of his studies, find reason to doubt what he began by believing; but in that case he doubts because he has a positive reason for it, and not on account of the Cartesian maxim (W 2, p. 212).[14]

'Positive reasons' (Peirce) or 'specific grounds' (Wittgenstein) are what is required to interrupt the natural attitude of trust which characterizes the background certainties of actions and practices (Perissinotto 2011). Something is needed for this interruption to occur: an accident, an

---

[12] See Menary (2003, pp. 230–231); Coliva (2010a, pp. 107–108); Tiercelin (2010, p. 16) and (2016, p. 183); Hamilton (2014, p. 226).

[13] See OC, §255.

[14] 'Some Consequences of Four Incapacities', 1868, also in CP 5.265.

unexpected event, a problem, or a surprise. Trust indeed is the natural environment of any process of growth and of primary learning or training, including the learning of language (Coliva 2010a, p. 110). Certainties are assimilated as indubitable, not as subject to doubt; it is only afterwards that they can be judged and doubted.

Wittgenstein repeatedly observes that in the process of learning, the child begins by belief, and only *after* belief is established can doubt arise. Indeed, the child normally *believes* the adult: this is how teaching and learning work. If a child immediately doubted what he is taught, that could only be a sign that something went wrong during his learning, or that he did not actually learn what they were teaching him (OC, §283).[15]

In this respect, what happens in the case of human beings is not so different from what happens in the case of animals. In fact, the following example by Peirce finds application both to humans and animals.

> Every decent house dog has been taught beliefs that appear to have no application to the wild state of the dog; and yet your trained dog has not, I guess, been observed to have passed through a period of scepticism on the subject. There is every reason to suppose that belief came first, and the power of doubting long after (CP 5.512).[16]

Another point is that for both thinkers it does not suffice to *want* to doubt in order to be able to genuinely doubt.[17] Doubt cannot be artificial, or voluntary, at least not in its ordinary manifestations. Peirce describes this very efficaciously by putting doubt and surprise side-by-side. Someone cannot decide to *surprise* themselves: if a surprise is genuine, it cannot be thought of in advance, it cannot be planned. A simple act of the will is not enough. In his view, something similar happens in the case of doubt: creating in oneself a genuine doubt is just as impossible as creating in oneself a state of surprise (CP 5.443).[18]

---

[15] See also OC, §§160, 288, 450.
[16] From 'Consequences of Critical Common-Sensism', ca. 1905.
[17] See Tiercelin (2010, p. 17) and (2016, p. 187), Hamilton (2014, p. 159).
[18] From 'Six Characters of Common-Sensism', ca. 1905. See also CP 5.524. Perhaps there is a bit of a stretch in the comparison here, in that in the case of surprise, deciding to surprise oneself

Chapter 2: Reasonable Doubts and Unshakable Certainties 67

Similarly, Wittgenstein asks himself, rhetorically, in OC, §221, whether one can doubt *at will*. As he already stated in PI, §84, we do not doubt simply because it is merely possible for us to imagine a doubt, or to think of a doubt. There seems to be no arbitrary choice involved in doubt. In a note written in 1948, Wittgenstein too makes a comparison in order to see the point more perspicuously; while Peirce evoked the theme of surprise,[19] Wittgenstein mentions mathematics. Just like a person can miscalculate only after having learnt to calculate, and making mistakes in calculating is not voluntary, a person can doubt only after having learnt certain things, and again doubting, he seems to suggest, is not voluntary (RPP II, §343).[20]

Finally, both for Wittgenstein and Peirce, doubt must have *consequences*; it must make a difference in a person's established beliefs and practices.[21] Wittgenstein imagines a situation in which a person doubts that the table is still there when no one sees it, and asks: 'How would his doubt come out in practice? And couldn't we peacefully leave him to doubt it, since it makes no difference at all?' (OC, §120). Peirce puts the matter in a more general way, stating: 'A true doubt is . . . a doubt which really interferes with the smooth working of the belief-habit' (CP 5.510).

I guess the array of similarities does not leave many *doubts* as to the effective vicinity between the two thinkers on these themes. Yet, some differences and nuances come to light once the analysis focuses on the role of doubt in scientific inquiry. For Peirce, doubt plays a primary role in the context of scientific research. Indeed, in this case, also 'feigned hesitancy' plays a great part, and even when it is feigned for mere amusement (W 3, p. 262).[22] There are two kinds of 'holding for true', Peirce specifies in 'The First Rule of Logic' (1898): the practical one, 'which alone is entitled to the name of Belief'; and the scientific one, in which 'the

---

makes surprise itself impossible, while in the case of doubt, it is not decision that makes doubt impossible; more simply, deciding to (genuinely) doubt is impossible.

[19] But also mathematics: see the complete note in 5.443.
[20] From MS 136, p. 140b, and also in Z, §§409–410. See Perissinotto (2011) for an analysis connected to OC.
[21] See Menary (2003, p. 230); Coliva (2010a, p. 106); Tiercelin (2010, pp. 15–16).
[22] 'How to Make our Ideas Clear', 1878, also in CP 5.394.

acceptance of a proposition... remains always provisional'. If a scientist adhered to a proposition in a definite manner, 'personally wedding his fate to it', he would cut himself off from science (EP 2, p. 56). In order to remain in the domain of science, a scientist must always self-consciously deal with hypotheses, be they apparently the most obvious or the most unlikely propositions. A probable hypothesis, indeed, is nothing but a hypothesis which agrees with our preconceived ideas: but the latter can always be wrong, and a good scientist is constantly 'gunning for' mistakes in preconceived ideas (CP 1.120).[23] This positive use of suspicion is what distinguishes a *critical* common-sensist from defenders of common sense, like Thomas Reid and the followers of the Scottish school.

> The Critical Common-sensist will be further distinguished from the old Scotch philosopher by the great value he attaches to doubt, provided only that it be the weighty and noble metal itself, and no counterfeit nor paper substitute. He is not content to ask himself whether he does doubt, but he invents a plan for attaining to doubt, elaborates it in detail, and then puts it into practice... (CP 5.451).[24]

It is only after a long and careful examination of the possible objections to a belief's indubitability, he explains, that the critical common-sensist will be disposed to declare the belief to be indubitable, and even then, after this examination, in any case he will be ready to acknowledge that 'it may be that some of his indubitable beliefs may be proved false' (*ibid.*). Therefore, for Peirce, in science, even apparently indubitable beliefs are hypotheses.

Wittgenstein instead distinguished sharply between the scientist and the philosopher. But this does not mean that he did not pay attention to science and scientific experimentation: on the contrary, there are many remarks on this, precisely in OC. Some of the certainties which are examined—for instance, the certainty that water boils at $100°C$—are the result of scientific experiments or are part of scientific theories, an aspect that Wittgenstein interestingly considers equivalent to their being part of

---

[23] Ca. 1896, also in SW, p. 54.
[24] From 'Six Characters of Common-Sensism', ca. 1905. See also CP 5.514.

school textbooks. But what Wittgenstein points out is that scientific inquiry is based on a framework of knowledge, practices, and instruments, the validity of which is necessarily never put in doubt. For example, a chemist can make experiments on some substances, but he will not doubt that in the same circumstances a given substance would always react in the same way to a given solicitation. Hence, when Lavoisier draws his conclusions, he would not say, 'it would happen otherwise another time'; he does not, because he has a steady world-picture, not invented but learnt when he was a child. This world-picture does not have a hypothetical nature, in that it constitutes the 'obvious foundation' (*selbstverständliche Grundlage*) of his inquiry (OC, §167). Doubt does have a role in science, but it rests on an apparatus which remains exempt from doubt. The scientist may have plenty of doubts, but not regarding the existence of the apparatus with which he works: this is taken for granted (OC, §337). The distinction envisioned here is at the core of OC. It is the distinction between empirical propositions and what commentators call hinges, using the term (*Angeln*) introduced by Wittgenstein just a few paragraphs later:

> ... the *questions* that we raise and our *doubts* depend on the fact that some propositions are exempt from doubt, are as it were like hinges on which those turn.
> That is to say, it belongs to the logic of our scientific investigations that certain things are *in deed* not doubted (OC, §§341–342).

It is worth noticing (and as far as I know the literature has largely ignored this[25]) that it is precisely in relation to *scientific inquiry* that Wittgenstein elaborates this famous image.

There is no reason to think that Peirce would not agree with these remarks.[26] Yet, as we have seen, in dealing with science and doubt, his aim is to underline that for the scientist, the acceptance of a proposition always remains open and provisional. In this sense, whereas for Peirce

---

[25] Hamilton (2014, p. 97) is an exception; nevertheless, he does not linger on this point.

[26] See Sections 'Wittgenstein's "hinges"' and '"Indubitables" and Regulative Assumptions in Peirce' (in this chapter) for a more cogent comparison on the theme of hinges.

the danger lies in believing too much (CP 5.517),[27] Wittgenstein would perhaps object that the danger lies in believing too little and always casting doubt on what is obvious.

Moore, Scepticism and Fallibilism

OC deals with doubt and certainty by working on two fronts: on the one hand, against scepticism; on the other hand, against G.E. Moore's attempt to defeat scepticism through the defence of common sense. The texts which Wittgenstein has in mind when writing the notes of OC are chiefly Moore's 'A Defence of Common Sense' (1925) and 'Proof of an External World' (1939).[28]

Very briefly, in the former article Moore lists and defends a series of propositions like 'There exists a body and it is my body', 'The earth existed for many years before my birth', 'I am a human being', and so on. Moore affirms that these propositions are rightly considered true but also that until now, contrary to what many philosophy have claimed, no one has really been able to analyse them. In his view, the analysis should lead to elementary propositions regarding sense data. The theme is partially resumed, though in a different perspective, in the latter essay, which opens with the Kantian statement that it is a 'scandal of philosophy' that the existence of things outside ourselves cannot be proved. Moore takes on the task himself, focusing on the idea that the existence of the external world

---

[27] But see also CP 5.451.
[28] Both republished in Moore (1959). According to M. Williams (2003), Wittgenstein generally refers to 'Proof of an External World' in the first 65 sections of OC, and to 'A Defence of Common Sense' in the rest of the notes. To be thorough, Moore's 'Certainty', published in the same 1959 volume but already known before (it was a conference Moore held in 1941), should be added to these texts, as well as another paper Moore read in 1939 at the *Moral Science Club*, now known with the title 'Being Certain that One is in Pain' (Moore 1993). Finally, some works by Malcolm might have had a role (see Malcolm 1942 and 1949), and also John Henry Newman's 1870 *An Essay in Aid of a Grammar of Assent* (Newman 1979; see Kienzler 2006; Pritchard 2015). On Moore and Wittgenstein, see Stroll (1994) and Coliva (2010a). On Moore and Wittgenstein's discussion in 1939 see Citron (2015b).

would be proved if the existence of 'things which are to be met with in space' were proved, which *is* effectively proved—according to his example—by the simple existence of two hands. The dissatisfaction of philosophers before this proof, Moore explains, derives from their desire to prove the premises of the argument, that is, the assertion 'Here is one hand, and here is another', uttered while showing one's hands. But this kind of proof cannot be given: according to Moore, it is possible to know things which cannot be proved, and among these things are the premises of the argument.

Before examining Wittgenstein's move, I would like to consider Bilgrami's (2004) proposal, which puts Moore's anti-scepticism and the pragmatists' anti-scepticism side-by-side. Building on Pryor (2000), Bilgrami sums up the sceptical challenge in the following dilemma. In order to affirm to know p with certainty, we must be able to exclude the possibility that q, where q is incompatible with the truth of p (q is, for instance, that we are dreaming). But if the grounds (for instance, perceptual grounds) for which we affirm to know p are based on the fact that q is false, and if q describes a condition which could obtain while we still possess those grounds, then we would never be able to affirm that we know p with certainty. According to Bilgrami, Moore replies by sustaining that in some cases, those in which we have the experience of p, we have a '*prima facie* immediate justification' to believe that p, and this suffices in order to say that we know p. More precisely, the *prima facie* condition characterizes the belief as justified, in the absence of further evidence, *even if it could be confuted* by further evidence. Bilgrami conceives the *prima facie* tactic as an application of the fallibilist–pragmatist strategy, which negates doubt as a starting point, but admits doubt as an open eventuality.

As Bilgrami takes it, there is a consonance between the Moorean-pragmatist position and the Wittgensteinian position, but it does not go very far. After reading Moore through the lenses of Pryor, he reads Wittgenstein through the lenses of Crispin Wright[29] and argues that for

---

[29] Wright (2004a) and (2004b). Interestingly, while working on perceptual justification, Coliva (2015) labels Pryor and Wright's positions, respectively, as 'liberal' and 'conservative': the former

Wittgenstein it is only the institutional and conventional character of the hinge proposition, 'the external world exists', that makes it indubitable. This is, in his reading, what guarantees the inference from 'I have the experience of a hand' to 'I have a hand' (and therefore to 'the world exists', in an inevitably circular reasoning). Bilgrami concludes that if, on the one hand, both for the pragmatists and for Wittgenstein doubt comes after certainty and hinge propositions cannot be doubted while the inquiry is underway, on the other hand, it is only for the pragmatists that a fallibilist option is valid: in the perspective of Wittgenstein, no doubt could ever jeopardize the indubitability of hinges, guaranteed by convention.

In my view, although Bilgrami's analysis of the pragmatist core in Moore's position is brilliant, his partial comparison with Wittgenstein is a lost opportunity. Unfortunately, he does not consider Wittgenstein's use of the example of the dream, which could offer an alternative perspective. Moreover, Wright's conventionalist reading of Wittgenstein, on which Bilgrami bases his work, finds no validation in Wittgenstein's writings.[30] According to the latter, what is at stake is *not* how to guarantee or justify an inference, nor how to find a conventionalist way out of the problem. Quite the opposite: Wittgenstein underlines that we do not need conventions because what 'solidifies' human agreement is the form of life within which it grows, and forms of life are not conventions, at least not in the ordinary sense of the word (Witherspoon 2003).[31] As I see it, some interpretations of Wittgenstein are vitiated by a strictly epistemological vision of our relationship with doubt and certainty. It is precisely by evading the game of true and false, the epistemic view, that Wittgenstein— as Perissinotto (1991, p. 83) notices—avoids *both* metaphysics *and* scepticism. What is required is not to reply to the sceptical doubt, but to realize that that doubt is an illusion because it is a grammatical impossibility

---

because it claims that an appropriate course of experience suffices to justify a belief about material objects, the latter because it claims that justification requires, besides the perceptual experience, a warranted assumption about the existence of the external world. Coliva's own position ('moderatism') claims that the assumption is needed, but it does not require in turn to be warranted (it is, in fact, unwarrantable).

[30] I agree with Coliva (2010a, p. 135 ff.) and (2015, p. 124) on this.

[31] See Section 'Secondary Literature: Relativism and Other Issues' in Chap. 5.

Chapter 2: Reasonable Doubts and Unshakable Certainties 73

(in the wide sense of 'grammar' to which Wittgenstein accustomed us). Whereas the sceptic says: I cannot investigate everything, but I should; Wittgenstein says: it is part of our method of doubting and investigating that certain things are considered absolutely fast (OC, §151). 'What is needed is to show them', as he put it in a conversation with Malcolm, 'that the highest degree of certainty is... something logical: that there is a point at which there is neither any "making more certain" nor any "turning out to be false"' (Malcolm 1958, p. 91).

Yet what is relevant is that *this does not imply infallibility*:

> It would be completely *misleading* to say: 'I believe my name is L.W.' And this too is right: I cannot be making a *mistake* about it. But that does not mean that I am infallible about it (OC, §425).

There is a form of fallibilism in Wittgenstein's position too, then, pace Bilgrami. What shape does it assume? Following Perissinotto (2011, pp. 170–172), I think that Wittgenstein's point is that the *physical* possibility of a failure of knowledge in these matters is not ruled out, and yet at the same time its *grammatical* possibility *is* ruled out in the logic of our words, that is, in the logic of our life. Let me elaborate a little. Although it is highly unlikely, it can turn out that my real name is actually different than I always thought—for instance, I may discover that according to the General Registrar's Office I have a middle name, or my name is spelled differently than I assumed. This is certainly possible. Similarly, it is possible that tomorrow, opening the door of my house, I would find myself in front of a ravine—a landslide might have occurred. But my acting with no doubt when I use my name or open the door and walk out in the morning manifests the logical impossibility of mistakes: it manifests that certainty is an inner trait of our life. To use Perissinotto's words (2011, p. 170),

> even if it can of course occur that the individual who doubts every day before opening his front door may just once (alas!) be right, this does not mean that we ought to consider the certainty with which every day and several times a day we open our front door to be hasty or stupid.

The verb 'can' in the quoted passage from OC, §425 is used *logically* and not *physically*, where 'logically' has to do with the grammar of our practices. As Wittgenstein also points out in another remark (OC, §155), in a sentence like 'in certain circumstances a man cannot make a mistake', if the verb 'can' is used 'logically', the meaning of the sentence is *not* that the man cannot say anything false. To repeat, the impossibility of mistakes on what Wittgenstein calls 'hinges' is compatible with a form of fallibilism. It is so in virtue of Wittgenstein's constant call to the way we use words, and by this to the way we live: in our practices, we act with a basic certainty that knows no mistakes because it is not a form of knowledge; while at the level of knowledge, the possibility of being wrong always remains open. This is the reason why we cannot make mistakes regarding the basic hinges governing our everyday activities, but at the same time we are not infallible.

What does the pragmatists' anti-sceptical fallibilism look like? The affinity, underlined by Bilgrami, with Moore's idea of premises which cannot be proved is perfectly clear in the following remark by Peirce.

> Indubitable propositions must be ultimate premises, or at least, must be held without reference to precise proofs. For what one cannot doubt one cannot argue about; and no precise empirical argument can free its conclusion altogether from rational doubt (CP 5.515).[32]

Later, Peirce also notices (CP 5.516) that when we look at our original beliefs with a critical attitude, the mind seems to pretend to have reasons for believing them and is prone to imagining that a sort of inductive proof or inductive process must exist, perhaps forgotten, which supports these beliefs. In his view, this is probably true, in a very generalized sense of induction, but 'this admission must be accompanied by the emphatic

---

[32] From 'Consequences of Critical Common-Sensism', ca. 1905. See also W 3, p. 24 (or CP 5.376).

denial that the indubitable belief is inferential, or is "accepted". It simply remains unshaken as it always was' (*ibid.*). Therefore, we do not arrive at original beliefs through inferences, but we simply find ourselves already having these beliefs. The non-inferential nature of original beliefs in this sense appears to support Peirce's anti-sceptical and fallibilist strategy.

Peirce's fallibilism, in conclusion, is simply another name for his critical common-sensism, according to which there are indubitable propositions and beliefs, and yet none of them can be absolutely and eternally certain. To use his own words:

[W]hile it is possible that propositions that really are indubitable, for the time being, should nevertheless be false, yet in so far as we do not doubt a proposition we cannot but regard it as perfectly true and perfectly certain;...while holding certain propositions to be each individually perfectly certain, we may and ought to think it likely that some one of them, if not more, is false (CP 5.498).[33]

What is striking in the comparison with Wittgenstein is that while the latter attempts to distance himself from the merely cognitive plane, Peirce places himself fully in that domain, albeit in a very broad sense of the word. This does not mean that Wittgenstein values and Peirce neglects the role of life, rather that Peirce (but not Wittgenstein) interprets human life as the life of an epistemic subject, himself a sign and interpreter in a world of signs and interpretations. In Wittgenstein, and in the 'Third' Wittgenstein in particular, this aspect tends to dissolve in the everyday traffic of practices and ways of doing.

The emphasis on the non-epistemic nature of certainties has been a common trait of many interpretations of OC ever since the first analyses published in the literature.[34] In this sense, those who conversely underline the sceptical aspect in Wittgenstein's reflection seem not to grasp the genuine bearings of his proposal because they remain on an epistemic terrain. Yet, there is a deep meaning in what Stanley Cavell, referring to

---

[33] From 'Pragmaticism and Critical Common-Sensism', 1905.
[34] See for instance McGinn (1989).

Wittgenstein, calls 'the truth of scepticism', or 'the moral of scepticism'[35]: its 'truth' does not consist of the discovery of a fallacy in our epistemic system, but rather of the acknowledgement that the primary relationship we have with the world, with other human beings and with ourselves is *not* epistemic in character.[36] As he puts it, the point is that 'the human creature's basis in the world as a whole, its relation to the world as such, is not that of knowing, anyway not what we think of as knowing' (Cavell 1979, p. 241). In this sense, those readings which see in scepticism either an ally or an adversary of Wittgenstein on the terrain of epistemology (and not, as in Cavell, on the *rough ground* of forms of life), both miss the point. This is the case, for instance, not only for Wright but also for the 'classical' Kripke (1982), as well as for Pritchard (2011) (while Pritchard 2016 proposes a somewhat different reading, as we shall see). In my view, it is partially so also in Tiercelin (2010) and (2016), though she acknowledges that in Wittgenstein the assent given to beliefs is not epistemic.[37] As she has it, Peirce and Wittgenstein refuse the sceptical scenario for the same reasons: its alleged general applicability, which makes it incomprehensible, and its alleged private and voluntary aspect (Tiercelin 2010, pp. 16–17).Yet, their respective strategies produce divergent outcomes: for Peirce, the result is realist (in the specific metaphysical sense of Peirce's realism), while for Wittgenstein, it is neo-Pyrrhonian, that is, it is a sceptical reply to scepticism. As she puts it in Tiercelin (2016, p. 201), it is only in Peirce that we find 'the living (and not merely regulative) rational hope to reach truth and knowledge', thanks to science and to the possibility of building a '*scientific realist metaphysics*'. By contrast, in her reading, in Wittgenstein's case, in no way is it possible to judge a rule, and the only instruments available to change a *Weltbild* and its form of life are persuasion and conversion. We shall come back to the themes of change and comparison between *Weltbilder* in Chapter 5. For now, suffice it to suggest that a Cavellian reading of OC could help to better understand

---

[35] Cavell (1979, pp. 7, 47–8, 241, 496).

[36] I find Bax (2013) illuminating on this. See also Putnam (2006) and Shieh (2006).

[37] See Tiercelin (2010, p. 25); Tiercelin (2016, p. 188).

Wittgenstein's reference to persuasion and conversion, which many have interpreted as a resignation to incommunicability.

Before turning to this, we need to further the comparison with Peirce on the other side of doubt: the side of certainty.

Wittgenstein's 'hinges'

'We know,' Wittgenstein states in OC, §340, 'with the same certainty with which we believe *any* mathematical proposition, how the letters A and B are pronounced, what the colour of human blood is called, that other human beings have blood and call it "blood"'. What is the nature of this certainty? Why does Wittgenstein equate mathematical certainty (and notice that he underlines the word 'any': he is not only concerned with propositions like 2 + 2 = 4 but with trust in mathematics in general) to linguistic capacity and the acknowledgement of something as basic as the fact that human beings have blood?

These questions lead to the core of the debate on OC. Indeed, one of the most discussed issues is the nature of the so-called 'hinge propositions'. Wittgenstein does not use this expression, which was first introduced into the debate by John W. Cook, in a much-criticized article (Cook 1980, p. 20); yet, according to those who adopt it, the expression was at least suggested by Wittgenstein in the remarks that follow the above-quoted passage. It is worth citing the metaphor more completely.

> That is to say, the *questions* that we raise and our *doubts* depend on the fact that some propositions are exempt from doubt, are as it were like hinges on which those turn.
> That is to say, it belongs to the logic of our scientific investigations that certain things are *in deed* not doubted.
> But it isn't that the situation is like this: We just *can't* investigate everything, and for that reason we are forced to rest content with assumption. If I want the door to turn, the hinges must stay put (OC, §§341–343).

Interestingly, the manuscript (MS 175, pp. 48r–48v) shows successive formulations of the first remark, in one of which Wittgenstein uses the term 'indubitability' (*Zweifelsfreiheit*) with respect to hinges. This is clearly a concept that Peirce uses very often. Both also write of certainties that are 'in deed' not doubted: Wittgenstein uses the words '*in der Tat nicht angezweifelt*' in the following remark, and Peirce speaks of beliefs that are 'not in fact doubted' in 'The Fixation of Belief' (W 3, p. 24; CP 5.376). I have already underlined that here Wittgenstein is concerned with *scientific* investigations—the natural environment of Peirce's reflections. Finally, to anticipate a passage that I will analyse in depth later, another terminological coincidence is worthy of note. In a late version of the pragmatic maxim, while explaining that pragmatism as he intends it is a method for ascertaining the meaning of 'intellectual concepts', Peirce uses the very same image of hinges. In fact, he defines intellectual concepts as 'those upon the structure of which arguments concerning objective facts may *hinge* (CP 5.467, my emphasis).[38] We shall come back to this.

One last note regarding words before proceeding. There is an oscillation in OC between the terms '*Sicherheit*' (sureness) and '*Gewissheit*' (certainty). As far as I understand, '*Sicherheit*' has less of an epistemological connotation than '*Gewissheit*', and Wittgenstein uses it as often as—if not more often than—the latter. Despite this, the English translation shows a bias towards 'certainty'. There may have been semantic nuances or philological reasons for this propensity, but it is a fact that the debate on OC has been strongly influenced by this emphasis, especially owing to the title given to Wittgenstein's notes.

The only other remark in which Wittgenstein makes use of the image of hinges is the following:

> The mathematical proposition has, as it were officially, been given the stamp of incontestability. I.e.: 'Dispute about other things; *this* is immovable—it is a hinge on which your dispute can turn' (OC, §655).

---

[38] From 'Pragmatism in Retrospect: a Last Formulation', ca. 1906, also in EP 2, pp. 401–402 and SW, p. 272. James uses the term 'hinge' as well, in connection with themes relevant to Wittgenstein: in discussing whether attention involves a 'principle of spiritual activity' or not, he affirms that this question is like a hinge on which our picture of the world swings between different perspectives (PP, p. 424).

Chapter 2: Reasonable Doubts and Unshakable Certainties 79

Like in OC, §340, the focus is on mathematical certainty and the point, like the following remarks in OC help clarify, is the (at least partial) comparability with other everyday certainties and with the 'confidence in the obvious' that speaking a language and being part of a form of life presuppose and ground.

It is curious that the cornerstone of the debate on OC consists of an image Wittgenstein uses only twice and that an in-depth debate is lacking on the issue which seems a priority in these two remarks, that is, the similarity between mathematical and everyday certainties. But as is well known, commentators use the expressions 'hinges' and 'hinge propositions' to refer more generally to the truisms Wittgenstein considers in OC, partly derived from Moore (such as 'Here is a hand' or 'The earth existed for a long time before my birth') and partly added by Wittgenstein himself (such as 'Water boils at 100°C', 'Books do not disappear when one puts them in a drawer' or 'I have never been on the moon').

Wittgenstein also uses other images to describe truisms. One of these is the metaphor of the riverbed of thoughts: although the riverbed can move slightly and change its shape by obeying the movements of the water, with respect to the latter it is fixed and represents its borders (its rules).[39] Other pictures are those of the axis of rotation of a body, immobile thanks to the movement around it (OC, §152); of things removed or pushed aside from the traffic (OC, §210); of the scaffolding of thoughts (OC, §211); of the 'rock bottom' (*Boden*: also ground, soil) and of the foundation-walls of a house, which are, as it were, 'carried' by the house itself (OC, §248). These images are not immediately overlapping. They may belong to a family, but there are differences among them—the function of something removed from the traffic is not the function of an axis of rotation or of a riverbed—and there are differences between the certainties Wittgenstein describes. According to Schulte (2005), for instance, Wittgenstein used the image of hinges when concerned with basic rules or notions, and the image of the axis when concerned with blatancies that go without saying. But here I'm not

---

[39] I shall come back to this in the last chapter.

interested in the relationship between the different pictures and the different examples, nor in a classification[40] of hinges: what matters is to bear in mind that the hinge metaphor is not the only nor perhaps even the best one. In my view, the image of the axis of rotation, which remains fixed in virtue of the movement around it, is particularly evocative and immediately suggests a novel approach to the vexed question of foundations.[41] Hence, it is only because it is so widely used in the literature that I am referring to the metaphor of hinges.

Hinges are those platitudes that, being at the very basis of our judging, acting, and living, constitute the standard of certainty itself. As Wittgenstein told Malcolm, they belong to our frame of reference: 'If I had to give *them* up, I shouldn't be able to understand *anything*' (Malcolm 1958, p. 92). For this reason, Moore is wrong to attempt to prove them or to find sensorial evidence supporting them, and he is also wrong to simply assert that he *knows* them. It is not a matter of *known* certainties, but of certainties which stand fast and are absolutely solid in that they are part of the very *method* of inquiry (OC, §151), they shape its framework. Precisely for this reason, it is inappropriate to say that one *knows* them (OC, §243). Indeed, if one says 'I know', one must be able to give grounds for this knowledge and demonstrate that what is claimed to be true is true. Asserting that we know a hinge amounts to accepting this duty (giving grounds), and thus, in the end, since it is not possible to give stronger grounds to what already constitutes a basic ground, it amounts to casting doubt on the very possibility of judging and knowing. The point is that by establishing the 'space' of doubts, that which makes doubts possible, hinges are not themselves objects exposed to doubt.

Before going onto the comparison with the pragmatists, I would like to briefly recall the main positions on hinges in the secondary literature. As mentioned, the expression 'hinge proposition' was introduced by Cook (1980), but already in 1972 G.H. von Wright had questioned the propositionality of *Weltbild* certainties, and spoken of *Vor-Wissen* or pre-knowledge:

---

[40] The most complete is probably in Moyal-Sharrock (2007, pp. 100 ff.).
[41] Besides Schulte (2005, p. 71), see Winch (1998, p. 198) and Hamilton (2014, p. 97).

Considering the way language is taught and learnt, the fragments underlying the uses of language are not originally and strictly *propositions* at all. The *Vor-Wissen* is not propositional knowledge. But if this foundation is not propositional, what then *is* it? It is, one could say, a *praxis*..., a pre-praxis..., and not yet full-fledged action (von Wright 1972, pp. 57–58).[42]

According to von Wright (1972, p. 52), the kind of certainty Wittgenstein is concerned with is 'a certainty in our practice of judging rather than in our *intellection* of the content of judgments'. Jerry Gill (1974) instead talked of tacit knowledge, he too connecting it with knowing-how and underlining that these certainties are generally *shown* and not *said*. In his view, since ordinary knowledge presupposes tacit knowledge, we generally know much more than what we can say. Some years later, in one of the first complete studies on OC, Marie McGinn (1989) highlighted the non-epistemic character of certainties, even in the sense of tacit knowledge. Wittgenstein's remarks on 'Moore-type propositions', she says, show that our relationship with them cannot be properly described in terms of knowledge: 'our certainty (...) is a form of practical confidence that is better expressed in the words "this is what we do" than in the words "this is true"' (McGinn 1989, p. 134).[43]

Another historically influential interpretation is that put forth by Avrum Stroll,[44] who proposed a foundational reading of hinges, though distinguishing Wittgenstein's strain from traditional foundationalism. For Wittgenstein's position, Stroll introduces the term 'rupturalist foundationalism', which discriminates between certainty and knowledge, asserting that certainty, located outside the language game, grounds knowledge. This categorical distinction, as we shall see, is at the origins of the difference that Stroll sees between Wittgenstein and Peirce. As for propositionality, according to Stroll Wittgenstein's position changes through time, from a propositional to a non-propositional view of hinges.

---

[42] This paper was republished with revisions in von Wright (1982).
[43] See also Rhees (2003, p. 89).
[44] See Stroll (1994) and (2004). Another foundationalist interpretation is Brice (2014).

Also Peter Winch, in an article published posthumously in 1998, affirmed that two ways of thinking are up against each other in OC: there are 'eggshells'[45] of Wittgenstein's earlier view of propositions, as well as a novel proposal centred on action and on judging itself as a form of action.[46]

Stroll's foundationalist interpretation is strongly opposed by Michael Williams (2005), who, calling attention to the centrality of contexts, highlights how a hinge certainty only works within one context, and can be criticized or undermined within another. A somewhat similar view is advanced by Wright (2004a, 2004b), according to whom—as already mentioned—we have an epistemic relationship with certainties which can be shaped in terms of a non-evidential warrant or, more precisely, a 'rational entitlement': we have the right to accept these certainties not because we have proof of their truth, but because, given the risk of any epistemic claim, we are entitled to make the necessary presuppositions and trust them. As Coliva (2010a, pp. 135–136) underlines,[47] this view is quite distant from that of Wittgenstein, who would negate the existence of anything 'risky' in the epistemic enterprise, and would probably also negate that what is at stake is an epistemic enterprise. Indeed, one of the quoted passages on hinges seems precisely to oppose this view, when Wittgenstein explains that the point is *not* that 'we just *can't* investigate everything, and for that reason we are forced to rest content with assumption' (OC, §343).

Another variant of the epistemic view (besides Williams' contextualism and Wright's rational entitlement) is the combination of epistemic externalism and Wright's approach which Pritchard (2011) calls 'neo-Mooreanism'. What Wittgenstein objects to in Moore—Pritchard states—is not the possibility of knowing hinges, but the possibility of

---

[45] Cf. Wittgenstein's MS 129, p. 181.

[46] As a forerunner of the later view, Winch cites PI, §§545–546, two remarks which, interestingly, sound reminiscent of William James' perspective on the bond between meaning and feeling. In the same manuscripts containing originally these remarks, MS 129 and MS 165, Wittgenstein makes explicit reference to James on contiguous themes and on a similar example. I will work on these references in Chapter 6.

[47] See also Pritchard (2016, pp. 77 ff.), whose criticism is not focused on Wittgenstein but on the validity of Wright's position as an anti-sceptical strategy.

Chapter 2: Reasonable Doubts and Unshakable Certainties 83

having a reflective access to this knowledge and its reasons. It is a position effectively reminiscent of Moore's, but, in my view, it does not mirror Wittgenstein's criticism, which is more radical and has to do with the epistemic nature of hinges in general, and not only with reflective accessibility. More recently, Pritchard (2016, pp. 90 ff.) has put forth a form of non-epistemic reading labelled '*nonbelief* reading'. In this view, hinges are not belief, but rational and ungrounded commitments, towards which we nevertheless can take a sort of 'belief-like' propositional attitude. Although not being in the market for rationally grounded knowledge, according to Pritchard, hinge commitments provide an essential ingredient for a successful anti-sceptical strategy.

Schönbaumsfeld (2016) too retains that epistemic readings go wrong in attributing epistemicity to hinges. She also retains that the pragmatic readings, like Moyal-Sharrock's (see below), err as well, because they do not realize that what is ruled out by Wittgenstein is the applicability of the very concept of certainty to hinges. In her view, certainty is a bipolar concept, just like knowledge, but when we *rely on* something, or take something *for granted*, we cannot (logically) be uncertain about it; hence, we cannot be certain either. She concludes that by misconstruing the role of hinges as a species of certainty, the pragmatic readings 'cannot but end up attributing some sort of (unpalatable) pragmatism to Wittgenstein' (2016, p. 180). I cannot see why this attribution (be it palatable or not) should follow from the misconstruction of the hinge as a species of certainty; yet, I agree with Schönbaumsfeld on the inappropriateness of applying the concept of certainty, if interpreted in a strict sense, to hinges.

Finally, the issue of propositionality vs non-propositionality and its connection with 'sayability' and 'non-sayability' have been the object of a debate between Danièle Moyal-Sharrock and Annalisa Coliva. Both hold a non-epistemic view, but while the former affirms that hinges are not propositions and they cannot be said, the latter affirms that they are propositions—though, she specifies, in a 'relaxed' sense of the term—and that they can be said.[48] More precisely, Moyal-Sharrock (2007, p. 72)

---

[48] Pritchard (2016) shows similarities with this position, albeit the two authors seem to differ on the issue of the rationality of hinges.

describes hinges as 'indubitable, foundational, nonempirical, grammatical, ineffable, in action' and introduces the notion of '*Doppelgänger*' (2007, pp. 140–141), in order to explain the cases in which an (apparent) hinge can be uttered. When this happens, for instance, when someone says, 'This is my hand', the sentence uttered is not the hinge, but an empirical double, which has a precise meaning in a particular context (in the example, the sentence is perfectly understandable if pronounced after a surgical operation). But in the case of real hinges, nothing meaningful can be *said*.[49] There is, in this sense, a continuity between the TLP distinction between saying and showing and OC, in which what cannot be said, but only shown, is the logic of the *Weltbild* and the background certainties that draw the boundary between sense and nonsense.[50] In this respect, Moyal-Sharrock talks of 'logical pragmatism'. Using Robert Brandom's distinction between a broad and a narrow conception of pragmatism (Brandom 2002), she claims that the later Wittgenstein is a pragmatist 'in the broad sense' and in particular that in OC he puts forth a form of logical pragmatism, which she defines as 'the view that our basic beliefs are a know-how, and that this know-how is *logical*—that is, that it is *necessary* to our making sense'.[51]

In Coliva's (2010a) alternative approach, the difference between hinges and empirical propositions does not lie in the non-propositionality of the former, and even less so in their ineffability, but in their normative nature.[52] But this does not block the possibility of meaningfully pronouncing a hinge precisely *qua* hinge (Coliva 2010a, p. 174): on the contrary, this is what happens when we teach the 'basics' of our culture or when we recall a moral norm to someone. To be sure,

---

[49] An even more radical view is that of Wolgast (1987), according to whom what is precluded is not only the possibility of uttering a hinge, but also of talking about it—which is the reason why Wittgenstein was unsatisfied with his own way of dealing with these issues; cf. OC, §358, and see also Rhees (2003, p. 58).

[50] See also Perissinotto (1991, pp. 148, 203) and McGinn (2001).

[51] Moyal-Sharrock (2003, p. 128), also in (2007, p. 173). On sense in relation to the normativity of hinges, see also Putnam (2000). For a criticism of Moyal-Sharrock's position, see Brice (2014, pp. 15 ff.).

[52] See also Kober (1996).

Moyal-Sharrock (2007, p. 67) admits that hinges can be said in heuristic circumstances; what Coliva adds is that only by acknowledging hinges with full propositionality are we able to grasp how they, once said, can fulfil a communicative function.[53]

As I see it, once the opposition between propositional and non-propositional is reinterpreted pragmatically—and pragmatistically: Pihlström (2012)—in non-dichotomic terms, Moyal-Sharrock and Coliva's views are not so distant from one another. Indeed, Wittgenstein *intentionally* leaves the notion of propositionality vague (OC, §320). The 'animal' certainty highlighted by Moyal-Sharrock represents a crucial aspect of OC[54]; yet, making it its principal characteristic risks oversimplifying Wittgenstein's remarks and overlooking his persistent interest in the linguistic and cultural nature of human beings and communities. Conversely, Coliva's insistence on the propositionality of hinges risks preventing us from seeing how normative understanding (but also propositional understanding in the strict sense) is from the very beginning a *practice* guided by *habits* and rooted in *know-how*.[55] This anti-dichotomic stance, so pervasive in pragmatism, is in harmony with Wittgenstein's urging us to free ourselves from the idea that concepts possess sharp and well-defined boundaries (Calcaterra 2003b, p. 135).

'Indubitables' and Regulative Assumptions in Peirce

Russell Goodman (2002, p. 19) identifies two features of OC that are most promising for the comparison with pragmatism (with James in particular): 'a sense that not all empirical propositions, or beliefs, play

---

[53] For a further reply by Moyal-Sharrock, see Moyal-Sharrock (2013a). More recently, while building on her understanding of hinges, Coliva (2015) proposes what she calls a 'hinge epistemology', without thereby offering—if I get her correctly—an epistemic reading of OC. Her view is that an appropriate conception of hinges as unwarranted and unwarrantable assumptions can ground a new approach to perceptual justification and rationality itself.

[54] See OC, §§359, 475.

[55] See Ryle (1945).

the same role; and a sense of the interrelation of action and thought'. While the latter aspect can be investigated through the perspective of the pragmatic maxim (see Chapter 4), the former concerns hinges, which can be compared to the pragmatists' approach to indubitable beliefs and common sense. Before extending the analysis to common sense, on which I will consider both Peirce and James, I would like to explore the more limited comparison which has been proposed between the Wittgensteinian notion and two Peircean ideas. Broyles (1965) and, later and independently, Johanson (1994) focus on hinges and what Peirce calls 'original beliefs' or 'indubitables'. More recently, Howat (2013) has compared hinges to the 'regulative assumptions' exemplified by the Peircean notion of truth. Both the proposals by Broyles and Johanson, and that of Howat, face some problems.

Let us start from Peirce's description of indubitable beliefs. Besides what one can read in the remarks already seen, Peirce works on this in the context of his writings on critical common-sensism (1905–1906). He lists three kinds of indubitability:

> [T]here are, besides perceptual judgments, original (i.e., indubitable because uncriticized) beliefs of a general and recurrent kind, as well as indubitable acritical inferences (CP 5.442).

Peirce does not linger on perceptual judgements; he defines acritical inferences as those in which the subject, though aware of the fact that one belief follows from another, does not realize that the reasoning proceeds according to some general principles (CP 5.441); while he dedicates more attention to original beliefs, with the aim of distinguishing his conception from that of the Scottish school of common sense. Original beliefs are instinctive (like acritical inferences) and common to all human beings. One could make a complete— though not absolutely fixed—list of these beliefs, but it would require hard work, 'for it is the belief men *betray* and not that which they *parade* which has to be studied' (CP 5.444, n1). Their being instinctive does not mean that they cannot change, slowly and imperceptibly, through time. Indeed, the Scottish school failed to recognize that 'they only remain indubitable in their application to affairs that resemble those of *a primitive mode of life*' (CP 5.445). Once evolution, and especially science and technique, refine human capacities and stimulate their critical attitudes, more and more situations occur in which the original belief does not have a grip anymore, because man *outgrows* the applicability of instincts (CP 5.511). Therefore, for instance, while the belief in the criminality of incest is still an indubitable belief, the belief that suicide is murder is not. In fact, it arose during the early period of the history of the Church, when martyrs were needed, and committing suicide was considered an 'abominable infidelity'. Nowadays, it has become possible to doubt this belief, and as soon as it is put in doubt, Peirce concludes, 'Reason will stamp it as false' (CP 5.445).

Hence, an indubitable belief can become dubitable and finally be declared false. But is the opposite also possible? More precisely: do indubitable beliefs grow out of dubitable beliefs? If today we have an indubitable belief that we did not have in ancient times—which is possible—it means that there has been a development. Yet, this does not imply that we have passed through a period of scepticism, nor that doubt preceded certainty, *in the process of learning*: belief is taught and learned as certain, not as doubtful (Peirce and Wittgenstein agree on this, as seen in Section 'Doubt').[56]

Another feature of original beliefs that common sense philosophers failed to see, according to Peirce, is vagueness. Vagueness is one of the most important concepts in Peirce's philosophy,[57] connected to the

---

[56] An anonymous reviewer has rightly observed that the history of science shows that most often doubt does precede certainty, and in particular that there is usually a phase of disbelief (presumably distinct from doubt) characterizing the attitude of a community towards a new scientific proposition before it becomes indubitable. Yet, I am not claiming that this does not happen; rather, the point is that when we learn basic certainties, including those deriving from science, like for instance that the earth rotates around the sun, we learn them as indubitable, and not as dubitable. As children, we are taught that this is the case, and not that perhaps this is the case. The fact that science develops by hypothesizing new propositions which first are scoffed at, and then progressively gain the status of indubitable beliefs, albeit clearly true, does not imply that the same happens in the process of learning.

[57] See Tiercelin (1992) on vagueness and realism in Peirce. As for the comparison with Wittgenstein, consider that Peirce affirms that logic cannot dispense with vagueness, just like mechanics cannot dispense with friction (CP 5.512), and that Wittgenstein makes use of a very similar image. In dealing with a logic which seeks purity, clear-cut concepts, the nature of 'the *real*

notions of generality, modality, and possibility, and to the fundamental categories of firstness, secondness, and thirdness. Here I can but hint at this, in relation to the themes we are dealing with. Vagueness characterizing beliefs is anchored, in his view, both in beliefs themselves and in the irreducible indeterminacy of reality. An example of indubitable belief, with unremovable remains of vagueness, is the belief that fire burns: one of our common sense beliefs, of which we are instinctively certain (CP 5.498).[58]

The critical common-sensist, moreover, unlike the traditional common sense philosopher, assigns a great value to doubt—to genuine doubt, of course, not to paper doubt. Only after an accurate analysis will a belief be declared indubitable; and even then, the critical common-sensist knows that nothing prevents that belief from being doubted in the future.[59] In other words, *indubitability does not entail truth*.

To sum up, Peircean indubitable beliefs are characterized by: their instinctive nature; a sort of universality connected to the primitive ways of life in which they emerged; gradual changes; vagueness; and always being potentially subject to criticism.[60]

As Broyles (1965) suggests, Peircean original beliefs are not indubitable because we see that they are self-evident and therefore true, but because in our present knowledge situation *we do not see that they are subject to doubt*. Their indubitability is not a sign of their absolute truth. This aspect—as Pritchard (2011, pp. 528–529) points out too—also characterizes the distance between Wittgenstein and traditional epistemology. And it is precisely the comparison between Peirce and Wittgenstein (and Malcolm) that interests Broyles. Writing *before* the publication of OC, Broyles examines PI, Malcolm (1952) and the conversations between Malcolm

---

sign' (PI, §105), he observes that when there is no friction, the conditions seem ideal, but they are only apparently so; in fact, on the slippery ice, we are actually unable to walk because there is no resistance. 'We want to walk: so we need friction—he affirms—Back to the rough ground!' (PI, §107).

[58] The same example of fire that burns is also proposed by Wittgenstein as an illustration of certainty (*Sicherheit*), for instance in MS 111, p. 121 (cf. BT, section 55).

[59] See CP 5.451, 5.498, 5.514 ff.

[60] On the latter aspect, see also Tiercelin (2016, p. 194).

and Wittgenstein recollected in Malcolm (1958); nevertheless, he is able to identify some themes which would be crucial in OC, like the opposition to Cartesian doubt, and more generally the idea of drawing *logical* limits to the notion of doubt. As he puts it, the point in the position of Wittgenstein and Malcolm

> ... rests on the relation between doubt and the notions of 'making sure' and 'turning out to be false'. Under circumstances where we really do not know what it would be like to make sure nor what one might mean by turning out to be false, doubt becomes unintelligible. Thus we may have our doubts about the apple in the bowl across the room. We could walk over and test it with our fingernail to see if it is wax. But there is no room for similar doubts about the apple we are presently consuming (Broyles 1965, p. 78).

According to Broyles, Peirce's later investigation on doubt is, like Wittgenstein's, logical and not psychological. Yet, Peirce's fallibilism is in contrast with Wittgenstein and Malcolm in that while for Peirce any belief, including indubitables, can eventually turn out to be false, for Wittgenstein and Malcolm, this does not make sense for some beliefs. In Broyles's reading, Peirce is concerned with *settled opinion* and not with the limits outside which it makes no sense to doubt. Peirce describes original beliefs as constituting 'the backdrop of the familiar, the expected, of "the way things are" that determines when reasons are required as well as what sorts of things shall count as reasons at all' (Broyles 1965, p. 87). In Broyles' view, this is not the point for Wittgenstein and Malcolm, who shed light on indubitability by means of an inquiry into the logical limits of doubt.

It must be said that Broyles' example of the apple is not perfectly fitting, as the indubitability of the apple we are eating is connected to experiential and sensorial aspects Peirce would have included in the category of perceptual judgements. What is more, it is concerned with the present moment, while a potential doubt has to do with the future. It must be said, moreover, that the role of the background of familiarity is crucial in Wittgenstein as well—an aspect that would emerge with most clarity in the notes of OC, which Broyles could not know. Yet, there is a core of truth in his analysis, in particular in his highlighting Wittgenstein's *logical* characterization of the role of hinges, a role that seems not to admit the least possibility of doubt.

Johanson (1994) too individuates Peirce's idea of what one may call 'the potential dubitability of indubitables' as a key point, which he efficaciously explains in these terms. In order to be considered indubitable, a belief must pass a 'very thorough examination' (Johanson 1994, p. 174). Although this may seem contradictory—either a belief is indubitable, or it is dubitable—it is not, because 'the process of examining alleged indubitables is not itself the creation of doubts' (ibid.); rather, the questioning concerns whether or not the belief *can* be put in doubt. Another interesting contribution Johanson offers is on the instinctive nature of original beliefs, which he illustrates with the help of Peirce's 'Philosophy and the Conduct of Life',[61] a piece in which the latter describes the instinctive and sentimental character of the 'marrowbones' of reason itself. When writing about *practical* infallibility, 'which is the only clear sense the word "infallibility" will bear' (CP 1.633), Peirce hints at the criminality of incest, which as we saw is an example of original belief:

> ...the man who would allow his religious life to be wounded by any sudden acceptance of a philosophy of religion or who would precipitately change his code of morals at the dictate of a philosophy of ethics—who would, let us say, hastily practice incest—is a man whom we should consider unwise. The regnant system of sexual rules is an instinctive or sentimental induction summarizing the experience of all our race (*ibid.*).

The instinctiveness of original beliefs, in this sense, is due to their constituting the present result of evolution. This result is not fixed once and for all: it can change, but it changes on the scale of evolution and not on the scale of the single human being, nor of the single culture.

---

[61] It is one of the Cambridge Conferences of 1898; see CP 1.616 ff. or RLT, pp. 105 ff.

Finally, Johanson makes explicit two more characteristics of Peircean indubitables. The first one is that they have a *hypothetical* nature: they are natural and instinctive hypotheses, which have been successful until now because they have been confirmed by the experience of the past generations, but as hypotheses, they are fallible. Broyles noticed this too, but Johanson's use of the adjective 'hypothetical' makes this aspect clearer. The second characteristic—and there is a difference here with Broyles—is that according to Johanson indubitables are *true*. Yet, they cannot be true in the sense that they are the final product of the inquiry of the community of researchers. If Peirce affirms that most indubitable beliefs are true—but Johanson does not offer textual evidence of this—this must mean that most likely there would not be experiential surprises contradicting them.

As for the comparison with Wittgenstein, Johanson highlights the affinity between the two on a number of themes: the idea of practical infallibility; the specification that the impossibility of a genuine doubt about certainties does not amount to the impossibility of imagining circumstances in which they can be doubted; the openness of certainties or beliefs to change; the existence of degrees of dubitability. More generally, both thinkers, in Johanson's view, refuse the alleged exigency of some sort of foundation for certainties. In other words, neither of the two feels the need to restrict true beliefs to self-evident propositions, or to propositions derived from them, nor feels the duty of an 'epistemic responsibility': in no way are we irresponsible if we accept *Weltbild* certainties or indubitables without justification.

Differences occur, according to Johanson, on other aspects: the hypothetical nature of Peirce's original beliefs, which finds no correspondence in Wittgenstein's certainties; Peirce's description of instinctive beliefs as the result of an inductive argument of the species, which Wittgenstein would probably refuse; and Peirce's original beliefs being described as true, which Wittgenstein would probably reformulate by saying that *Weltbild* certainties constitute the *standard* of truth. The latter aspect, Johanson observes, is the outcome of a broader difference between the two on the issues of truth and reality: while for Wittgenstein truth is relative to a frame of reference, for Peirce it is the result of the community of researchers' activity. As a consequence, while for Wittgenstein it would never be possible to have a rational method to decide who is right, for instance, between those who believe in oracles and those who believe in physics, for Peirce, this method does exist, and it is the scientific method, warranted by the effective existence of an objective truth and by human beings' instinctive capacity to grasp it.

In my view, what is interesting in Johanson's proposal is its highlighting the affinity between the two philosophers on the theme of foundations. Both oppose the exigency of a foundation for our belief, but (as will be clearer in Chapter 5) in neither case does this lead to an anti-foundationalist position tout court. Conversely, what I find weak in Johanson is the characterization that emerges from his work on the differences between the two, which depicts Wittgenstein quite hastily as a relativist thinker and Peirce as an anti-relativist.

Other commentators share this view of the contraposition between a relativist Wittgenstein and an anti-relativist Peirce.[62] On the other hand, Avrum Stroll's reading is at odds with it:

> [Peirce] agrees with Wittgenstein that not everything can be doubted at once, yet he denies that anything is certain. In that respect he differs from Wittgenstein who states that . . . there is such a thing as certainty. Looked at from a Wittgensteinian perspective, Peirce seems to have held that we never get outside of the language game . . . (Stroll 1994, p. 139).[63]

In Stroll's view, Peirce has it that every possible context belongs to the language game and therefore that 'doubt is distributively possible over the totality of items belonging to such contexts' (*ibid.*). Conversely, Wittgenstein's distinction between the language game and its external support, that is, certainty, according to Stroll, provides a novel insight which prevents the attribution of relativism to Wittgenstein. Peirce lacks a similar distinction and therefore cannot defend himself from this accuse.

Hence, the same charge of relativism that Johanson addresses to Wittgenstein, Stroll addresses to Peirce. The existence of such diverse

---

[62] For instance, Tiercelin (2010) and Haack (1982).
[63] See also Stroll (1994, pp. 149, 156, 161 and 169).

Chapter 2: Reasonable Doubts and Unshakable Certainties

interpretations shows we are still far from achieving any clarity with respect to these themes. I would like to suggest that the *similarity* between Wittgenstein and Peirce on the issues of foundations and objectivity could offer a better starting point for this comparison because it shows that both *escape* the dichotomy of relativism vs. anti-relativism, as well as the dichotomy of foundationalism vs. anti-foundationalism. While postponing further analyses on this (see Chapter 5), what remains to underline is a difference that both Broyles and Johanson let emerge, a difference that confirms what was already perceived in the work on doubt: Peirce and Wittgenstein share a fallibilist perspective, but their fallibilism assumes different forms. In Peirce, between dubitability and indubitability there is a gradualism, if not a continuity; in Wittgenstein, there is a categorical distinction depending on the role the proposition plays. It is the distinction between empirical and grammatical which he describes through the metaphor of the riverbed, where he observes: '...I distinguish between the movement of the waters on the riverbed and the shift of the bed itself; though there is not a sharp division of the one from the other' (OC, §97). This discrepancy has to do with the different attitude Wittgenstein and Peirce (and James) show regarding the relationship between science and philosophy. We shall come back to this.

As mentioned, besides Broyles' and Johanson's readings, which put the Wittgensteinian notion of hinges side by side with Peircean indubitable beliefs, there is a more recent proposal advanced by Howat (2013), which places hinges alongside another notion derived from Peirce, the idea of regulative assumptions.

In order to arrive at Howat's position, we must start from Peirce's acritical inferences, which are one of the three kinds of indubitables in his classification. These inferences are acritical in the sense of unexamined: those making the inference do not realize that they are guided by a general principle, a habit, or a guiding rule. In 'The Fixation of Belief', Peirce described them in this way:

> That which determines us, from given premises, to draw one inference rather than another, is some habit of mind, whether it be constitutional or acquired.... The particular habit of mind which governs this or that

inference may be formulated in a proposition whose truth depends on the validity of the inferences which the habit determines; and such a formula is called a *guiding principle of inference* (W 3, p. 245).[64]

Peirce deals with the same theme in many other writings. The SW collection gathers several works that Peirce dedicated to it under the title 'What is a Leading Principle?'. Here one can read, for instance: 'A habit of inference may be formulated in a proposition which shall state that every proposition *c*, related in a given general way to any true proposition *p*, is true. Such a proposition is called the *leading principle* of the class of inferences whose validity it implies' (SW, p. 131).[65] In the 'Leading Principles' entry which Peirce prepared for *Baldwin's Dictionary of Philosophy and Psychology* (1902), he affirmed that it is part of the essence of reasoning that those who reason proceed according to a habit or method that, they retain, from true premises will lead to a true conclusion or to an approximation of truth. The effect of this habit, he added, can be stated in a proposition, which is called 'the leading principle of inference' (SW, p. 133). There is, therefore, a somewhat ineludible belief in the validity of reasoning in general. It is perhaps the same idea that Peirce was after in the passage in which, as we have seen, he used the verb 'to hinge'. On that occasion, he stated that pragmatism in concerned with 'intellectual concepts', defined as 'those upon the structure of which arguments concerning objective facts may hinge'.[66]

Is it possible, then, to compare Wittgensteinian hinges with Peircean guiding principles of inference? This is the challenge taken up by Howat (2013). His aim is to present Wittgenstein's concept as a sort of ally for strengthening the notion of regulative assumption, by means of which Hookway (2000) and Misak (2004) defended the Peircean idea of truth.

Howat (2013, p. 451) formalizes the Peircean conception of truth in the following statement:

---

[64] Also in CP 5.367. See also W 3, p. 246 (or CP 5.369).
[65] From 'On the Algebra of Logic', 1880, also in W 4, p. 165.
[66] See the previous section.

(T) If a hypothesis H is true, then (if inquiry into H were pursued long enough and well enough, then H would be believed).

He clarifies that this is not a definition, rather a 'pragmatic elucidation' saying what consequences should be expected when 'true' applies to a hypothesis. In order to defend this criterion, in Howat's reading, both Hookway (2000) and Misak (2004) appeal to a notion of regulative assumption, which Howat (2013, p. 453) describes as follows:

> We Peirceans do not assert (T), nor are we committed to saying we can have adequate justification to do so. Our claim is that (T) is a *regulative assumption of inquiry*, i.e. one must assume (T) in order to inquire rationally into the truth of any hypothesis. If one did not assume (T), then there would be no point inquiring.

Although there is no justification for believing (T), one has the right to assume that (T) is true, and we cannot but do so if we intend to investigate any hypothesis.

According to Howat, the comparison with Wittgenstein's hinges offers the opportunity to clarify and qualify this approach, which he finds insufficient from an epistemological point of view. The symmetry between Wittgenstein's treatment of claims to *know* in OC, and Peirce's treatment of claims to *doubt* in 'How to Make Our Ideas Clear', permits the hypothesis of a single, shared view of inquiry and of the structure of reasons. Just like hinges, (T) is *indubitable*, although it does not appeal to knowledge, foundations, or grounds. Howat (2013, p. 457) concludes that the Peircean claim (T) works as a hinge proposition in Wittgensteinian terms, and that the latter's conception provides 'the best way to explain and to justify the appeal to regulative assumptions'. By considering (T) as a hinge proposition, in his view, we can therefore account for regulative assumptions of inquiry in a more satisfactory way, explaining their special epistemic status and showing the difference between them and other ordinary propositions. For this reason—he adds—it may even be better to drop the expression 'regulative assumption' altogether and adopt 'hinge proposition' (Howat 2013, p. 457n22).

Howat's position is susceptible to objections both from the Peircean and the Wittgensteinian sides, and he considers and replies to some of them in the paper. For instance (T) does not seem to be vague, as Peircean original beliefs are, nor obvious, as Wittgenstein's hinges are. Besides these (albeit relevant) objections, a more radical problem concerns the characterization of the 'structure of reasons' which according to Howat is at the root of both Peirce and Wittgenstein's approaches. In particular, in my view, Howat's description of Wittgenstein, largely derived from Pritchard's (2011) reading, suffers from the same gaps that have been highlighted with respect to Wright's conception of rational entitlement. Wittgenstein is not interested in justifying any kind of apparently unjustified 'right', but simply in taking note of how we operate ordinarily. There is no leap, so to speak, no vacuum beyond which to jump, no epistemic risk, and no need to *presuppose* anything. It seems to me that Wittgenstein is trying to show that feeling in need of a justification is precisely part of the problem.

Perhaps there is some distance here between Wittgenstein and Peirce. Remember that on the only occasion in which the former mentioned the latter,[67] he remarked that instead of asking *how it is possible* that we are able to do something, we should ask *how we do* it. The idea of an epistemic risk and the exigency of a justification is more present in Peirce, especially if we consider the reading proposed by the two authors, Misak and Hookway, on whom Howat based his argument. Both link this issue to Peirce's way of dealing with Kant, transcendentalism and 'indispensability'. Misak (2011) also highlights how pragmatists have always made use of arguments of indispensability. In the middle of the 1870s, William James started to work on the idea that (very roughly speaking) if we need to believe something, then we should believe it, a reflection that eventually led to the final version of WB. According to Misak (2011), in Peirce the issue of indispensability assumes the form of regulative assumptions that must be accepted in order for cognitive practices to proceed.

---

[67] See Section 'Wittgenstein Reader of Peirce?' in Chap. 1.

Chapter 2: Reasonable Doubts and Unshakable Certainties   97

Yet, as Hookway (2000) notices, at a certain point Peirce partially changes his perspective on this. Like Kant, Peirce aimed to explain the possibility of scientific research and the legitimacy of its rules (Hookway 2000, pp. 184–185). In 'The Fixation of Belief', he showed that the fundamental hypothesis of science—that there are real things independent from our beliefs, though their characters can be discovered through scientific research—is itself presupposed whenever a logical question is raised. In later years, he would refuse Kantian transcendentalism and equate regulative principles to *hopes* (Hookway 2000, pp. 186, 190)—a term which suggests the risky nature of the cognitive enterprise and the role of warrant that regulative principles play even more clearly. He would explicitly distance himself from the transcendentalist perspective:

[W]hen we discuss a vexed question, we hope that there is some ascertainable truth about it, and that the discussion is not to go on forever and to no purpose. A transcendentalist would claim that it is an indispensable 'presupposition' that there is an ascertainable true answer to every intelligible question. I used to talk like that, myself...(CP 2.113).[68]

In this sense, Peirce (but James displays the same attitude) intends to naturalize Kant, assigning a human and low profile to arguments of indispensability (Misak 2011, p. 265).[69] The reason which pushes us to trust regulative assumptions is '*desperation*' (Misak 2011, p. 266), says Peirce: if we do not adopt the assumptions which inquiry requires us to adopt, 'however destitute of evidentiary support' they may be (CP 7.219),[70] we will end up unable to know any positive fact at all, and the consequence would be a sort of 'insanity' (W 6, p. 206).[71]

---

[68] From 'Partial Synopsis of a Proposed Work in Logic', 1902. See also Misak (2011, p. 265).
[69] Gava (2014, pp. 80, 156–157) proposes a different yet somewhat related reading, according to which Peirce rejects transcendentalism as a justificatory and foundational perspective, but adopts a form of 'explanatory transcendentalism'.
[70] From 'The Logic of Drawing History from Ancient Documents', ca. 1901.
[71] From 'A Guess at the Riddle', 1887–88; also in CP 1.405.

To conclude, based on Misak and Hookway's readings, Howat identifies the regulative assumption on truth as a cornerstone of Peirce's thought, and in particular of his description of the structure of reasons. The same kind of interpretation is proposed, based on Prichard's reading, for Wittgenstein's notion of hinges and his own characterization of the structure of reasons. Given the alleged possibility of overlapping the two approaches concerning the structure of reasons, Howat proposes overlapping the notions of regulative assumption and hinge proposition, with the aim of offering a fuller characterization of the former with the help of the latter. The argument works if all its steps work. But in my view, there is a weak link in the chain: the description of Wittgenstein's approach as anchored to an idea of rational entitlement. This is far from his spirit and writings.

Concluding Remarks

In this chapter, I have begun to investigate what may 'sound like pragmatism' in Wittgenstein's OC, examining the affinity between Wittgenstein and Peirce on the themes of doubt and certainty. Starting from an anti-Cartesian attitude, both thinkers highlight doubt's belonging to an environment of certainty and undisputed beliefs. I lingered over the particular form of fallibilism they both—with some reservations—adopt, and the way in which they distance themselves from scepticism. Regarding certainty, after illustrating the Wittgensteinian notion of hinges, also with the help of secondary literature, I analysed two comparisons which have been attempted by commentators: one on Peircean indubitable beliefs, the other on his conception of the guiding principles of reasoning, interpreted as regulative assumptions. This analysis highlighted not only the convergences but also some divergences between the two approaches, which are not always detected by critics. Remaining within the same general subjects—doubt and certainty—I would now like to extend the investigation to the broader theme of common sense, with the focus on some open questions, and by doing so, also bring William James back into the discussion.

Chapter 3: Common Sense and *Weltbild*

Preliminary Remarks

The subject of common sense[1] involves dense themes such as—to mention just a few—the relationship between knowledge, prejudices, and ideology, the changes in ways of living through time, the intertwinement of social, natural, cultural, and aesthetic elements, the roles of science and philosophy, and their capacity to distance themselves from their historical context. In what follows, I shall analyse how common sense is presented in the perspectives of Peirce, James, and the later Wittgenstein, in order to gain a vaster point of view on the boundaries of the comparison.

The starting point will be Peirce's account of common sense. Since his view was already largely described in the previous chapter, I will limit myself to some notes on the influence of Thomas Reid and some hints at emerging consonances with Wittgenstein. I shall then examine how William James picks up some of Peirce's suggestions and elaborates a vision of his own, connected to the themes of language, Kantian categories

---

[1] Part of this chapter is a reworking of Boncompagni (2012a), and is published here thanks to the kind agreement of the editors of the journal *Cognitio—Revista de Filosofia* (São Paulo).

and evolutionism. On the Wittgensteinian side, after noticing that again the reflections of OC are prefigured in some remarks from the first half of the 1930s, I will focus on what Wittgenstein prefers to call *Weltbild*, or picture of the world. Once the main features of the three approaches have been highlighted, it will be possible to compare them more fully. The analysis will rotate around the systemic and holistic nature of common sense. It will come to light with even more clarity that the distance between Wittgenstein and the pragmatists has to do with the relationship between science and philosophy, and their vicinity has to do with a shared move towards a novel approach to foundations, objectivity, and rationality.

Peirce's Critical Common-Sensism and James' 'Mother-Tongue of Thought'

Whereas Wittgenstein's reflection on common sense is stimulated primarily by G.E. Moore, Peirce's reflection is stimulated primarily by Thomas Reid,[2] who sees common sense as the totality of the principles and criteria one cannot help adhering to, by nature. For Reid, therefore, believing in something contrary to common sense amounts to being in conflict with human nature. Beliefs and principles of common sense form a coherent system, which is generally mirrored in ordinary language. When the syntactic structures of different languages show some common features, in particular, they are the signs of a shared common sense conception of the world, which is inborn in human beings. According to Reid, this means that in philosophy, those who sustain theses against common sense must meet the burden of proof: until proven otherwise, it is correct to believe in what common sense suggests. Hence, for instance, it is not necessary to *reply* to a sceptic because the natural plausibility of common sense is sufficient in itself. Common sense is the prerequisite for

---

[2] See in particular *An Inquiry into the Human Mind on the Principles of Common Sense*, 1764 (Reid 1997), and *Essays on the Intellectual Powers of Man*, 1785 (Reid 2002), both also in Reid (1863). For a comparison between Reid and Wittgenstein see Wolterstorff (2000); for a comparison between Reid and Moore, see Holt (1989).

rational thinking: anyone undertaking an argumentation must necessarily take some principles for granted. Common sense principles concern both necessary truths—among which grammatical, logical, and mathematical rules but also the axioms of morality and aesthetics—and contingent truths, like the existence of what is directly perceived or the fact that what we remember did effectively happen. In both cases indeed, says Reid, the truths are immediately believed without the need to gather proofs.

Peirce's critical common-sensism is indebted to Reid mainly for the theory of perception, the concepts of belief and habit, and realism (CP 5.444).[3] For Reid (1863, p. 328), belief is 'the main spring in the life of a man'; for Peirce, belief, conceived as a rule of action or a habit, constitutes a 'general principle working in a man's nature to determine how he will act' (CP 2.170).[4] For both thinkers, belief precedes doubt and it is closely connected to action. Moreover, Peirce's critique of 'paper' doubt (let alone Wittgenstein's critique of the disease of philosophy) is clearly prefigured by Reid's critique of 'closet' doubt or closet belief: philosophers may entertain beliefs contrary to common sense in their private life, but 'if they should carry [them] into the world, the rest of mankind would consider them as diseased, and send them to an infirmary' (Reid 1863, p. 110).[5]

As for the differences between critical common-sensism and Reid's approach, these were seen in part in the previous chapter, because they chiefly concern the characterization of doubt and certainty. In particular, Peirce lists six elements which differentiate his own approach from Reid's[6]: the inclusion of indubitable *inferences* among indubitables; the acknowledgement that indubitables can change through time, albeit slowly; the recognition that they remain indubitable only when they are relative to primitive ways of living; the irreducibly vague character of indubitables; the positive value of genuine doubt; and the *critical* attitude of the new common-sensist. This critical attitude can be read as the result

---

[3] See Tiercelin (1989) and Pich (2012, pp. 281–282).
[4] From 'Why Study Logic?' ca. 1902.
[5] See also (1863, p. 184); cf. Tiercelin (1989, p. 214).
[6] See CP 5.440–52, 'Six Characters of Common-Sensism', 1905. See also CP 5.505–25.

of the application of a broadly Kantian kind of criticism to the common sense perspective, though within a historical and fallibilist view.[7]

Peirce also specifies that part of his conception is the denial of an infallible introspective power, allegedly capable of distinguishing between belief and doubt (CP 5.498). His opposition to introspection and to the full self-transparency of the subject is a clear point of contact with Wittgenstein. For both, it is outside and not inside the subject that certainties lie: certainties are what they are because the meaningfulness of language finds its environment in a constitutively intersubjective dimension.

Other aspects of Peirce's thought can be also interesting for the comparison with Wittgenstein. Peirce too, for instance (like James, as we shall see shortly), retains that beliefs form a system and sustain each other, and that they grow, as it were, by grafting onto one another, each offering a justification and needing one too.[8] Besides, there is in Peirce the conviction that common sense certainties (to be more precise, the certainties of 'common experience')—which, more than any sort of 'new facts', are the proper object of philosophy—are usually not put in doubt because there is simply no awareness of their existence and pervasiveness:

> [S]uch new facts, however striking they may be, afford weaker support to philosophy by far than that *common experience* which nobody doubts or can doubt, and which nobody ever even *pretended* to doubt except as a consequence of belief in that experience so entire and perfect that it failed to be conscious of itself; just as an American who has never been abroad fails to perceive the characteristics of Americans; just as a writer is unaware of the peculiarities of his own style; just as none of us can see himself as others see him. (CP 5.120)[9]

A couple of more similarities concern mathematical certainty, and the biographical certainty of a sentence like 'My name is...'.

---

[7] On this attempt, see Gava (2014, pp. 195 ff.). Gava reads Peirce, in general, along Kantian-transcendental lines.

[8] See, for example, EP 2, p. 454, from 'A Sketch of Logical Critics', 1911.

[9] 'The Three Kinds of Goodness', part of the *Harvard Lectures on Pragmatism*, 1903.

Manifesting what one may call, to a certain extent, an 'anthropological' approach, in 1898 Peirce underlines that mathematics, just like geometry and deductive reasoning in general, although 'theoretically' infallible, is not exempt from errors 'practically'. So if on average a man makes a mistake every thousand additions, 'and if a thousand million men have each added 2 to 2 ten thousand times, there is still a possibility that they have all committed the same error of addition every time', so much so that—Peirce even goes so far as saying—twice two is four is no more certain than the existence of phantasms. Yet, he adds, 'the certainty of mathematical reasoning... lies in this, that once an error is suspected, the whole world is speedily in accord about it' (CP 5.577).[10]

Hence, Peirce would agree with Wittgenstein on there being a paradigmatic use of mathematics as a criterion of certainty, and on this paradigmatic nature as consisting of the fact that 'the whole world' is involved when it comes to this kind of certainty. Though the two approaches do not overlap, the connection between mathematical certainty and shared practices *is* (also) a Wittgensteinian theme, as for Wittgenstein too mathematical certainty consists of the fact that mathematicians normally agree (PPF, §341). Indeed, in OC he affirms that the mathematical proposition bears a sort of the stamp of 'incontestability' (OC, §655), and nothing but human practices have given it that stamp. Indeed, the 'actions' of mathematics do not differ from the actions of any other domain of our life, and exactly like those, they are subject to 'forgetfulness, oversight and illusion' (OC, §651).

Wittgenstein compares mathematical certainty with biographical certainty:

> The propositions of mathematics might be said to be fossilized.—The proposition 'I am called...' is not. But it too is regarded as incontrovertible by those who, like myself, have overwhelming evidence for it. And this not out of thoughtlessness. For, the evidence's being overwhelming consists precisely in the fact that we do not need to give way before any

---

[10] 'The First Rule of Logic', 1898.

contrary evidence. And so we have here a buttress similar to the one that makes the propositions of mathematics incontrovertible. (OC, §657)[11]

Although a mathematical proposition and a sentence like 'My name is LW' have very different structures and only the former seems to be fixed and hardened, for the owner of the name LW, the certainty characterizing them both is the same: incontrovertible and not in need of any other proof. Once more, it is possible to find a parallel passage in Peirce, who in the context of a reflection on probability observes: 'I regard it as *sufficiently* proved that my name is Charles Peirce, and that I was born in Cambridge, Massachusetts, in a stone-colored wooden house in Mason Street' (CP 2.663).[12] Yet, he goes on and acknowledges that even regarding his own name, which is what he is most sure of, there remains a very small probability that he may have got it wrong. Memory has lapses, we are not able to remember the episode of our birth, nor can we specify the occasion in which we were informed by someone else on the circumstances and place of our birth. Therefore, how can we exclude the possibility that we have been deceived? 'How can I be so sure as I surely am that no such reason [for deceiving me] did exist?'—Peirce asks. His answer is: 'It would be a theory with no plausibility; that is all' (*ibid.*).

His position is not weak. He is saying that, in spite of the fact that *no decisive empirical evidence* seems to support the belief that this is my name, no plausible theory supports the opposite view, and, most importantly, that this is all we need.

What is at stake here is the compatibility between certainty and fallibilism, which as we saw both philosophers retain possible, though from different perspectives.[13] In particular, while Wittgenstein uses mathematics as a touchstone for biographical certainty and *Weltbild* certainty in general, underlining its *human and therefore certain* character, Peirce seems to

---

[11] See also the following remark, OC, §658.

[12] From notes added in 1910 to the article 'The Doctrine of Chances', published in *Popular Science Monthly* in 1878. The notes were also published in SW, pp. 157 ff.

[13] Calcaterra (2014) offers an insightful analysis centred on first-person certainty and testimony.

highlight the *human and therefore fallible* character of first-person beliefs, mathematics, and common sense.

This aspect, as well as the critical attitude towards common sense, emerges progressively in Peirce's thought. As Hookway (2000, Chap. 8) notices, in this respect, in 1893 and then in 1903 Peirce adds interesting remarks to 'The Fixation of Belief' (1877), reported as footnotes in CP. In these remarks, he recommends a general inquiry into the origins of our opinions; he states that it is not possible to exclude that doubts on alleged indubitables can arise as time passes; he underlines that even after having established something as indubitable, mental action can still have a self-critical function. According to Hookway, these notes are the very germs of critical common-sensism, in which a primary role is played by the 'critical acceptance of uncriticizable propositions' (CP 5.497).[14]

The coexistence of trust in common sense and legitimacy of doubt is also a trait of William James' approach (surely indebted to but not parasitical on Peirce), to which I now turn.

It was not until the beginning of the century that James got interested in common sense, and not until P that he dedicated full attention to it. To be sure, some ideas connected to common sense *can* be found in earlier works, but James used them instrumentally. For example, in 1897, James stated that in ordinary circumstances we are not able to doubt propositions like 'that I now exist before you, that two is less than three, or that if all men are mortal then I am mortal too' (WB, p. 21)—notice that the examples are not chosen at random: they express perceptual evidence, mathematical certainty, logical syllogisms—yet, James specified, it is only because of a sort of 'scholastic'[15] legacy that we believe them so indubitably, or that we are such 'absolutists by instinct' (WB, p. 22). Its utility notwithstanding, this instinct is 'a weakness of our nature from which we must free ourselves' (*ibid.*). The connection with instinct resurfaces in VRE, where, in

---

[14] Quoted in Hookway (2000, p. 207). See also Tiercelin (2016) on this. I take this tendency to be compatible with another tendency in Peirce, highlighted by Fabbrichesi (2004), to attribute a foundational character to habit (more on this soon). In a sense, it is perhaps because of the epistemologically fallible aspect of certainty that Peirce moves towards a more behavioural and externalist account.

[15] In PP, p. 960 James defined scholasticism as 'common sense grown articulate'.

discussing how the value of a religion and of saintliness should be judged, James affirms that we are inevitably guided by prejudices, instincts, and common sense, and adds: 'such common sense prejudices and instincts are themselves the fruit of an empirical evolution' (VRE, pp. 263–264).

The awareness of the philosophical significance of this theme begins to emerge in 1903. In a letter to Schiller, James writes: 'From the pragmatistic point of view an ode has yet to be written to common sense' (Perry 1935 II, p. 501). Again in 1903, in a draft of the introduction to the projected but never completed volume 'The Many and the One', he states that intellect often destroys the work of 'the God of common sense', which brings the world into a sort of 'genuine inner unity' (MEN, p. 9).[16] James' hope is to find a way of criticizing common sense without destroying its good outcomes (MEN, p. 11). Two passages written in 1905 (the same year in which Peirce's articles on critical common sense appeared) placed the connection between common sense and action in the foreground, defining common sense as a stage or a 'halting-place of thought' having purposes of action (MT, p. 73; ERE, p. 73).

All these themes reappear and are further refined, probably also taking Peirce's articles into account, in lecture V of P, 'Pragmatism and Common Sense'. The starting point is how knowledge grows. According to James, it grows 'in spots':

> [L]ike grease-spots, the spots spread. But we let them spread as little as possible: we keep unaltered as much of our old knowledge, as many of our old prejudices and beliefs, as we can. We patch and tinker more than we renew.... Our past apperceives and co-operates; and in the new equilibrium in which each step forward in the process of learning terminates, it happens relatively seldom that the new fact is added *raw*. More usually it is embedded cooked, as one might say, or stewed down in the sauce of the old. (P, p. 83)

The growth of knowledge—James adds—can be painful because it may require a reconsideration of beliefs previously taken for granted. Our way of dealing with this epistemic suffering and of minimizing traumas

---

[16] James would later use this text for the P lecture on common sense.

is to let old beliefs act on new ones as well, so that there is a reciprocal influence between them: what is new determines changes, but what is old decides how changes are to be interpreted. Hence, the whole body of common sense knowledge constitutes a complex system, which James describes in holistic terms, emphasizing that a new belief can be accepted within the system only in virtue of the affinity and the links that it can boast with the net of previous beliefs. Something too radically new would not be considered at all.

Biological evolution, James observes, has equipped us with some still indispensable instruments, like the five fingers, but has also left us with parts of the body we do not use anymore, like a rudimentary caudal appendage. Likewise, the evolution of our knowledge has left us with both vital ways of thinking, and remainders now fallen into disuse (P, p. 83). In a Darwinian vein, James states that the discovery of useful tools and methods happens by chance and is perpetuated by natural selection.[17] Our ancestors ran into ways of reasoning which proved useful for the adaptation of the species to the environment, and these ways of reasoning have reached our times, shaping what we call common sense. Thus, common sense represents the sedimentation of uses that have progressively grown solid:

> *[O]ur fundamental ways of thinking about things are discoveries of exceedingly remote ancestors, which have been able to preserve themselves throughout the experience of all subsequent time.* They form one great stage of equilibrium in the human mind's development, the stage of *common sense* (*ibid.*).

Talking of 'discoveries', James offers a characterization of common sense in terms of knowledge. This is even more patent a few pages later, where he compares remote common sense discoveries to more recent ones, citing the conceptions of Democritus, Berkeley and Darwin. Just like philosophers and scientists' conceptions, common sense categories were originally discoveries of exceptional individuals, who understood the adaptive value of their ideas before everyone else. These categories

---

[17] On this theme see also 'Great Men and Their Environment' (in WB).

fossilized into *language* (remember Reid), and since common sense gives shape to thinking by means of the structure of language, it can be defined 'the natural mother-tongue of thought' (P, p. 88). As a corollary, from within a language it is extremely difficult, if not impossible for us to imagine a radically alternative form of life (to borrow a Wittgensteinian term to which I will return at length).[18] Yet, we can imagine its *possibility*—we can imagine that, were our biological conformation different, the fundamental categories of thinking would be different (P, p. 84).

In describing the fundamental concepts of common sense, James makes use of the German expression '*Denkmittel*', translating it as 'means by which we handle facts by thinking them' (P, p. 84).[19] What is at stake here is the classic problem of the relationship between thought and perception, and indeed James mentions Kant[20] and speaks of categories. Impressions of sensory experience are understood once they are integrated in a conceptual system (P, p. 84), whose most important common sense categories are: 'Thing; The same or different; Kinds; Minds; Bodies; One Time; One Space; Subjects and attributes; Causal influences; The fancied; The real' (P, p. 85). Yet, differently from Kant, and in agreement with the Peircean approach, categories are not a-historical, rather, they are concrete instruments which can change in the course of the natural history of the species. Even space and time, Kant's pure *a priori* intuitions, in James' view are 'constructions as patently artificial as any that science can show' (P, p. 87).

For this reason, there is nothing completely fixed, and no clear-cut distinction can be drawn between old and new categories. At times, it will happen that old common sense is no longer able to offer an apt way of thinking and living for our world. New stages of knowledge may appear. The distant, apparently abstract concepts of science may turn out more useful than common sense, says James, as scientific and

---

[18] See, for instance, James' description of the concept of permanently existing things as 'one of the foundations of our life' in MT, pp. 42–43.

[19] See also 'The Sentiment of Rationality': 'Every way of classifying a thing is but a way of handling it for some particular purpose. Conceptions, "kinds", are teleological instruments', WB, p. 62.

[20] Peirce did the same, for instance in 'Consequences of Critical Common-Sensism', CP 5.525.

technological progress demonstrates. Moreover, the stage of critical philosophy can lead to a more satisfactory intellectual gratification. These three stages of human knowledge—common sense, science, and critical philosophy—are each provided with some advantages over the others in their respective spheres, but none of them is provided with a general truth which overcomes the other two systems in every context. This is an example of his conception of truth. When different systems or types of knowledge claim to possess truth, the simple idea of truth as a sort of duplication of an independent and given reality by the mind proves unsatisfactory as a test for judging which is the best system (P, p. 93). More complex criteria are needed, because each system can prove more powerful than the others in some domains or circumstances. A good conception of truth must be able to preserve the compatibility between the different systems.

Common sense itself, although the more consolidated system, cannot claim to possess the truth. On the contrary, James' conclusion—in spite of what the 'ode to common sense' imagined in 1903 might have suggested—is a *warning against* common sense:

> We have seen reason to suspect it, to suspect that in spite of their being so venerable, of their being so universally used and built into the very structure of language, its categories may after all be only a collection of extraordinarily successful hypotheses... Retain, I pray you, this suspicion about common sense. (P, p. 94)

In lecture VI of P, 'Pragmatism's Conception of Truth', 'things' and 'relations' of common sense are considered the bases of the mental processes leading, through verification, to truth. James affirms here that truth lives on a 'credit system': our beliefs and thoughts 'pass' so long as they are not challenged, just like banknotes pass so long as nobody refuses them (P, p. 100). Common sense, one may add, 'passes' so long as nobody doubts it.

In order to see the roots of James' attitude towards common sense, it is worth examining his concept of belief in the light of his psychology.

The difference between imagining something and believing its existence, James explains in PP,[21] is that in the case of belief the object is not only present in the mind but is also thought of as real. By belief, James means 'every degree of assurance, including the highest possible certainty and conviction' (PP, p. 913). Equated to the sense of reality, belief, 'in its inner nature, ... *is a sort of feeling more allied to the emotions than anything else*' (*ibid.*), and it is similar to 'consent'—a term used in the psychology of volition, which emphasizes the active aspect of believing. When a belief is entertained, theoretic agitation ceases, and motor effects and practical activity are likely to follow.

In his description of the belief concerning something's being real, James lingers over the example of a newborn having an experience for the first time, this experience being the visual impression of a lighted candle. The immediate feeling of the baby before the image is belief: 'What possible sense (for that mind) would a suspicion have that the candle was not real? What would doubt or disbelief of it imply?' (PP, p. 917). For *us*—James continues—it would be meaningful to say that the candle is unreal or imagined, but not for the newborn mind, whose only experience is the image of the candle.

> The sense that anything we think of is unreal can only come, then, when the thing is contradicted by some other thing of which we think. *Any object which remains uncontradicted is ipso facto believed and posited as absolute reality.* (PP, p. 918)

The similarity with Peirce's reasoning on the impossibility of starting with doubt is patent. 'As a rule we believe as much as we can' (PP, p. 928), says James. It is when more objects and more worlds—the world of sense, that of science, of ideal relations, of the 'idols of the tribe' (that is, 'illusions or prejudices common to the race'), of the supernatural, of individual opinions, and of madness (PP, p. 921–922)—collide, that we acknowledge the reality of only *some* things. The things whose reality we cannot doubt are those having '*intimate and continuous connection with*

---

[21] In particular in Chap. XXI, 'The Perception of Reality'.

[our] life' (PP, p. 926), and in particular, those attracting our attention: sensations in the first place, then what stimulates emotions and actions and what satisfies intellectual and aesthetic needs. The point of James' account is that belief precedes doubt and it intimately *concerns* us, so much so that an object is believed to be real whenever it possesses a close connection with us. The connection can actually also be far away in time and in space (provided the object interests us). Indeed, things and events are governed by a principle of continuity, so that nothing is completely separate from its surroundings, and around every believed thing there is a *fringe* of vagueness that connects it to us: 'The word "real" itself,' James concludes, 'is, in short, a fringe' (PP, p. 947).

Belief is therefore rooted in a principle of continuity which blends together—without confusing them—subject and object. Ultimately, this is a corollary of the Jamesian notion of the stream of thought. Yet, James' appeal to the subject does not derive from an idealistic position: it is, more properly, an appeal to the first person, which in every moment calls us back to our active, present, potential, and vital nature. Indeed, the conclusion of the PP chapter on the perception of reality is an exhortation to believe and to act in accordance with belief so that, becoming a habit, action itself can contribute to the reality of what is believed.

The issue of belief, then, leads to the issue of the will, another key topic in James' thought. In this context (but see Chapter 4 for a fuller account), suffice it to remember the spirit of WB, one of the most controversial works by James. Before an existential dilemma in which it is not possible to suspend judgement, and in the absence of evidence in favour of either hypothesis, according to James we are legitimated to choose on the basis of emotions and preferences. In this sense, belief can be rational even when there is no evidence in its favour; moreover, belief can contribute to creating the conditions for the believed facts to effectively be the case. A classic example is the belief in one's own capacities, which can help improve a performance. James extends this principle to religious belief, arguing in favour of the right to adopt a believing attitude in the name of a rational criterion based on the positive consequences of believing, given the absence of proof for or against God's existence.

Attention to consequences as a pragmatic criterion for judging beliefs brings the discussion back to common sense, which James associates with religion. Indeed, common sense is a guide for judging the value of a religion 'by its fruits': common sense helps us to see the usefulness of religious beliefs, in the wide sense of their responsiveness to human needs. James clarifies this from the very beginning of VRE, where he warns his readers that although some of his remarks may sound odd or excessive, he would always connect them to 'other principles of common sense' (VRE, p. 6). Yet common sense is not an immutable stock of certainties. The idea of immutability is openly rejected by James, who recommends 'recogniz[ing] that all the insights of creatures of a day like ourselves must be provisional' (VRE, p. 267). He also points out, just like Peirce, that the acknowledgement of the dubitability of one's beliefs, far from entailing scepticism, is a pragmatic *response* to scepticism. 'To admit one's liability to correction is one thing, and to embark upon a sea of wanton doubt is another' (*ibid.*), he states. Hence, common sense judges religious beliefs, but it can also be judged and it can undergo changes. It is, ultimately, a pragmatic criterion that governs both religious and common sense beliefs, a criterion which, precisely by hinging on fallibility, represents the best antagonist to scepticism.

Common sense is also invoked in VRE within a discussion on the relationship between science and religion. According to James, 'in the name of common sense', it should be recognized that both science and religion are 'genuine keys for unlocking the world's treasure-house for him who can use either of them practically' (VRE, p. 104–105), because from the practical point of view one does not exclude the other.

To conclude on James, his concept of belief is embedded in an idea of the person which highlights the vital and intimate character of the flux of our experience, that is, of our reality. At the same time, James' concept is grounded in a fallibilist and, for this very reason, melioristic notion of human knowledge. Accordingly, common sense is thought of as a set of consolidated but not immutable beliefs, which have proved useful for the life of human beings, from an evolutionistic and historical perspective. What originally were unusual discoveries, thanks to the confirmations of experience and to practice, have become truths and even platitudes. Yet, this sort of practical satisfaction does not eliminate a theoretical worry, and James constantly invites us not to trust consolidated truths blindly.

It is not difficult to see the affinity between James and Peirce's conceptions of common sense, although differences in their overall approaches are also present (Peirce is chiefly interested in generality, James in individuality and concreteness). Their attitude towards doubt and belief is one and the same, with the accent put on the primacy of belief and the rejection of the 'wanton' doubt of scepticism. They both highlight the role of indubitable yet fallible beliefs and of *Denkmittel* or ways of thinking we cannot dispense with. James links the concept of belief to a fringe of vagueness: vagueness is one of the features of Peirce's indubitables. Finally, both offer an evolutionistic account, which somewhat de-transcendentalizes logical principles and Kantian categories[22] and sees common sense as a sedimented corpus of knowledge, inherited over the centuries and millennia, but not qualitatively different from scientific knowledge.

Wittgenstein's *Weltbild*

A couple of preliminary remarks are in order prior to exposing Wittgenstein's view. First, Wittgenstein shows an interest in the issue of common sense well before the writings of OC. Second, in OC, although one of the constant targets is Moore's defence of common sense, Wittgenstein does not make use of the expression 'common sense', but uses '*Weltbild*', world-picture, and one may wonder why, and whether or not they are synonyms.

Wittgenstein first focuses on the relationship between philosophy and common sense during the first half of the 1930s. Notice that Moore's 'Defence' was published in 1925, and that Moore attended Wittgenstein's lectures between 1930 and 1933. In Wittgenstein's perspective, common sense is a sort of home or fatherland to which the philosopher needs to go

---

[22] On the relationship between the pragmatists and Kant on common sense see Maddalena (2010). It is impossible to deal here with the fascinating topic of Kant's approach to common sense. Let me just mention that his attitude is on the one hand critical (towards common sense intended as *gemeinen Menschenverstand*) and on the other hand sympathetic (towards common sense intended as *sensus communis* or *Gemeinsinn*, especially in the third Critique), and that in this respect neither the pragmatists nor Wittgenstein seem distant from him. See Ameriks (2005) and Mosser (2009).

back. Yet, common sense is not able to offer first-step answers to philosophical problems. It must be understood and clarified philosophically so that its nature and potentially misleading pictures are comprehended. More properly, if one intends to defend common sense against the attacks of philosophers, one would only be able to do so by *first* solving or dissolving the philosophers' puzzles. Upon seeing that their puzzles were senseless—or common-senseless, as Jolley (1998, p. 53) puts it –, the philosophers would cease to feel the need to attack common sense. It would be completely pointless, conversely, to try defending common sense by simply restating its views. This can be interpreted as a criticism levelled at the Moorean strategy.

The perspective, touched on in *The Blue Book*,[23] is further developed in a 1934 lecture:

> Philosophy can be said to consist of three activities: to see the commonsense answer, to get yourself so deeply into the problem that the commonsense answer is unbearable, and to get from that situation back to the commonsense answer. But the commonsense answer in itself is no solution; everyone knows it. One must not in philosophy attempt to short-circuit problems. (LCA, p. 109)

These lines, I think, bear an interest that goes beyond the theme of common sense because they clarify an often overlooked aspect of the Wittgensteinian methods. When the latter, in the course of his inquiries, lets imaginary adversaries speak, walks deliberately through dead-end streets, reverses his decisions, pushes himself towards the limits of sense, he is obeying the maxim of 'not short-circuiting problems'. For non-philosophers, for common sense people, there is nothing wrong in trusting common sense: on the contrary, it is a perfectly sane and healthy attitude, as the German expression for common sense, *gesunder* (healthy) *Menschenverstand* (understanding of men) manifests. But the philosopher is a peculiar creature, who 'has to cure many intellectual diseases in himself

---

[23] See BBB, pp. 58–59. Venturinha (2012) analyses the criticism Sraffa levelled at this passages and other related remarks in 1941.

before he can arrive at the notions of common sense' (CV, p. 44). For a philosopher, it is necessary to delve into the problems in order to be able to come out of them, and it is not sufficient to put oneself into the hands of common sense. Wittgenstein's therapeutic method, in this case, takes the shape of a sort of vaccine: only by assuming a small amount of poison, is it possible to create the antidote.[24]

Another passage from the *The Blue Book* can be connected to OC more directly. Here Wittgenstein deals with the temptation to say that subjective sensorial experiences are the material of reality. If we are trapped by this idea, he observes, then it might seem that our language is too coarse to describe phenomena, and that we need a subtler language (arguably, the target of this remark is Wittgenstein himself just a few years earlier). He explains:

> We seem to have made a discovery—which I could describe by saying that the ground [*Grund*] on which we stood and which appeared to be firm and reliable was found to be boggy and unsafe.—That is, this happens when we philosophize; for as soon as we revert to the standpoint of common sense this *general* uncertainty disappears. (BBB, p. 45)

The link between common sense, *Grund* (ground, terrain, fundament, and reason), and certainty and uncertainty (notice the adjective 'general' underlined by Wittgenstein) is already present, as is the destabilizing nature of a philosophy attempting to undermine common sense.

Given these premises, how can philosophy defend common sense, the naturalness of the *Grund, without using the words of common sense*?

On the one hand, the Wittgensteinian philosopher's objective is to describe platitudes which no one has ever doubted and which could not be disputed. This enacts a paradoxical change in perspective for philosophy. While previously the common sense man reacted to the words of the

---

[24] I borrow the suggestion of seeing Wittgenstein's technique as a vaccine from Rosso (1999: cxxix), who quotes Wittgenstein himself: 'I know that I have to drink in logical poison—in order to be able to overcome it' ('Ich weiß dass ich logisches Gift in mich hineintrinken muss—um es überwinden zu können'), MS 108, p. 193, June 1930. See Gómez Alonso (2012, pp. 71–72) for an analysis of OC as an example of 'rational therapy', broadly in line with this reasoning.

philosopher by thinking that the philosopher was uttering 'plain nonsense', now, in front of the Wittgensteinian philosopher, the common sense man would think that his words are 'pure and simple platitudes'. In both cases—Wittgenstein observes—the common sense man is right, but what has happened in this development is that 'the aspect of philosophy has changed',[25] and it has changed in a fundamental way. Philosophy, one might say, has switched from nonsense to platitudes.

On the other hand, gathering platitudes does not amount to reasserting common sense truths: rather, it amounts to trying to show them from a different point of view, at the same time showing the ambiguous role of ordinary language. Wittgenstein is neither endorsing nor contesting common sense: 'We never dispute the opinions of common sense,' he affirms in a slightly later remark, 'but we question the expression of common sense' (PO, p. 247).[26] What he is opposing, in particular, is the use of common sense to defend common sense itself.

The very same strategy is at work in OC. Yet, it is worthy of attention that, as mentioned, here Wittgenstein does not use the expression 'common sense' at all, in spite of his notes being heavily stimulated by Moore's writings which explicitly address this topic. Though without explaining why, he seems to prefer the word '*Weltbild*', world-picture. This suggests that his point was to highlight that these kinds of certainties form a general idea of the world. They depict the environment within which we live, or better, they build, as it were, the conceptual environment within which we live. As I see it, a relevant feature of a *Weltbild*, which also marks a difference with respect to the concept of *Weltanschauung* (on which see Chapter 6), is that one is born and grows up within a *Weltbild* without usually being aware of it. A *Weltbild* cannot normally be chosen, adopted or negated. A *Weltanschauung*, instead, is a vision of the world under a certain theoretical perspective, it is the fruit of a philosophical system or in any case of a political (in the widest sense) point of view. As such,

---

[25] I am here referring to an interesting and quite unknown note in TS 219, pp. 5–6, a short typescript dating back to 1932–1933.

[26] From MS 149, p. 43 (1935–1936). See also MS 137, pp. 11b, 1948.

it can be chosen, defended, contrasted and so on. To be sure, the boundary between the two concepts is blurred. Yet what is relevant in the idea of *Weltbild* is that it emphasizes that these certainties offer us an overall coherent system encompassing the logic and practices of our whole life, in such a way that we live naturally within the system without paying attention to it. In this sense, our grammar is wise and expert in virtue of its being unconsciously lived and practised, as we are not even aware of possessing it and of being constantly guided by it. This coherent system is kept together by the mutual support of its intertwined parts: as Wittgenstein puts it, 'these foundation walls are carried by the whole house' (OC, §248).

Weltbild certainties derive their sureness not much from the fact that 'every single person is certain of [them]', but from the fact that 'we belong to a community which is bound together by science and education' (OC, §298). It is not the agreement of single opinions or convictions that counts, but this sort of solidification coming from the belonging to a community. The *Übereinstimmung*, the agreement, is a consonance, a harmony of voices towards a *sense* which is in *common*, in that it is already linguistically and practically at the basis of sharing.[27] It is an agreement we inherit as a background and a horizon for our ways of acting and thinking. We do not adopt it because it satisfies our need for 'correctness'; rather, it is precisely against this background that we distinguish between true and false (OC, §94), and in this sense, it is the background that implicitly provides the criteria of correctness itself.

The expression *gesunder Menschenverstand* lacks this communitarian and holistic connotation, although it suggests other interesting aspects, like healthiness. Moreover, the expression *Weltbild* perhaps aims to highlight the grammatical or logical character of common sense certainties, which are *embedded within* and at the same time *emergent from* ordinary experience, and cannot be equated to a simple set or an archive of natural perceptions and knowledge items. Far from reducing knowledge or culture to common sense, Wittgenstein read in common sense,

---

[27] On the concept of agreement see also Sections 'Form of Life in Wittgenstein's Writings' and 'A Human Objectivity' in Chap. 5.

interpreted as a *Weltbild*, the place in which grammatical paradigms express themselves. The term *Weltbild* therefore shifts the conceptual perspective from a traditional vision of common sense, evident (also) in Moore's insistence on the knowledge value of certainties, towards a new framework. Indeed, it is by contesting Moore's use of 'I know', through an analysis of the logical role this phrase holds in ordinary language, that Wittgenstein tries to suggest a different viewpoint. While Moore's pointing out of common sense certainties has the merit of highlighting the distinct role some propositions have, his application of the 'I know' to them tends to hide this very distinctiveness, by levelling out the difference from empirical sentences in which the use of 'I know' is effectively kosher. A logical distinction between empirical propositions and propositions belonging to our *Weltbild* must be kept in mind.

In Wittgenstein's perspective, moreover, common sense is a whole picture [*Bild*], as it were, a *painting*, rather than just its *framework*[28]: not only does it prescribe rules from the outside but it also manifests itself in how we apply the rules in our praxes.

> We do not learn the practice of making empirical judgments by learning rules: we are taught *judgments* and their connexion with other judgments. A *totality* of judgments is made plausible to us. (OC, §140)

Weltbild certainties, with which we do not have a strictly epistemic relationship, are the rules governing the totality of judgements *from the inside*, operating as a grammar of knowing-how[29]—an aspect which may also shed some light on Wittgenstein's neither fully transcendentalist nor fully naturalist perspective.[30] We shall come back to this in the last two chapters.

---

[28] The expression 'framework', or more precisely 'frame of reference', only appears once in OC (§83), although many interpreters often bring up this concept. The 'framework reading' is in fact one of the kinds of readings of OC according to the classification proposed by Moyal-Sharrock and Brenner (2005).

[29] Here I will not venture into the debate on the epistemic or non-epistemic nature of knowing-how, but see Harrison (2012) for a Wittgensteinian and yet epistemic outlook.

[30] See Lear (1986) and Pihlström (2003).

Outlines for a Comparison

Before tackling the comparison, I would like to set out few lines on Wittgenstein's possible acquaintance with the pragmatists' texts dealing with these topics. Peirce wrote on critical common-sensism in articles published or republished in CP (chiefly in volume 5, which appeared in 1934) and in SW (New York and London, 1940). No textual evidence proves that Wittgenstein knew them. Yet, potentially he could have accessed both collections. Moreover, the latter includes (like CLL) 'The Probability of Induction'—a fragment of which, as we saw, was discussed with Rhees in 1943—and other writings on doubt, certainty, fallibilism, guiding principles of reasoning, vagueness, and the pragmatic maxim. The CP were also read in the UK in those years. For instance, it is documented that Wittgenstein's pupil Gilbert Ryle had a copy of them, as they are part of the bequest he left to the Oxford University library.[31] Concerning James, as already noticed, no document attests that Wittgenstein read P, though it is likely that he had at least indirect knowledge of some parts of it, while his familiarity with VRE is certain.

That said, it is time to point out the main similarities and differences between the three thinkers' perspectives on common sense.[32] One of the issues touched on is vagueness. Peirce makes it one of the features of indubitables. In his view, the attempt to define the contours of an indubitable belief amounts to losing its vagueness, and also its very indubitability. Indeed, in so doing, the belief is somehow translated into another belief, with more precise contours, which is now dubitable; while the original belief, so long as it is vague, remains intact and exempt

---

[31] Indeed, the library catalogue (http://solo.bodleian.ox.ac.uk) lists volumes 1, 3, 5, and 6, belonging to the Ryle Collection and still available in the Linacre College Library. Ryle and Wittgenstein first met in 1929 (Monk 1991, p. 275). Ryle was one of his most famous pupils, and although Wittgenstein did not show particular interest in his work (Hacker 1996b, p. 169; but see also Bouwsma 1986, p. 50), it is likely that the two had at least occasional conversations, for example, when Wittgenstein was staying with Elisabeth Anscombe, roughly from April 1950 to January 1951 (Bouwsma 1986, p. 57).

[32] A more specific comparison between Wittgenstein and James is outlined in Boncompagni (2012a).

from doubt. Vagueness and certainty therefore, far from being in contradiction with each other, are perfectly compatible; rather, the certainty of the indubitable *implies* vagueness. A complete account of Peirce's notion, central to his overall system, is beyond the scope of this work. What is relevant here is the continuity both with James and Wittgenstein's attitude. The former often emphasized the role of this concept in his philosophy, so much so that in PP he affirmed that what he was 'anxious to press on the attention' was 'the re-instatement of the vague to its proper place in our mental life' (PP, p. 246). It is in describing one of the fundamental characters of consciousness, continuity, that he introduced the image of the stream (PP, p. 233), which, in his intention, has to convey the thought that any idea in the mind is completely immersed in what surrounds it, precisely as if it were in a flux of water. To acknowledge this is to acknowledge the role of vagueness. With the aim of accounting for this intrinsic and constitutive vagueness, as hinted, James proposes the concept of a 'fringe' that surrounds ideas, a halo owing to which they do not possess precise boundaries, but slowly merge into each other. This theme has profound echoes in the later Wittgenstein, in many respects. It finds correspondence in the latter's attention to vagueness itself (Fairbanks 1966), the variability of meanings, the physiognomy of experiences and the associations they suggest.

Besides, Wittgenstein's notion of meaning as bound to the contexts of the use of words, and metaphorically described with the image of family resemblances, has VRE as one of its sources. Indeed, as Goodman (2002, p. 53) and others have noticed, in VRE James offered an account of the concept of religion in terms of a 'collective name' which does not denote any essence:

> Let us not fall immediately into a one-sided view of our subject, but let us rather admit freely at the outset that we may very likely find no one essence, but many characters which may alternately be equally important to religion. (VRE, p. 30)

In the PI remark in which he proposes the conceptual instrument of family resemblances, just after listing different games sharing one feature or another, Wittgenstein puts it like this:

Chapter 3: Common Sense and *Weltbild* 121

I can think of no better expression to characterize these similarities than 'family resemblances'; for the various resemblances between members of a family—build, features, colour of eyes, gait, temperament, and so on and so forth—overlap and criss-cross in the same way.—And I shall say: 'games' form a family. (PI, §67)

It is interesting to see that this remark from PI is also an example of an affinity between Wittgenstein and Peirce. Indeed, Wittgenstein continues his description by making the example of numbers, and saying that we call something a 'number' when we notice some similarities with other things that we call so. What happens is that we extend our concept like we were spinning a thread by twisting fibres together. 'And the strength of the thread—Wittgenstein comments—resides not in the fact that some one fibre runs through its whole length, but in the overlapping of many fibres' (*ibid.*). Once again, a common image testifies a consonance with Peirce: the image of a thread or of a cable which, though in different contexts, both describe as being strong in virtue of the intertwinement of the many fibres composing it. Indeed, in claiming that philosophy should follow the methods of science, and therefore 'trust rather to the multitude and variety of its arguments than to the conclusiveness of any one', Peirce affirmed:

> Its reasoning should not form a chain which is no stronger than its weakest link, but a cable whose fibres may be ever so slender, provided they are sufficiently numerous and intimately connected. (W 2, p. 213)[33]

Both for Peirce and for Wittgenstein (and, one may obviously add, also for James) thinking is not made of discrete mental states, but it is a living process, in which concepts partially overlap, evolve, and refer to each other in complex ways. From this point of view, in both perspectives vagueness is not a weakness, but a strength.[34] In more general terms, Rorty (1961, p. 210) observed:

---

[33] From 'Some Consequences of Four Incapacities', 1868, also in CP 5.265.

[34] The same image is also the starting point for Bambrough (1981).

Wittgenstein, like Peirce, is insisting on the reality of vagueness. When he argues against Frege and 'Ockhamists' generally that a concept's having vague boundaries does not prevent it from being used (PI, §71), he is articulating the germ of Peirce's thesis that realism (in the sense of the irreducibility of the indeterminate) and pragmatism reciprocally entail each other.

For both thinkers, the indeterminacy of intensional reference is counterbalanced by the determinacy of the pragmatic operations that assign words their particular meanings. Moreover, as Fabbrichesi (2004) also underlines, the same connection that Peirce sees between indubitability and vagueness can be found in Wittgenstein's notes on *Weltbild* certainties, which, although manifested in our actions constantly and without hesitation, we are not able to justify rationally.

The vagueness of certainties and beliefs, Wittgenstein and the pragmatists teach us, go hand in hand with their being in a *continuum* together with other certainties and beliefs, so that each finds its foundation and scaffolding in the others, but no one of them would be able to stand on its own, let alone carry the whole system. It is in this holism of common sense that Goodman (2002, pp. 24 ff.) identifies a remarkable similarity between James and the Wittgenstein of OC. In his view, James' 'ancient' common sense beliefs are the equivalent of Wittgenstein's 'inherited' *Weltbild*, against which one distinguishes between true and false.

For Wittgenstein, perhaps even more than in James, and more similarly to Peirce's conception of the guiding principles of inference, the systematic aspect of the *Weltbild* constitutes the bare bones of any reasoning. It is always within a system that all the activities aimed at testing and verifying hypotheses take place, but the system itself must not be considered as a point of departure, in the traditional sense of a proposition (be it axiomatic, or perhaps subject itself to doubt) from which all the reasoning originates. The system is not a starting point but rather an environment, it is 'the element in which arguments have their life' (OC, §105).[35]

---

[35] See also OC, §§142, 144.

Chapter 3: Common Sense and *Weltbild*

For this very reason, a completely new element, independent and unconnected to already given experiences and beliefs, would not be immediately included in the system. In James' words:

> [A] new idea is then adopted as the true one. It preserves the older stock of truths with a minimum of modification, stretching them just enough to make them admit the novelty, but conceiving that in ways as familiar as the case leaves possible. An *outrée* explanation, violating all our preconceptions, would never pass for a true account of a novelty. (P, p. 35)

In Wittgenstein's:

> Might I not believe that once, without knowing it, perhaps in a state of unconsciousness, I was taken far away from the earth—that other people even know this, but do not mention it to me? But this would not fit into the rest of my convictions at all.... (OC, §102)[36]

As we saw, in Wittgenstein this is also reflected in our being part of a community which is kept together by science and education (OC, §298). In this regard, the vicinity with Peirce (and with Dewey) is more evident than that with James. Not only because of Peirce's emphasis on the community of researchers, but more generally because of the (roughly) externalist perspective in which both Wittgenstein and Peirce work when concerned with thought. Their anti-Cartesianism indeed consists of this: disconnecting certainty from the subjective ego, and reconnecting it to the community (Calcaterra 2014). If the *pars destruens* of this anti-Cartesianism also involves William James' generally positive attitude towards introspection in the criticism, the *pars construens* finds an ally in James when the latter notes how common sense is 'deposited' in language and thereby constitutes the 'mother-tongue of thought'. Similarly, the Peircean accent on community and the intersubjectivity of knowledge combines with

---

[36] In another passage, significantly reminiscent of James' theme of the stream of thought, he uses these words: 'I am in England.—Everything around me tells me so; wherever and however I let my thoughts turn, they confirm this for me at once....' (OC, §421). Notice that this remark immediately precedes the lines on pragmatism.

a semiotic perspective in which community itself wears the clothes of an interpretant; and similarly, Wittgenstein describes *Weltbild* hinges as certainties that are part of a *mythology* (OC, §95).[37] Hence, the communitarian dimension is one and the same as the linguistic dimension. Without resorting to the Wittgensteinian argument against private language, suffice it to underline the full consonance between Peirce and Wittgenstein on an anti-mentalism that, far from negating 'internal' phenomena, instead negates the possibility of a private ostension of emotions or sensations as an ultimate guarantee of certainty, allegedly grounded in the self-transparency of the subject. In particular, introspection is for Peirce 'wholly a matter of inference', just like all cognitions (CP 5.462),[38] and although this marks a difference from Wittgenstein (owing to the suspicion with which the latter usually deals with issues such as inference and interpretation), it is also the sign of a deep attunement. For both, indeed, the attempt to identify the foundation of knowledge in an interior certainty turns out to be not only impossible but also senseless, the outcome of misplaced desires of epistemic faultlessness.

As for the foundational or non-foundational character of common sense / *Weltbild*, without giving away too much about a topic I will tackle in more detail in Chapter 5, let me just add that in my view neither Wittgenstein nor the pragmatists can be said to endorse either the foundationalist or anti-foundationalist position. Not only because in both cases what prevails is an anti-dichotomist stance, which already softens the extremes, but also and more interestingly because the rejection of the alternative is a consequence of their general philosophical perspectives. The search for a unique and certain foundation for knowledge, be it an interior self-transparency or an external anchorage independent from the subject, is indeed the result of a dualism between subject and object that both Wittgenstein and pragmatism oppose, in the name of the pervasiveness of the linguistic-interpretative categories guiding any knowledge endeavour. Yet, this does not amount to a

---

[37] Using similar words, Wittgenstein wrote a few years earlier: 'An entire mythology is stored within our language' (RF, p. 133, from MS 110, p. 205).

[38] See also 'Questions Concerning Certain Faculties Claimed for Men', W 2, pp. 193 ff., CP 5.213 ff.

pure and simple denial of the possibility of objective knowledge, rather it suggests the reshaping of the very concepts of knowledge, objectivity and rationality,[39] a reshaping which is, in the end, the only appropriate answer to the sceptical challenge. Indeed, scepticism is rooted in a metaphysical conception of knowledge as a mirror of nature, which had ceased to exercise its supremacy in philosophical reflection for both Wittgenstein and pragmatism.[40]

To be sure, they all use words and examples evoking metaphors of foundations, but at the same time these very metaphors suggest—though with some differences—the revisability and fallibility of the foundational certainties of beliefs.

Starting from Wittgenstein and James, both speak of layers in order to show the different density of beliefs and the existence of a basic stratum on which other less stable layers of beliefs are deposited, graft and grow. This is the relationship that James sees between common sense, the basic stratum, and science and philosophy, the more sophisticated and changeable modes of knowledge. In PI, Wittgenstein, in turn, used the image of the 'bedrock' of actions where, once justifications come to an end, '[the] spade is turned' (PI, §217). In OC, he also introduced the image of the river bank, composed by different parts subject to different degrees of alteration (OC, §99). Yet, neither thinker considers basic certainties or beliefs an absolute foundation.[41] In James, the fallibility of common sense beliefs results in an invitation not to trust them blindly, but to be always suspicious of them. In Wittgenstein, the grounding role of bedrock actions and practices is accompanied by their ungrounded character so that the language game is 'something unpredictable... it is not based on grounds. It is not reasonable (or unreasonable). It is there—like our life' (OC, §559). Surprisingly, it is Wittgenstein more than James that

---

[39] See Calcaterra (2003a, Chap. 3). On the feasibility of a novel conception of rationality on the basis of OC, see Coliva (2015). In my view, the attunement with pragmatism is much deeper than what she retains (see pp. 121 ff.), but I need to leave the development of this point to a future work.

[40] As is well known, this is the point for Rorty (1979). See also Gómez Alonso (2012, p. 65).

[41] In spite of some attempts among Wittgensteinians to read OC as a foundationalist work, like Conway (1989) and Stroll (1994, 2004).

underlines the pragmatic character of *Weltbild* certainties. Indeed, whereas James seems to remain anchored to an epistemic account of common sense (Hamilton 2014, p. 80) in which categories—though called *Denkmittel*—are ultimately *discoveries*, Wittgenstein deems the distinction between certainty and knowledge and the shift of the former towards a praxiological level a way of subtracting certainties from sceptical doubt and accepting, from scepticism, a subtle (perhaps unintentional) lesson—the awareness that our primary relationship with the world is not played within the epistemic domain.

That James deals with common sense in (roughly) epistemic terms is surprising because in a sense he himself elaborated conceptual instruments that could have been used to advance a different vision. The concept of habit, the relevance of automatisms, the importance of the background of actions, are all ideas he put forth in PP, but they find no application in his P lecture on common sense; while they do find application in Wittgenstein, as Goodman (2002, pp. 33–34) also underlines.[42]

Regarding Peirce, in spite of his frequent appeal to instinct (for example, on acritical inferences), his attention again usually remains focused on knowledge. Yet, in some of his later writings, the relevance of action and habit emerges with more clarity, especially in connection with the theme of foundations. Fabbrichesi (2004) highlights that in their later years, both Wittgenstein and Peirce turn towards a more pragmatic approach which tends to account for certainty in terms of actions, forms of life, habits and practices. In this sense, Peirce speaks of habit as the final logical interpretant, which closes the chain of semiosis. It can be expressed in the form of a conditional proposition: 'If so and so were to happen to any mind this sign would determine that mind to such and such *conduct*' (CP 8.315).[43] In a note written in 1907, he is even more explicit:

---

[42] In this sense, in Boncompagni (2012a) I argued that Wittgenstein is even more of a pragmatist than James on these themes.

[43] From a 1909 letter to James.

It can be proved that the only mental effect that can be so produced and that is not a sign but is of a general application is a *habit-change*; meaning by a habit-change a modification of a person's tendencies toward action, resulting from previous experiences or from previous exertions of his will or acts, or from a complexus of both kinds of cause. (CP 5.476)[44]

To a certain extent, Wittgenstein's reflections on how justifications end is not far from this. In describing how, and by means of what, empirical propositions are tested, and referring in particular to a *Weltbild* proposition, he asks:

What *counts* as its test?—'But is this an adequate test? And, if so, must it not be recognizable as such in logic?'—As if giving grounds did not come to an end sometime. But the end is not an ungrounded presupposition: it is an ungrounded way of acting. (OC, §110)[45]

According to Fabbrichesi—and the same was argued by Bouveresse (1987, p. 576)—Wittgenstein and Peirce face the same problem: how to stop the chain of interpretations. As I see it, it is not precisely the *same* problem, as Wittgenstein not only rejects the chain of interpretations but *interpretation* itself as the first move of the game: it is this move that, by its very nature, creates the chain, in a modern version of the ancient Third Man Problem. His reflections on 'seeing-as', indeed, can be read as an attempt to offer a non-interpretative notion of understanding.[46] Moreover, there is a difference in the outcomes of this line of reasoning between Wittgenstein and Peirce, that is, between the ideas of form of life and habit: the latter is a much wider and stronger concept in Peirce's philosophy, as it includes the laws of nature, thereby showing its belonging to a whole cosmology.[47] Similarly, the concept of instinct, which in Wittgenstein accounts for the 'primitive' and 'animal' aspect of man and language,[48] is imbued in Peirce

---

[44] From 'A Survey of Pragmaticism'.
[45] See also OC, §204.
[46] See section XI of PPF.
[47] On habits and forms of life see the next chapter.
[48] On instinct and animality in the later Wittgenstein see OC, §§357–359, 475.

with a metaphysical tone, and, especially in his later writings, it becomes a reflex of synechism, the principle of continuity in virtue of which from the very beginning man is in tune with nature and its development. Habit and instinct are therefore manifestations of the synechist realism endorsed by Peirce. According to this perspective, the advancement of science manifests an underlying logic, which 'indisputably proves... that man's mind must have been attuned to the truth of things in order to discover what he has discovered' (CP 6.476).[49] It is this natural and instinctive attunement which, in the end, constitutes 'the very bedrock of logical truth' (*ibid.*).

In spite of the use of the same image of the bedrock, in this case there is a difference between the two thinkers: while in Wittgenstein the bedrock corresponds to ungrounded actions, in Peirce it corresponds to the continuity between the mind and the truth of things.[50] This complex form of realism, especially its metaphysical tones, is extraneous to the Wittgensteinian outlook. Nevertheless, it is undeniable that both philosophers identify habits and practices as the place where the search for explanations must cease.[51]

One last aspect of common sense deserves attention: its link to religion, acknowledged by James and Wittgenstein. The latter recognizes the similarity between the roles of religious faith and of *Weltbild*, while also emphasizing that, for certain aspects, religious belief is different from ordinary belief, and that the use of 'I believe' in the two cases follows different rules.

In a 1938 lecture, he considers the example of a man who has an unshakable belief in the Last Judgment, and makes of it the guidance for his life (LC, pp. 53 ff.). The role of this belief and its features do not derive from any kind of argumentation nor from an appeal to ordinary empirical

---

[49] From 'A Neglected Argument for the Reality of God', 1908.

[50] Interestingly, Descartes also used a similar image against scepticism in his *Discourse on Method*: 'Not that I imitated the skeptics, who doubt only for the sake of doubting, and always affect irresolution; for on the contrary, my whole plan was only to assure myself, and to reject shifting earth and sand in order to find rock or clay' (Descartes 2001, p. 24, quoted in Perissinotto 1991, p. 112).

[51] Notice also the curious remark of OC, quite neglected (to my knowledge) in the literature: 'It is always by favour of Nature that one knows something' (OC, §505).

grounds: they are manifest in the way in which the belief regulates the man's life. One might say that this is 'the firmest of all beliefs'. Yet, Wittgenstein observes, only to a certain extent would the man say that his belief is 'well-established'. Indeed, a belief like this one, manifesting a faith, 'does not rest on the fact on which our ordinary everyday beliefs normally do rest' (LC, p. 54).

Wittgenstein then distinguishes religious belief from empirical beliefs because only for empirical beliefs is it appropriate to speak of opinions and knowledge:

> ...one would be reluctant to say: 'These people rigorously hold the opinion (or view) that there is a Last Judgement'. 'Opinion' sounds queer.
> It is for this reason that different words are used: 'dogma', 'faith'.
> We don't talk about hypothesis, or about high probability. Nor about knowing. (LC, p. 57)[52]

In OC, there are remarks which explicitly put religious belief side by side with *Weltbild* certainties. For instance, Wittgenstein notices that although normally people believe that every human being has two human parents, 'Catholics believe that Jesus only had a human mother'; they also believe that 'in certain circumstances a wafer completely changes its nature' although it is normally believed that things do not change their nature in this way (and Catholics themselves acknowledge that it is contrary to evidence) (OC, §239). Moore's assertion that he 'knows' that the wafer remains a wafer, or that the wine remains wine, would not convince them.[53]

More generally, I think that one can safely assume that for Wittgenstein the lack of foundations in the traditional sense, accompanied by the presence of beliefs or certainties themselves constituting a new kind of foundation, is a common trait between *Weltbild* certainty and religious belief. Not coincidentally, as Kienzler (2006) and Pritchard (2015) have underlined, one of the sources of Wittgenstein's reflections on these

---

[52] See also LC, p. 60.

[53] See also OC, §459, where Wittgenstein seems to say that it is religious belief that he has in mind when he deals with belief.

themes may have been Cardinal John Henry Newman's *Grammar of Assent* (Newman 1979).[54] In it, in order to defend religious beliefs from the attacks of the empiricists, Newman noticed that many of our commonest certainties, like for example that Great Britain is an island or that there is an external world, precisely like religious beliefs, are not grounded in empirical experience but in our upbringing and education.

According to Kober (2005), too, Wittgenstein's conception of religion sheds light on how *Weltbild* certainties should be understood. Kober also emphasizes the relevance of William James in the development of Wittgenstein's ideas on religion, which do not undergo deep changes between 1912 (when he read VRE) and 1950–51 (when he wrote the notes of OC). For James, like for Wittgenstein, religious belief is neither true nor false, but expresses the attitude of the believer towards life and the world. Neither thinker is interested in belief *per se*. Rather, they are interested in the *practised* belief, or in how belief can transform the person's life. Like and prior to Wittgenstein, James stressed that the truth of faith has nothing to do with argumentation or rationality. Kober (2005, p. 237) quotes a passage not actually by James, but part of a quotation James himself inserted in his text. Yet, since James seems to endorse it and since it belongs to a part of VRE that is undoubtedly important for Wittgenstein, it is worth recalling:

> Various dogmatic beliefs suddenly, on the advent of the faith-state, acquire a character of certainty, assume a new reality, become an object of faith. As the ground of assurance here is not rational, argumentation is irrelevant. (VRE, p. 200–201)[55]

For Kober (2005, pp. 245–246), who borrows the expression from Glock (1996, p. 321), beyond offering (in his remarks on religion) a non-cognitive 'theology for atheists', Wittgenstein offered (in OC) a non-cognitive

---

[54] James also knew Newman; he mentions him for instance in VRE, PP, and WB.

[55] The quote is from Leuba (1896). That these pages by James are important for Wittgenstein is testified, for instance, in LE, p. 41, where Wittgenstein talks about the feeling of being 'absolutely safe': James described the same experience here by saying that one feels sure 'to be saved now and forever' and that this state is characterized by 'the loss of all the worry' (VRE, pp. 200–201).

'theology for epistemologists', with the aim of achieving a deeper understanding of the epistemic stance of certainty. The certainty attitude, manifesting itself in taking things for granted, is a peculiar state of the person, a state 'already there' before any action: it is the inherited background which constitutes the basis of every human activity (Kober 2005, p. 248).

Putnam (1991, p. 66) went further than Kober in underlining that the main point for Wittgenstein (as well as for Kierkegaard; but let me add, also for James) is that 'understanding the words of the religious person properly is inseparable from understanding their religious form of life, and this is not a matter of "semantic theory" but a matter of understanding a human being'. The religious stance, precisely like the *Weltbild*, is a substantial part of the human being and it is a key that, once understood, gives access to what is most intimate in the person, that is, to our unique way of seeing the world and our life, which is reflected in our unique way of doing things—whatever we do.

One last point that can be made regarding the affinities between *Weltbild* and religious belief is that when, in dealing with the issue of conflicting *Weltbilder*, Wittgenstein makes reference to the concept of persuasion, his example shows that what he has in mind is precisely religious conversion (OC, §612).

While the similarities between religious faith and *Weltbild* certainty are undeniable, the differences must nevertheless not be forgotten, in order not to imprison the interpretation of OC in too narrow an analogy. Indeed, it seems blatant to me that the certainty of 'this is my hand' is *not* the certainty characterizing (for instance) faith in the Eucharist, and only to a certain extent can the latter help to clarify the sense of the former. There is no faith, no leap, so to speak, in the sureness of 'this is my hand', while religious belief in the Eucharist or God's existence are held in the awareness of a leap. To entrust oneself to faith is to risk, to know that nothing but faith sustains belief. Conversely, we do not have faith in the certainties or hinges governing our everyday activities, rather, we carry those out in the way we are used to. Therefore, if on the one hand religious beliefs show deep affinities with *Weltbild* certainties, and these affinities help to see what distinguishes both religious belief and *Weltbild* certainties from empirical knowledge, on the other hand the analogy should not be pushed so far as to suggest that the everyday *trust* in *Weltbild* certainties is completely understandable in terms of a kind of *faith*. Wittgenstein's constant attention to differences, I submit, would prevent such a claim.

One example of this attention to differences is his reflection on the grammar of 'I believe', which is not identical in everyday and in religious contexts. The following remark also shows some dissimilarities with the pragmatists regarding the connection between religion and common sense. In LC, Wittgenstein notices that ordinarily one can say 'I believe this', meaning 'I don't know this for sure, I only believe it'. This is not the case when (for instance) it comes to the existence of God. Believing, 'only' believing, and not believing assume a different meaning, and the consequences are different.

> Also, there is this extraordinary use of the word 'believe'. One talks of believing and at the same time one doesn't use 'believe' as one does ordinarily. You might say (in the normal use): 'You only believe—oh well...'. Here it is used entirely differently; on the other hand it is not used as we generally use the word 'know'. (LC, p. 59–60)

Belief in God, Wittgenstein seems to say, is neither a case of 'only believing' as opposed to knowing, nor a case of knowing. Similarly, a few pages before he affirmed, as we saw, that it sounds queer to talk of hypotheses and opinions for religious beliefs. What is at stake is, again, the distinction between certainty and knowledge, this time articulated for the specific case of religious belief. If I am correct, the pragmatists would hold a different point of view on this. In the name of the epistemic continuity (derived from the ontological continuity) between the domains of science, religion and the everyday, and in the name of fallibilism, they would consider belief, including religious belief, opinion and knowledge, on the same footing. Indeed, they seem to suggest that the relationships between these domains are fluid and that they trespass into each other seamlessly.

In this sense, to go back to the relationship between common sense, philosophy and science, for the pragmatists there are no categorical differences either between the epistemic bearings of common sense and science, or between the nature of scientific and philosophical activities. More radically, the *denial* of these categorical divisions is one of the distinctive characteristics of the pragmatist philosophical stance on the whole, a stance aimed on the one hand at highlighting the fallible aspect of any epistemic activity, and therefore the continuity between common sense and the most refined scientific knowledge; on the other hand, and again in the name of continuity, aimed at envisioning for philosophy a methodological proposal not distant from the scientific one. There is no longer any accord between this and the Wittgensteinian approach. On the contrary, there is a neat difference, manifesting itself in both the relationship between common sense and empirical-scientific knowledge, and the relationship between science and philosophy.

On the former point, it is Wittgenstein's terminological choice to use '*Weltbild*' that signals the distance and the implicit refusal to deal with common sense as traditionally intended. Knowledge incorporated in a *Weltbild*, even supposing that it is knowledge, has a logical-grammatical nature, that is, it does not pertain to knowledge but the *mode* of knowledge, proving to be intrinsic to epistemic and non-epistemic human practices (the sense in which Moyal-Sharrock talks of logical pragmatism). For this reason, a characterization of common sense in terms of hypotheses, like that of James, cannot fit Wittgenstein's vision. Through the denial of the hypothetical character of *Weltbild* certainties, Wittgenstein more generally marks the difference from traditional epistemologists (McGinn 1989, p. 112), a move that the pragmatists do not make, at least not with this emphasis.

The defects of the epistemic approach are pointed out as such in OC:

> This situation is thus not the same for a proposition like 'At this distance from the sun there is a planet' and 'Here is a hand' (namely my own hand). The second can't be called a hypothesis. But there isn't a sharp boundary line between them. (OC, §52)[56]

The boundary between hinges and empirical propositions, states Wittgenstein, is not neat, and indeed it is easy to fall into the traditional epistemologist's (and the sceptic's) position, and treat sureness as a propositional attitude. The use the pragmatists make

---

[56] See also OC, §55.

of terms like 'hypotheses', 'opinions', and 'belief' is exposed to the same criticism, although one must remember that Wittgenstein himself is not so univocal. On some occasions, indeed, he *does* use expressions more in harmony with those of Peirce and James. Beyond OC, §410 ('Our knowledge [*Wissen*] forms an enormous system'), he does so in a couple of passages (OC, §§210–211) in which the echoes of James' view seem to resound, when he states that what in our time seems fixed and is part of our *Weltbild* perhaps 'was once disputed' and then slowly came to belong 'to the scaffolding of our thoughts'.

The crucial difficulty is how to account for the evolutive and historical change of the 'scaffolding': if, with Wittgenstein, one intends to draw a distinction between scaffolding and ordinary thought, it remains to be explained how the latter can have a role in the development of the former. That the two levels somehow interact is recognized by Wittgenstein in the metaphor of the river (OC, §§95–99). In it, he points out in particular that the 'mythology' constituted by our *Weltbild* certainties 'may change back into a state of flux', that 'the river-bed of thoughts may shift'. Yet he also adds: 'But I distinguish between the movement of the waters on the river-bed and the shift of the bed itself; though there is not a sharp division of the one from the other' (OC, §97).

Like in OC, §52, Wittgenstein underlines that there is not a *sharp* division, but nevertheless that *there is* a division. It is, ultimately, the distinction between the logical or grammatical and the empirical level, and the whole of Wittgenstein's later (perhaps not only later) reflection can be said to aim to offer glimpses of this unstable boundary. Wittgenstein's insistence on this point is strictly correlated with a critique he constantly addresses to James, often charged with the fundamental mistake of confusing grammatical and empirical, *a priori* and *a posteriori*, logical and experiential. It cannot be by chance, then, that Wittgenstein chooses the metaphor of the river to illustrate the distinction. Indeed, he speaks of the riverbed *of thoughts* (*Flussbett der Gedanken*), an image immediately recalling James' image of the *stream of thought*. In my view, here Wittgenstein is resuming *and* criticizing James' metaphor. In Chapter 6, I will briefly show that there is textual evidence in Wittgenstein's *Nachlass* supporting this interpretation.[57]

Paralleling Wittgenstein's criticism of James, Broyles (1965, p. 86) criticizes Peirce for not distinguishing beliefs that are indubitable because they are corroborated by scientific inquiry (empirical level) and those that are indubitable because they are presupposed in any inquiry (grammatical or logical level). However, Peirce *does* make a distinction among indubitables which resembles the distinction between empirical and grammatical:

> True, it is conceivable that what you cannot help believing today, you might find you thoroughly disbelieve tomorrow. But then there is a certain distinction between things you 'cannot' do, merely in the sense that nothing stimulates you to the great effort and endeavors that would be required, and things you cannot do because in their own nature they are insusceptible of being put into practice. (CP 5.419)[58]

There is a similarity here with Wittgenstein. Yet, according to Peirce, the belonging of a belief to the second kind (shall I call it 'grammatical certainty'?) is, in turn, an experientially based hypothesis. Peirce has the exigency to acknowledge a sort of non-empirical indubitability, and at the same time to make this indubitability part of a wider conception of the empirical. In this way, the continuity of the different kinds of belief is guaranteed. Accordingly, he associates common sense indubitables to scientific results, again in the name of evolution:

> [T]hose vague beliefs that appear to be indubitable have the same sort of basis as scientific results have. That is to say, they rest on experience—on the total everyday experience of many generations of multitudinous populations. (CP 5.522)[59]

---

[57] See Boncompagni (2012b) for a fuller account.
[58] 'What Pragmatism Is', 1905. See also 'The Fixation of Belief', W 3, p. 246 and CP 5.369, and compare these remarks with OC, §155 on the logical use of 'can'.
[59] 'Consequences of Critical Common-Sensism', 1905.

Critical common-sensism, as Hookway (2000, Chap. 8) observes, responds to a strategy to keep faith with two seemingly contradictory assumptions: on the one hand, the acknowledgement that rationality requires a corpus of beliefs, principles, and inferences whose acceptance does not depend on the results of future scientific research; on the other hand, the denial of the existence of non-scientific knowledge, or in other words the exigency that propositions be considered meaningful only in so far as their truth implies a difference for future experience.

The distinction between grammatical (or logical) and empirical, intentionally softened by the pragmatists and intentionally emphasized by Wittgenstein, is reflected in the parallel distinction between philosophy and science. In fact, differently from James, Wittgenstein 'never abandons his commitment to the idea that his philosophical observations are also logical investigations, and that logic brings a different kind of certainty than most of what we call "knowledge"'; and conversely, '[i]f Wittgenstein's commitment to logic sets him apart from James, then James' commitment to science . . . sets him apart from Wittgenstein', as efficaciously summed up by Goodman (2002, pp. 27, 30), in a reasoning whose second part at least can easily be extended to Peirce. Hence, if philosophy must be scientific, it clearly will deal with opinions, hypotheses, and verifications, just like science does. James and Peirce's attitude towards the continuity between common sense, science, and philosophy is perfectly coherent with their approach, if not strictly *required* by their approach. I shall examine the questions arising from these issues in depth in the last chapter.

Concluding Remarks

Beginning from Peirce's indubitables, this chapter has examined his conception of critical common-sensism, to then pass to James' approach and focus on his 1907 lecture on common sense, published in P. The later Wittgenstein's position on *Weltbild* was interpreted as an attempt to overcome the epistemic point of view on common sense. The three thinkers' perspectives were then compared, and similarities and differences emerged. Among the similarities: the compatibility between certainty and vagueness, the holistic nature of common sense / *Weltbild*, the communitarian dimension, a new approach to the theme of foundations, the connection with action and the connection with the religious domain. Among the differences: the way of dealing with the distinctions and relationships between empirical and grammatical and between science and philosophy.

In the next chapter, I shall make a fuller analysis of one of the similarities just mentioned, the bond between certainty and action. The starting point will be the pragmatic maxim, which Peirce directly connected to common-sensism, asserting that the latter, even if elaborated before a complete account of the former, could be intended as a consequence of it (CP 5.438–439). I will argue that surprisingly similar ideas, though expressed in a different style of reasoning, are put forth by Wittgenstein in OC.

Chapter 4: Action and the Pragmatic Maxim

Preliminary Remarks

On the topic of action, the proximity between pragmatism and Wittgenstein is even more evident than on the topics of doubt, certainty, and common sense, just examined. But in the case of action, paradoxically, a more cautious attitude is recommended. Indeed, not only would it be too easy to simply point at the fact that the later Wittgenstein stresses the relevance of action, and that action is one of the main themes in the pragmatist tradition: by doing so, we would also risk not to see that both Wittgenstein and pragmatism had something new and interesting to say about it. If we are to avoid generic comparisons and stereotyped accounts of pragmatism, we will have to pay close attention to the texts of pragmatism's founding fathers, and to the effective way in which they, as well as Wittgenstein, dealt with some key issues. Only in this way will it be possible to capture the elements of novelty which mark out both Wittgensteinian and pragmatist philosophy from traditional approaches. What does it mean, indeed, to place action in the foreground? What *is* action? How is it possible to make it the hinge of inquiry, without falling prone to ancient dichotomies, such as the mind/body dilemma, or to easy but empty analyses, such as the distinction between

© The Author(s) 2016
A. Boncompagni, *Wittgenstein and Pragmatism*, History of Analytic Philosophy, DOI 10.1057/978-1-137-58847-0_5

facts and values? Wider attention to the texts, I hope, will help to pinpoint the profoundest and less evident aspects on which both perspectives converge.

While bearing this theoretical warning in mind, let us go back to the reasoning developed in the previous chapter, and to the link between critical common-sensism and the pragmatic maxim. It is time to outline more precisely this conception. The pragmatic maxim is, more appropriately, a *method*, at the core of pragmatism both in Peirce, who first elaborated it, and in James, who developed his own version and contributed to its broader treatment in the philosophical debate. Roughly, it is the connection between the meaning of a conception and its practical effects, thanks to which we can claim to know something completely only insofar as we know its effects in factual and/or behavioural terms. This is a necessarily imprecise characterization, given that there are several versions of the maxim, but I hope it catches a salient feature of it.

As regards OC, my interpretative proposal is the following. There is a quite substantial group of remarks, written by Wittgenstein approximately during the week 15–22 March 1951, which are significantly suggestive of the maxim. Wittgenstein himself described this period as particularly fertile and productive for his work. The group of notes includes OC, §422, 'So I am trying to say something that sounds like pragmatism. Here I am being thwarted by a kind of *Weltanschauung*.' My hypothesis is that Wittgenstein was sufficiently aware of the fact that his own reflections revolved around the very themes and techniques used by the pragmatists. This suggests that Wittgenstein knew more of the pragmatists' texts than he was willing to admit; that the similarity with pragmatism, which he perceived with annoyance, was real, especially in the notes from this period; and that this similarity can be identified in a precise and not generic way with the pragmatic maxim.

My focus on the pragmatic maxim and on Wittgenstein's reading of it in the following pages will enable us to deal more extensively with the topic of meaning as use, which was touched on in the first chapter. This will also offer a starting point from which to widen the inquiry towards the general topic of action, while avoiding the vagueness that sometimes surrounds it in Wittgensteinian literature. Action is neither for Wittgenstein nor for the pragmatists a real object of study: rather, it is an interpretative instrument on many levels and for many issues—linguistic games, meaning, belief, knowledge, and the dialectic of doubt and certainty. However, this does not mean that they fail to outline action as a concept. As we shall see, when they do describe action, although it does not happen often, both Wittgenstein and the pragmatists highlight its belonging to a form of life, a habit, a set of rules and uses, a background of praxes and practices, partly natural partly cultural, which action itself at the same time manifests and produces.

The chapter begins with an examination of the different formulations of the pragmatic maxim offered by Peirce and James; it then proceeds with an analysis of Wittgenstein's reflections about the links between knowledge, truth, and consequences, and more generally about understanding and meaning, and closes by shifting the comparison to the wider terrain of action.

The Pragmatic Maxim

The pragmatic maxim makes its first appearance in the philosophical arena (though, in this context, without being labelled as 'pragmatic maxim') in the aforementioned article, 'How to Make our Ideas Clear' by Peirce, published in 1878. Here are the relevant excerpts.

> ... [T]he whole function of thought is to produce habits of action; ... To develop its meaning, we have, therefore, simply to determine what habits it produces, for what a thing means is simply what habits it involves. ... It appears, then, that the rule for attaining the third grade of clearness of apprehension is as follows: Consider what effects, that might conceivably have practical bearings, we conceive the object of our conception to have. Then, our conception of these effects is the whole of our conception of the object. (W 3, pp. 265–266)[1]

Although this is the classical formulation to which scholars normally refer and to which Peirce himself usually refers, it must be noticed that in a later writing he dated the first formulation of the maxim to 1871

---
[1] Also in CP 5.400–402.

(EP 2, p. 465). It is around the beginnings of the 1870s, indeed, that these ideas make way in his thought, probably stimulated by the Metaphysical Club discussions which were at the origin of pragmatism (Menand 2001). During the meetings of the Club, Nicholas St. John Green, Chauncey Wright's fellow student, then lawyer and professor of Law at Harvard, and strong supporter of the idea that beliefs and knowledge have an active character, stressed the importance of adopting Alexander Bain's definition of belief as what one is ready to act upon:

> The relation of Belief to Activity is expressed by saying that *what we believe we act upon*.... The difference between mere conceiving or imagining, with or without strong feeling, and belief, is acting, or being prepared to act, when the occasion arises. (Bain 1868, p. 372)

This kind of approach, hinging on the fact that we judge what someone believes on the basis of her actions—*faith by works*, according to the Epistle of James, from the Old Testament, cited by Bain; or *by their fruits ye shall know them*, according to the New Testament, cited by Peirce and James—made a powerful impression on the members of the Metaphysical Club, so much so that Peirce later said that pragmatism on the whole was nothing but a corollary of Bain's definition of belief (CP 5.12, ca. 1906).

'The Fixation of Belief', the first of the articles belonging, together with 'How to Make our Ideas Clear', to the series published in *Popular Science Monthly* (and later in CCL and SW, besides CP and W), particularly shows traces of the impact of Bain's conception. In it, Peirce states that 'the feeling of believing is a more or less sure indication of there being established in our nature some habit which will determine our actions' (W 3, p. 247).[2] The concept of habit is Peirce's fundamental contribution to and qualification of Bain's idea of belief, in which it was perhaps implicit but not so evident (Wu 1994). I will come back to this later.

---

[2] Also in CP 5.371.

In 'How to Make our Ideas Clear', Peirce proposes the maxim as a rule or a criterion for achieving a reflexive clarity on the contents of ideas, concepts, propositions, beliefs, hypotheses, and so on: by applying the maxim, it is possible to know what the contents of ideas effectively are. One of the goals is to illustrate that certain hypotheses or concepts do not bear any cognitive content at all, and hence to avoid the mistakes of a metaphysics one is not aware of, but which is nonetheless underpinning the picture (Hookway 2012, Chap. 9). It must be underlined, moreover, that Peirce's aim is *not* to offer a real definition of meaning or a maxim having the character of generality, that is, sufficient in order to identify meaning univocally and completely. Understanding and meaning itself, in fact, have three aspects, namely there are three grades of clarity, and the pragmatic maxim constitutes the method to grasp the *third* aspect or grade of clarity. The former two aspects or grades are familiarity with the object or notion (Descartes' 'clear' ideas, Mill's denotation) and the definition of its contents (Descartes' 'distinct' ideas, Mill's connotation).[3] The contribution offered by Peirce, fully aware that he is aiming to complete a subject already handled by previous thinkers, consists precisely of specification of the third aspect of meaning, the pragmatic aspect. In this sense, the process of understanding a meaning can be said to be complete when the third aspect is *also* considered: that is, when we know what consequences to expect if the hypotheses containing the term in question are true.

The relevance of the third aspect, usually neglected in philosophy, is, among other things, that it is a criterion for the identity of meanings: if two concepts produce the same practical effects they are to be regarded as equivalent. This is one of the points on which Peirce, but also James, would linger in the following years, and it is one of the reasons why application of the maxim to the philosophical field is particularly fruitful: to affirm that two ideas are equivalent when their effects are the same is only to acknowledge meaningfulness in those conceptions which can have practical bearings, to eliminate those which do not have any, and to

---

[3] See Misak (2004, pp. 12–14).

declare equivalent those which produce the same effects.[4] A significant simplification, which in any case must be read together with the specification of what is meant by 'practical consequences', 'practical effects', 'practical bearings', and 'practical conduct'. It is Peirce himself who feels unsatisfied on this, as manifested by his need to repeatedly reformulate the maxim, always looking for a better expression. Chiefly, it is the psychological aspect linked to belief and truth which Peirce's retrospective outlook finds insufficient. In 1903, for instance, he affirms that it is unsatisfying to reduce belief to psychological facts and that every attempt to do so has proven to be shallow (CP 5.28).[5] On the matter of practical consequences, he is cautious. 'The only doubt—he states—is whether this is all that belief is, whether belief is a mere nullity so far as it does not influence conduct' (CP 5.32).

To a certain extent, the whole of Peirce's reflection can be interpreted as a more and more wide-reaching attempt to clarify the nature of the practical bearings of concepts, partly in opposition to the parallel but distant reflections made by James; a deepening that leads him progressively to stress the *potential* nature of practical consequences:

> Pragmatism is the principle that every theoretical judgment expressible in a sentence in the indicative mood is a confused form of thought whose only meaning, if it has any, lies in its tendency to enforce a corresponding practical maxim expressible as a conditional sentence having its apodosis in the imperative mood. (CP 5.18)

In other words, a theoretical principle or a judgement only has meaning insofar as it produces a practical maxim of the kind: 'If conditions C arise, then you'll act in way A'. This is rather different from asserting that the entire meaning of a conception consists of its practical effects, because (apart from the accent on conduct, as we shall see) it introduces a conditional form: *potential* effects must also be considered. Why did Peirce feel the need to clarify this? Not only because he was unsatisfied

---

[4] See CP 5.196, from 'Pragmatism and Abduction', 1903.
[5] In 'Pragmatism: The Normative Sciences'.

with the psychological tone of the preceding definition but also because he wanted to distance himself from what pragmatism was becoming, in the scholarly community, under the impulse of William James' personality.

So let us now take a look at James' position: it is mainly by examining the dialectic between the two thinkers that their respective attitudes can be better understood (Hookway 2012, Chap. 10).

As Koopman (2014, p. 163) notes, contrary to what is normally argued, James adhered at least implicitly to pragmatism already in 1881, when he underlined that 'if two apparently different definitions of the reality before us should have identical consequences, those two definitions would really be identical definitions' (WB, p. 99) and, in a note, added a reference to the 'admirably original' 'How to Make our Ideas Clear' by Peirce. But it is especially in 1898, with the article 'Philosophical Conceptions and Practical Results', that James' distinct way of making use of the maxim emerges. He writes:

> Thus to develop a thought's meaning we need only determine what conduct it is fitted to produce; that conduct is for us its sole significance.... To attain perfect clearness in our thoughts of an object, then, we need only consider what effects of a conceivably practical kind the object may involve, what sensations we are to expect from it, and what reactions we must prepare. (P, p. 259)

These effects, he states very clearly, determine 'the whole' of the meaning that we are looking for. In the following lines, after attributing the maxim to Peirce, James partly differentiates his own position, affirming that in his view the principle should be expressed more broadly, that the change in our conduct must be stimulated by the expectation of a change in experience, and that 'the effective meaning of every philosophic proposition can always be brought down to some particular consequence', stressing the relevance of particularity (*ibid.*). This accent, which in James is also an accent on the *individual*, is of course very far from the tone of the Peircean approach. Peirce indeed—beyond the cited passage in which he explains that the maxim should be expressed in a conditional form—will again specify the meaning of his words in order to avoid assimilation with James' position. For instance, he will offer a semiotic version of it, talking about meaning as the 'intended interpretant of a symbol' (CP 5.175),[6] and he will link the maxim to the logic of abduction by affirming that 'the maxim of pragmatism, if true, fully *covers* the entire logic of abduction': in this case, the maxim is a rule for the admissibility of hypotheses as 'hopeful suggestions' for the explanation of phenomena (CP 5.196).[7]

A connection which will become more and more explicit is that with the concept of habit, and in this case, the comparison with James again helps to clarify the reasons for this accentuation. In 1903, Peirce argues that the end of an explanatory hypothesis, which works by means of experiments, is 'to lead to the avoidance of all surprise and to the establishment of a habit of positive expectation that shall not be disappointed' (CP 5.197).[8] A couple of years later, he explicitly rejects James' characterization of pragmatism, and given the notoriety that the term has already gained, he coins the new expression 'pragmaticism'—a name ugly enough to be safe from kidnappers, as he famously said (CP 5.414).[9] In this period, the connection between conduct and generality is constantly reaffirmed. In 'Issues of Pragmaticism' (1905), for example, pragmaticism is described as the position according to which 'the purport of any concept is its conceived bearing upon our conduct' (CP 5.460), and more extensively:

> [t]he entire intellectual purport of any symbol consists in the total of all general modes of rational conduct which, conditionally upon all the possible different circumstances and desires, would ensue upon the acceptance of the symbol. (CP 5.438)

The concept of habit embodies the conditional, potential, and dispositional aspect of the connection between meaning and practical agency, and indeed, Peirce highlights precisely the exigency of not talking about

---

[6] In 'Three Types of Reasoning', 1903.
[7] In 'Pragmatism and Abduction', 1903.
[8] Again in "Pragmatism and Abduction'.
[9] In 'What Pragmatism Is', 1905.

a single action, nor about a set of actions, as consequences of a concept, but of a habit of conduct, that is of a *general* determination which includes not only what happens but what *could* happen.[10]

A letter Peirce wrote to *Nation* and *The Atlantic Monthly* a couple of years later confirms that the issue of habit was one of the essential differences between his and James' visions. In emphasizing that the two perspectives differed 'only' in that the latter did not restrict meaning to a habit, but allowed that percepts have a role, Peirce affirmed: 'practically, his view and mine must, I think, coincide, except where he allows considerations not at all pragmatic to have weight' (CP 5.494).

What for Peirce were 'considerations not at all pragmatic' were at the core of James' conception. In his P, the relevance of perceptions, concreteness, and individuality are even more evident. Moreover, James picks up and adapts the technical-methodological aspect of the maxim to his approach, which makes it an instrument for leaving aside useless discussions, empty conceptions, and abstract metaphysical temptations. He says:

> The pragmatic method is primarily a method of settling metaphysical disputes that otherwise might be interminable.... If no practical difference whatever can be traced, then the alternatives mean practically the same thing, and all dispute is idle.... The whole function of philosophy ought to be to find out what definite difference it will make to you and me, at definite instants of our life, if this world-formula or that world-formula be the true one. (P, pp. 28–30)

James insists on the practical difference that a philosophical perspective—a vision of the world one might say—makes *for you and for me*, in a concrete, specific situation. It is not just a form of contextualism: it is a point of view according to which a philosophical perspective (and *a fortiori* any everyday belief) is not only adopted but *espoused*, lived, embodied. In his *doing* philosophy, and not only in his idea of philosophy, James expresses himself in the first person. Once philosophy is an object of study, for James, it is also an object and instrument of communication

---

[10] See CP 5.504, from 'Consequences of Critical Common-Sensism', 1905.

with the other, an invitation to assume different points of view: second person. The third person, the philosophy which says how things are, is not eliminated, but it becomes parasitical with respect to its personal nature and to its communicative, hortatory, educational function. This wideness of vision and approach implies that uncertainties can—and perhaps must—have the positive task of casting doubt over any claim with a hint of the absolute. It is in this sense, reading his thought as broadly existentialist and hortatory, that, in my opinion, James' personal mode of 'practicing pragmatism' is to be taken.[11]

If, then, according to the pragmatic maxim, the meaning of a thought is in the conduct it produces (P, p. 29), pragmatism in the Jamesian perspective is above all a criticism of abstractions and general conceptions, and an appeal to the concrete, to particulars and to the practical aspects (P, pp. 31–32).

Peirce's writings in that very same year (1907) point clearly in the opposite direction. As we saw:

> I understand pragmatism to be a method of ascertaining the meanings, not of all ideas, but only of what I call 'intellectual concepts', that is to say, of those upon the structure of which, arguments concerning objective fact may hinge.... Intellectual concepts... convey... the 'would-acts', 'would-dos' of habitual behaviour; and no agglomeration of actual happenings can ever completely fill up the meaning of a 'would-be'. (CP 5.467)[12]

Generality, potentiality and habit are the trademarks of Peircean pragmatism. The idea of habit when applied to the behaviour of a human being not only represents the key for understanding the meaning of the concepts held true by the person, but it also constitutes the *totality* of what we can possibly know about that belief. Here we find again, under a different light, that principle of externalism with respect to minds which, as I mentioned, constitutes another topic on which a comparison with Wittgenstein would prove interesting.[13] Indeed, not only the

---

[11] See Calcaterra (2012) and Marchetti (2015a).
[12] From 'A Survey of Pragmaticism', 1907; also in EP 2, pp. 401–402, and SW, p. 272.
[13] Yet, in my view, the expression 'externalism' (like any other 'ism') needs qualification when referred to Wittgenstein, as his reflections cannot easily be put under this label. See in particular

'living comprehension' (CP 6.481)[14] of the meaning of a concept resides in the habits of conduct deriving from belief in the truth of the concept but also, as Peirce would say later, 'as long as it is *practically certain that we cannot* directly, nor with much accuracy even indirectly, observe what passes in the consciousness of any other person..., it is much safer to define all mental characters as far as possible in terms of their outward manifestations', and this maxim is, 'roughly speaking, equivalent to the one that I used to call the "rule of pragmatism"' (EP 2, p. 465).[15]

Perception and Conduct, Truth and Belief

In both Peirce and James' version of the maxim, there seems to be an ambivalence. On the one hand, the maxim states that the meaning of a concept lies in the practical conduct stemming from it, and on the other hand, it states that meaning lies in the expected perceptive consequences. This ambivalence in Peirce's formulations is particularly underlined by Hookway (2012, Chap. 9), who talks of a 'pragmatist dimension' and a 'verificationist dimension'. The first dimension, Hookway argues, is more evident in the 1878 version of the maxim and later in the 1903 and 1905 writings (see the already cited passages); formally, it can be put in these terms:

(I) If the circumstances are C and you have desires D, then (you ought to perform) an action of type A. (Hookway 2012, p. 169)

We can see the first dimension also in the subtler formulation of 1907, which Hookway renders as follows:

(II) If E were experienced to be the case, then the object a would behave in way B. (Hookway 2012, p. 170)

---

the remarks on the internal and the external in LW, which show a very sophisticated and unconventional outlook.

[14] From 'A Neglected Argument for the Reality of God', 1908.

[15] From 'An Essay toward Improving our Reasoning in Security and Uberty', prob. 1913.

The second dimension, a form of verificationism, according to Hookway, cannot be found in any explicit formulation of the maxim, but it can be found in many examples Peirce offers and in many writings in which he refers to the experimental method. For instance, in 1907, Peirce affirms that 'all pragmatists will . . . agree that their method of ascertaining the meanings of words and concepts is no other than that experimental method', and that this method is 'nothing but a particular application of an older logical rule, "By their fruits ye shall know them"' (EP 2, pp. 400–401).[16] He also refers to the fact that any hypothesis must be tested through the experimental method and that 'nothing that might not result from experiment can have any direct bearing upon conduct' so that 'if one can define accurately all the conceivable experimental phenomena which the affirmation or denial of a concept could imply, one will have therein a complete definition of the concept' (CP 5.412).[17] Hookway formalizes this second dimension in these terms:

(III) In circumstances C, if I were to do A, then I would experience E. (Hookway 2012, p. 173)

The pragmatist and verificationist aspects are connected, and Hookway himself notices that the very idea that 'nothing that might not result from experiment can have any direct bearing upon conduct' builds a bridge between them, suggesting the hypothesis that our reasons for acting might have something to do with what can be experienced. Formulation (II), which Hookway adds to (I) as an example of the pragmatic dimension, already makes reference to what can be experienced and so, implicitly, to the verificationist dimension. Yet, according to Hookway, this connection between acting and experiencing had worried Peirce for a long time, and he was never completely satisfied with his way of dealing with the matter.

In my view, not only are the two aspects connected, but they are also connected precisely in virtue of what makes pragmatism what it is, that is—to go back to the origins, in 1877–78—the idea that belief is a habit of action. Believing something, for instance, believing that A is true,

---

[16] From 'Pragmatism', 1907.
[17] 'What Pragmatism Is', quoted in Hookway (2012, p. 173) from EP 2, p. 332.

implies a habit of action and this very habit constitutes, non-reductively, the verification of the belief: a verification which remains open just like a behavioural habit remains open to change, correction, evolution. Peirce himself concludes his *Harvard Lectures* on the maxim (1903) with a remark that puts the two aspects together in a natural and unproblematic way:

> The elements of every concept enter into logical thought at the gate of perception and make their exit at the gate of purposive action; and whatever cannot show its passports at both those two gates is to be arrested as unauthorized by reason. (CP 5.212)

The distinction traced by Hookway[18] in Peirce's thought finds an echo in an older discussion regarding the (alleged) existence of two not just logically independent but even contradictory aspects in James' thought. It is a criticism Arthur O. Lovejoy levels against James in 1908, and it is interesting to examine it.

> The 'effects of a practical kind'... may consist in either: (a) future experiences which the proposition (expressly or implicitly) predicts as about to occur, no matter whether it be believed true or not; or (b) future experiences which will occur only upon condition that the proposition be believed. The consequences of the truth of a proposition... and the consequences of belief in a proposition, have been habitually confused in the discussion of the pragmatic theory of meaning. (Lovejoy 1908, p. 8)

In the former sense, Lovejoy continues, only genuine predictive propositions, referring to specific sensations or situations in the concrete experience of a consciousness, have meaning; in the latter sense, meaning has nothing to do with propositions pointing to the future: all that is required is that in the believer's mind, propositions, once believed, imply different experiences from those that the mind would otherwise have had.

---

[18] But see also Wu (1994).

It is easy to see that the pragmatic maxim's job is precisely to establish a link between the two senses. As Rydenfelt (2009) says, in the maxim the two sides are intrinsically connected: to believe something to be true is to be ready to act consequently and is *at the very same time* to expect particular experiences and perceptions. James' words, as many have noted, are easily misinterpreted, and he sometimes fostered misinterpretations: in this case, for instance, in a letter he even affirmed that Lovejoy was right (Rydenfelt 2009, pp. 84). Nevertheless, I agree with Rydenfelt in identifying this aspect as the core of the pragmatic maxim, and maybe of the pragmatist proposal itself. James' version of the maxim, in connection with his conception of truth, is open to criticism; yet once the central issue of belief is examined, I think it appears much closer to the Peircean version than both authors were willing to sustain. The point is that the ambiguity highlighted by Hookway between the verificationist and the pragmatic aspect in Peirce is similar—though not identical—to the ambiguity between the consequences of the truth of a proposition and the consequences of deeming a proposition true, as highlighted by Lovejoy in James.[19] The closeness emerges clearly when one considers that, for both, belief results in effects on conduct. Deeming something to be true (belief) establishes a habit of conduct which produces not only behavioural effects but, *in the long run*, real and hence perceptive effects; these in turn act upon conduct and belief. The Peircean clause 'in the long run' is naturally central, and James himself resorts to it when he needs to defend his approach.[20] This clause is what permits the two formulations to be considered similar. On the other hand, if the clause is to be neglected, this loosens the degree of kinship between them, highlighting the distance between the pragmatic *realist* Peircean perspective, in the complex sense in which 'would-bes' are part of reality; and the pragmatic (let me say) *existentialist* Jamesian perspective, appealing to an 'ethos of contingency' hinging upon individual responsibility which, through ideas and actions, gives a human directive to events (Calcaterra 2012).

---

[19] On this topic see also Putnam (1992a).
[20] See for instance MT, pp. 4, 143.

Of course, it is not within my aims to further investigate these aspects. For the moment, let me just add that, as we shall see, this way of assembling truth and belief, perceptive effects and behavioural consequence that joins Peirce and James, can be compared with Wittgenstein's view on knowledge and meaning, particularly in OC.

Meaning and Consequences: The 'Pragmatist Week'

The theme of the connection between meaning and consequences appears many times in Wittgenstein's writings. When he first mentioned pragmatism, as we saw in Chapter 1, he was working on the relationship between perceptive expectation, action, and truth. Similar issues emerge in later remarks concerning meaning, understanding, behaviour, rules, but also the virtues and the limits of considering consequences as criteria for grasping meaning.[21] But it is in OC that Wittgenstein develops specific reflections, which in my perception suggest his acquaintance with some of the pragmatists' writings on the pragmatic maxim.

At the end of February 1951, Wittgenstein, together with Doctor Bevan, whom he was staying with in Cambridge, decided to give up the therapies he was following against cancer. He affirmed with relief: 'I am going to work now as I have never worked before' (Monk 1991, p. 577). On 16 April, he wrote to Norman Malcolm: 'An extraordinary thing has happened to me. About a month ago I suddenly found myself in the right frame of mind for doing philosophy.... It's the first time after more than two years that the curtain in my brain has gone up' (McGuinness 2012, p. 479). Of course, the lucidity and self-transparency of a terminally ill person (Wittgenstein died on 29 April) should not be taken for granted. Yet, his work in those last months was surely fertile.

The remark which opens the fourth section of OC bears the date of 10 March. The initial part of this section, which is the longest one in the volume

---

[21] See PR, §230g; BT, p. 95 and in general sec. 32 and sec. 60; PI, §§80–81, 268–269, 543, 578; RPP I, §306; LW II, pp. 81 ff.

(remarks from §300 to §676), contains some key points: the categorical distinction between knowledge and certainty (§308), the remarks on empirical propositions and logical or methodological ones (for example §318 and §319), and the hinges metaphor (§§341–343). Starting from 15 March, during what we might call the later Wittgenstein's 'pragmatist week', many remarks concerning the topic of consequences begin to appear.

Wittgenstein focuses in particular on what it means to say that one 'knows' something, and makes examples regarding everyday platitudes. For instance:

> I KNOW that this is my foot. I could not accept any experience as proof to the contrary.—That may be an exclamation; but what *follows* from it? At least that I shall act with a certainty [*Sicherheit*] that knows no doubt, in accordance with my belief. (OC, §360)

The connection that he points out is that between knowing something and acting with certainty on that basis, including—as he explains in OC, §395—speaking about the things which are believed. Developing the example above, he asks himself whether being certain of the consequences is not 'the whole point' of knowing that this is a foot (OC, §409), where being certain of the consequences would consist (among other things) in being able to tell someone else who was doubtful: 'You see? I told you so!'. In this sense, the whole point of knowledge is that it is a clue or a rule that we use in our everyday actions, predicting, perhaps even without an explicit awareness, how things in the world would be or behave. Knowledge itself (and supposing that it is knowledge that we are talking about) would not be necessarily explicitly held. 'Of course—Wittgenstein observes—I do not think to myself 'The earth already existed for some time before my birth', but do I *know* it any the less? Don't I show that I know it by always drawing its consequences?' (OC, §397).

How, then, should one account for these basic certainties? Acting in accordance with them and being able to predict consequences assume a primary role. It was so for the pragmatists and it is so for *this* Wittgenstein. Like he did in the early 1930s, when he reflected on the distinction between propositions referring to sense-data and hypotheses referring to the future, he now replies to Moore's strategy—which *is*, after all, based on sense-data—and states that it is not enough for someone to say that he or she *knows* something and to try assuring the listener of this self-confidence (OC, §426). The starting point must be different from sense-data and self-assurance. 'We need to show—he finally affirms—that even if he never uses the words "I know...", his *conduct* exhibits the thing we are concerned with' (OC, §427, my emphasis).

The remark about pragmatism and the 'thwarting' *Weltanschauung* (OC, §422) is found in these same days: written on 21 March, within a train of thought concerning the certainty of a proposition such as 'I am now in England', which if, on the one hand, *cannot be a mistake* (OC, §420), on the other hand, does not guarantee that, by pronouncing that phrase, I am *infallible* as to this (OC, §425). The remarks which surround OC, §422, once seen in the light of the fundamental themes of pragmatism, reveal rather deep consonances. Here we find, indeed, not only the particular form of fallibilism just mentioned, but also reflections on the relevance of the community as a criterion for the truth and the reasonableness of assertions (see OC, §420 on normality and madness), a contextualist approach (OC, §423), and more generally remarks with a pragmatic tone on doubt, certainty, and belief. But it is probably the topic of the connection between knowing something and knowing its consequences, found in a considerable amount of Wittgenstein's thoughts in those days, the main reason for the appearance of the word 'pragmatism' in OC, §422.

I do not think that what emerges is a complete overlap between a sort of Wittgensteinian version of the pragmatic maxim and the original version, but I do think that there is a significant closeness. It is not an overlap first of all because the terms in question are partly different: (1) Wittgenstein speaks chiefly about certainty, sureness, and knowledge, not of belief, and he repeats that in these cases we *cannot* speak of belief; (2) besides, he does not deal with meaning, but with assertions about what one knows. Yet, as for the former point, it must be remembered that for a fully fallibilist position like that of the pragmatists, knowing something and believing something are one and the same: everything we know, we believe we know, because our knowledge is always fallible, even when it is certain, with the fast certainty of common sense. In Wittgenstein's case, things are more complicated, as one of the thematic issues of OC is precisely that for some of our certainties it is not *grammatically* correct to say that we know them, nor *a fortiori* that we believe them. So whereas the pragmatists assimilate knowledge, belief, and certainty, Wittgenstein sets knowledge against certainty. Here is where the fallibilism of the pragmatists and of Wittgenstein differ: the former is part of an epistemic approach, however wide, anchored in the priority of inquiry; while the latter is an attempt to get away from this kind of perspective, by fixing the certainties of the *Weltbild* in the priority of life.

As for point (2), it must be also considered that Wittgenstein is actually *asking himself* whether it is appropriate or not in certain circumstances to claim to know something, and he is trying to understand if this kind of assertion can be substituted by something else: by our acting and our being able to predict, in practice, the consequences of what we say we know. At this point, Wittgenstein had not yet reached a conclusion—as the many question marks in these remarks show—but he seems to be testing the idea that the question about knowing the consequences of something could equate to (and maybe substitute) the question about knowing something. In other words, instead of trying to demonstrate that we know what we say we know, as an attempt to reply to the sceptic which nevertheless remains on an epistemic level (and hence risks not being able to face up to the challenge), we could, perhaps, limit ourselves to ascertaining that we already *show* our certainty in acting and predicting the consequences. Thus, in a sense, in OC the distinction which characterized the *Tractatus*, between saying and showing, resurfaces, but while previously the distinction pertained to the terrain of logic ('logic must take care of itself', TLP 5.473), it now pertains to the terrain of action ('the practice has to speak for itself', OC, §139).[22]

There is also another difference between the classical version of the maxim and Wittgenstein's 'version', which stands out in particular if we are to consider some of Peirce's formulations. The latter, indeed, sometimes insists on the fact that the maxim concerns intellectual concepts

---

[22] The presence of the saying/showing distinction in OC, only in part comparable to the Tractarian distinction, is not a new topic in literature; see for instance Gill (1974), McGinn (2001), Moyal-Sharrock (2007, pp. 48, 94 ff.), Boncompagni (2014).

and generalizations. Conversely, Wittgenstein has a propensity for the world of the ordinary and makes use of everyday examples. This difference should not be neglected; yet, upon a closer look, it appears weakened in this case as well. What Peirce calls intellectual concepts are, in fact, the most important and common logical operations of reasoning, the fundamental categories of thinking.[23] Peirce, like Wittgenstein to a certain extent, is interested in the connection between these operations and the everyday world. Intellectual concepts, Peirce explained, are those upon which arguments concerning objective concepts, that is, factual judgements, hinge. Mathematical judgements may be an example, as well as the concept of causality: innumerable factual judgements depend upon the employment of these categories. The fact that here Peirce uses the term, dear to the 'Third-Wittgensteinians', 'to hinge', is clearly a coincidence, but an interesting one, suggesting that we re-examine the way in which Wittgenstein uses the same image. In the propositions we saw about hinges in OC, Wittgenstein is in fact speaking about something very similar: he is relating some kinds of certainties, like mathematical ones, to other kinds, usually considered distant from the former; and he is saying, of both types, that they are like the hinges around which ordinary judgments rotate. The image of hinges is preceded by another interesting remark.

> We know, with the same certainty with which we believe *any* mathematical proposition, how the letters A and B are pronounced, what the colour of human blood is called, that other human beings have blood and call it 'blood'. (OC, §341)

Also in the following remark (OC, §342), and in the other one regarding hinges (OC, §655), Wittgenstein refers to *scientific inquiries* and again to *mathematics*, focusing on something Peirce would not hesitate to include among intellectual concepts. Wittgenstein's point, rather, is that to these concepts it is possible to assimilate other ones we learn when learning a

---

[23] But see the different opinion of Chauviré (2003, p. 96), who underlines the closeness to scientific conceptions.

language ('how the letters A and B are pronounced', 'what the colour of human blood is called'). Hence, what is relevant in the comparison is not the fact that Peirce highlights intellectual concepts whereas Wittgenstein concentrates on certainties belonging to the ordinary world: Peirce highlights intellectual concepts and Wittgenstein what we may call grammatical certainties, and in both cases these aspects constitute the background of everyday life. Differences remain, but they are not so deep, and they are not exactly where we thought they were.

Let us dwell on one last point, which will finally take us back to the double aspect of the maxim shown in the previous section. The consequences Peirce and James describe have to do, on the one hand, with what happens in the world of facts and perceptions, and on the other hand, with actions, practices, and habits. In Wittgenstein's remarks too predictions concern *both* the world of facts *and* the conduct of the person who holds the certainty in question. In OC, §§360, 395, 427, indeed, certainty shows itself in the way an individual acts 'in accordance with her belief', in the way she speaks, in her conduct, and in OC, §397 and §409 in 'always drawing the consequences', and therefore in correctly predicting how things will be. Predicting consequences correctly, Wittgenstein clarifies, even when they belong to the factual world, is always shown in the actions, because it is through her actions that one can see if a person was able to predict facts correctly: it is in her moving without hesitation, in her not tripping up, that one can see that she knew where to put her feet, where obstacles were. In Wittgenstein too, belief, or rather certainty, is indissolubly bound to action. 'Would my knowledge still be worth anything if it let me down as a clue for action?', he asks himself in OC, §409, echoing with the expression '*Richtsnur des Handelns*', precisely that 'rule of action' with which Peirce, in 'How to Make Our Ideas Clear', identified both belief and habit.

To conclude, although Wittgenstein's and the pragmatists' approaches do not overlap, Wittgenstein's remark in OC, §422 ('So I am trying to say something that sounds like pragmatism. Here I am being thwarted by a kind of *Weltanschauung*') turns out to be perfectly natural if it is hypothesized that he had sufficient knowledge of pragmatism and could see the consonance between his reflections and the pragmatic maxim. The indissolubility of the bond between thought and action highlighted by his remarks is also a fundamental trait of the maxim, although perhaps it does not exhaust its meaning. Hamilton (2014, p. 247) has it that for Wittgenstein 'it is not that thought must make a direct impact on life' (which is what the pragmatists say, in his view); 'rather, there is no such thing as thought at the propositional level, divorced... from "the actions of life"', and, he states, '[t]hat is not pragmatism'. In my view, Hamilton is right *in general terms* in noticing that the embeddedness of thought within practices and forms of life is a wider theme, which one cannot sum up by simply labelling it 'pragmatism'. Yet, if one examines the remarks we have just considered in the light of the pragmatic maxim, it becomes clear that they *do* capture something essential to pragmatism as expressed in the maxim, and that is the motive behind Wittgenstein's concerns in OC, §422.

The reflection just set out contains a possible direction of inquiry I would like to look into further, as it leads to a theme I have already touched on, and can now be contextualized with more accuracy. This is the theme of meaning as use, which we saw with reference to the connection between use and usefulness, but which can also be considered with reference to the pragmatic maxim. Indeed, the maxim connects understanding something to understanding its consequences. To what extent is this relevant for Wittgenstein's perspective on meaning?

Meaning and Understanding

The issue of use with respect to the pragmatist tradition is at the centre of the analysis carried out by Schulte (1999), who particularly emphasizes the relevance of the *contexts* of use, in the broad sense, as a common trait in Wittgenstein's and the pragmatists' conception of meaning. According to this perspective, in order to know the meaning of a word, it is necessary to know its *possibilities* of use, that is, to be able to indicate the possible contexts of use, to imagine the concrete situations in which these uses are embedded. This sometimes, but not necessarily, implies an *instrumental* use of words and propositions. There is indeed an instrumentalist aspect in Wittgenstein's concept of meaning, as we saw in the first note on pragmatism in 1930. For Schulte, this can be compared to pragmatism, considering pragmatism as an approach which highlights the instrumental nature of language for the solution of problems connected to our needs and desires. Something similar can be found in Wittgenstein, for instance, when he affirms that what matters in a verbal or non-verbal language is its *Dienst*, that is, the service it performs (RPP I, §§265–266).[24] But according to Schulte there is also a difference: when Wittgenstein invites us to look at the use of words and sentences, his aim is not to underline the search for possible uses with the purpose of adapting oneself to new exigencies; rather, his aim is an inquiry into the already existent, but perhaps unacknowledged or misinterpreted features of our grammar. Not that Wittgenstein resolutely denies the connection between meaning and use as usefulness—as we saw, in some cases he even emphasizes this very connection. Schulte helps us to add another example to the brief survey presented in Chapter 1:

> It is said: It's not the word that counts, but its meaning, and in saying this one always thinks of meaning as if it were a thing of the same kind as the word, yet different from it. Here is the word, here the meaning. (Money, and the cow that one can buy with it. But on the other hand: money and its profit [*Nutzen*]). (BT, p. 58)[25]

Language is here compared to a credit system (is there anything more instrumental?) and the relationship between word and meaning is compared to the relationship between money and its counter value, its utility.[26] Yet, it must be remembered that Wittgenstein, as we saw, opposes a *generalized* explanation of this kind, limiting himself to the admission that *sometimes* it is correct to describe meaning in terms of utility. In Schulte's interpretation, the Viennese philosopher is able to disconnect, in a very refined manner, the reflection on *use* from a vision

---

[24] From MS 131, p. 70.
[25] Originally in MS 110, p. 231 (1931), quoted in Schulte (1999, p. 318).
[26] Notice that William James repeatedly compares truths and the banknotes of the credit system (see for instance P, p. 100), and remember his metaphor of the 'cash value' (P, p. 32).

of the world which can derive from the emphasis on *usefulness*, a vision shaped by the ideals of progress and the improvement of society, which the pragmatists would endorse.[27] In addition, Schulte suggests that Wittgenstein is able to disconnect this reflection from the naturalistic and causalistic explanations which would be implied in the pragmatist conception. Although Wittgenstein's remark, according to which some linguistic forms are part of our natural history just like walking and eating (PI, §25), can sound pragmatist, indeed it must not be forgotten that Wittgenstein puts the emphasis on something else: the aim is not to look for the causes of phenomena, but to show that small-scale differences (in linguistic games) are signs of differences on a large scale (grammar), without thus purporting to offer a general system. We will come back to the issue of naturalism in the last chapter.

In order to go deeper into the matter of the connection between the pragmatic maxim and meaning as use, I would like to examine a claim advanced by Richard Rorty, which will also help to see other aspects of the relationship between Wittgenstein and Ramsey. In a famous article, Rorty (1961, p. 198) asserted that Wittgenstein and the pragmatists' intuitions about language were very similar in certain respects, and in particular that '[t]he similarity of their insights about language reflects the fact that the slogans "don't look for the meaning, look for the use" and "the meaning of a concept is the sum of its possible effects upon conduct" reciprocally support each other'. According to Rorty, the affinity between the two perspectives has to do with the anti-reductionism which characterizes both, and, in turn, this has to do with the value that in both cases is assigned to vagueness.

Both approaches, indeed, emphasize the role of vagueness, which constitutes one of the qualities of common sense beliefs. Regarding its link with meaning, it is impossible not to see the relevance that some remarks by James had in Wittgenstein's thought: I am referring in particular to the idea of the *fringe*, which we have already encountered. But Peirce comes to mind too, both owing to the reciprocal influences that the two founding fathers of pragmatism had on each other on the

---

[27] On the difference between use and usefulness, see also Moyal-Sharrock (2007, p. 171).

theme of the continuity of thought,[28] and because Peirce's attitude, with its insistence on generality and virtuality, resembles Wittgenstein's invitation to imagine the *possible* uses of words in order to understand their meanings. As Peirce says:

> I do not think that the import of any word (except perhaps a pronoun) is limited to what is in the utterer's mind *actualiter*.... It is, on the contrary, according to me, what is in the mind, perhaps not even *habitualiter*, but only *virtualiter*, which constitutes the import. (CP 5.504)[29]

I therefore agree with Rorty on the similarity between Wittgenstein's idea of looking for meaning in use and the conception of meaning which emerges from the pragmatic maxim, and on pinpointing this similarity in vagueness and in a certain kind of contextualism. Yet, the pragmatist's conception of meaning also has other aspects from which Wittgenstein's approach seems more distant. Here some clarifications are needed. I am referring to two issues in particular. The first one relates to the Peircean passage cited earlier in which he writes about what 'is in the mind'. This expression must not suggest that Peirce was, to use a more recent label, *mentalist* about meaning: the pragmatic maxim has precisely the sense of pointing out that the 'place' of meaning lies in visible external factors, be they of a perceptual or behavioural nature. In order to better understand the reference to the utterer's mind, these lines should be interpreted within the wider horizon of Peirce's semiotics, a task which is outside our goals. But we must not forget that one of the themes on which Wittgenstein criticized the other pragmatist, James, was the characterization of the flux of experience in exclusively psychological terms; chiefly, Wittgenstein opposed the way in which James connected

---

[28] Compare the chapter on the stream of thought in James' PP (1890, originally appearing in 1884 as an article) with Peirce's metaphor of thought as a melody in 'How to Make Our Ideas Clear' (1878), and also with Peirce's article 'The Law of Mind', 1892 (W 8, pp. 126–157, CP 6.102–163, CLL, pp. 202–237).

[29] From 'Consequences of Critical Common-Sensism'. A similar characterization of thought can be found in 'Some Consequences of Four Incapacities', where Peirce affirms that the meaning of a thought is virtual and not actual (W 2, p. 227, CP 5.289). We will examine this passage in next chapter.

intention and sensation, for instance, in the cases of the feeling of 'tending' and the sensation of the 'atmosphere' of a word.[30]

The conviction that meaning has to do *essentially* with the mental state of the speaker and the intentionality in what she is saying, was also the subject of conversations between Wittgenstein and Ramsey. This is what Rush Rhees maintains, in his interpretation of PI, §511[31]:

> What does 'discovering that an utterance doesn't make sense' mean?— And what does it mean to say, 'If I mean something by it, surely it must make sense'?—If I mean something by it?—If I mean *what* by it?!—One wants to say: a sentence that makes sense is one which one can not merely say, but also think.

This quote is part of a reasoning about intending and understanding in which Wittgenstein highlights the insufficiency of the process of *intending* something when uttering a sentence in order for the sentence to have meaning. PI, §514, for example, criticizes the philosopher who tries to understand the sentence 'I am here' by thinking about something while uttering it, without considering the way or the circumstances in which it is uttered. According to Rhees, the quoted remark refers to the conversations with Ramsey because, in those conversations, which were about the infinite and set theory, to Wittgenstein's affirmation that 'This is senseless', Ramsey replied: 'No, I am sure I mean something by it'. Meaning— Wittgenstein sustained then and also later—is not the mental activity through which words receive their sense.

That the PI remark does refer to the conversations with Ramsey is confirmed by examining some other passages from the manuscripts: Ramsey's name appears several times in association with the idea that if, by pronouncing a sentence, one means something, then as a result the sentence has meaning. For example, in a remark belonging to MS 112 (1931), Wittgenstein opposes Ramsey's affirmation according to which the mere 'thinkability' of a man who never dies or of a wheel which

---

[30] See for example PI, §§591, 633; PPF, sec. vi; RPP II, §§242–243.
[31] Rhees (2003, p. 32). The original formulation of PI, §511 is in MS 110, p. 292 (1931).

never stops turning justifies the possibility of an extensional infinity (MS 112, p. 120r); after a few pages, Ramsey is mentioned again in connection with the idea that, when we say or hear a proposition expressing a contradiction, we nevertheless have the *sensation* that there is a sense, albeit degenerate (MS 112, p. 126r).[32] Similar reflections also occur in other writings.[33] In sum, the point is that, even if one emphasizes the relevance of purpose and use in meaning, as Ramsey and the pragmatists did, for Wittgenstein much work still needed to be done to clear the field of the idea of intention considered as an inner mental state. 'Over and again—he observes—we're inclined to think of the sense of a proposition, i.e. its application (its use) [*seine Verwendung (seinen Nutzen)*], as concentrated in a speaker's mental state', while we should concentrate on 'calculating with it, operating with it, replacing it with this or that picture as times goes by' (BT, p. 84).

In addition, the pragmatist conception of meaning is prone to another kind of interpretation that Wittgenstein considers problematic: and here we come to the second issue on which there is a distance. Since the pragmatic maxim focuses on *consequences*, one could intend this perspective in terms of *cause and effect*. When Peirce affirms that 'the elements of every concept enter into logical thought at the gate of perception and make their exit at the gate of purposive action' (CP 5.212), it is possible to see him (not to the letter perhaps, but that is not the point) as affirming that perception is the cause of meaning, and action is its effect. The causalist interpretation of meaning, brought to the centre of the philosophical debate also by two publications which were very well known in the 1920s and 1930s, *The Analysis of Mind* by Russell and *The Meaning of Meaning* by Ogden and Richards,[34] was, again, not extraneous to Ramsey, and was an option Wittgenstein refused.[35]

---

[32] Ramsey wrote about tautologies and contradictions as 'degenerate cases' of propositions in 'The Foundations of Mathematics', 1925 (see Ramsey 1990, Chap. 8).

[33] See MS 153, p. 40v (1931); MS 116, p. 51 (circa 1937–1938); MS 119, p. 87v (1937); the same themes can be found in some typescripts: TS 211, pp. 521, 529 (1932); BT, p. 340; TS 228, p. 10 (1945–1946); TS 233, p. 56 (1945–1946).

[34] Russell (1921), Ogden and Richards (1960), first edition 1923.

[35] See Egidi (1983). On Russell's book and Wittgenstein see Engelmann (2012).

While opposing both the mentalist and the causalist interpretations of meaning, already at the beginning of the 1930s the latter tended towards a conception according to which meaning rests within the system of grammar:

> I want to say that signs have their meanings neither by virtue of what accompanies them, nor because of what evokes [*hervorruft*] them—but by virtue of a system to which they belong—one, however, in which when a word is uttered nothing need be present other than the word.[36]

That 'nothing need be present other than the word' does not imply that grammar remains, so to speak, trapped in itself: as would emerge in later years with more clarity, in Wittgenstein, grammar is intertwined with the form of life to which it belongs. Similarly, in Peirce, the system of signs and interpretations is intertwined with the behaviour and habits which constitute its expression and its limit.

We can now draw some conclusions about meaning and the pragmatic maxim. Wittgenstein's suggestion to look for meaning in use does not precisely overlap with the suggestions made by the pragmatic maxim, according to which the meaning of a concept lies in its practical consequences; yet, in virtue of some important underlying affinities, particularly on vagueness and contextualism, the two approaches do share some common features. The consonance is clearer once some issues are put aside that are connected to certain interpretations of pragmatism, rather than to pragmatism itself: a sort of mentalism focused on the sensation of understanding, and the association with a cause-and-effect approach to meaning.

One last theme related to the pragmatic maxim requires further investigation. I said that the practical consequences to which the maxim refers materialize in perceptive expectations and, eventually, outcomes which have to do with action. What did the pragmatists and Wittgenstein mean, more precisely, by terms such as 'action', 'practices', 'conduct', 'habit', and 'behaviour'?

---

[36] BT, p. 155. See also BT, sec. 10 and LCL, pp. 63–64.

'Im Anfang war die Tat'

Admirers of Goethe, both James and Wittgenstein quote *Faust*, '*Im Anfang war die Tat*', 'in the beginning was the deed'. James does it in 'Bergson and his Critique of Intellectualism', one of the PU lectures, published in 1909 (but he cites Goethe on other occasions as well[37]). Wittgenstein does it in OC, among the remarks from the 'pragmatist week' (but he also cites Goethe on other occasions as well[38]). Clearly, this is a famous quote and they are not the only ones to have used it, but it is of interest that both were struck by the very same words, and probably for similar reasons[39]: although in different contexts, both indicate action, rather than the word, as the starting point of philosophical activity. Now the point is to understand to what extent the two aspirations share a common vision.

In the pragmatist tradition, it is James, more than Peirce, who emphasizes the theme of action; this is actually one of the acknowledged divergences between the two thinkers. Beyond working on it in connection with the pragmatic maxim, James mainly deals with action in the context of psychology. The description of action in PP puts two aspects in the foreground. On the one hand, it underlines how instincts, reflex actions and voluntary and deliberate actions are not distinguishable from each other in a clear-cut way, but rather gradually dissolve one into another. As James says: 'the animal's reflex and voluntary performances shade into each other gradually' (PP, p. 26); 'decisions with effort merge

---

[37] *Faust* is mentioned again in the PP chapter on the will; other quotes can be found for instance in 'Reflex Action and Theism' (WB, p. 61), in 'The Sentiment of Rationality' (WB, p. 90), in VRE. On Goethe and James cf. Richardson (2006, sec. 12).

[38] The same quote is in MS 119, p. 47 (then in CV, p. 31), but many citations appear in his notes, from the 1930s until the last manuscripts. On Goethe and Wittgenstein, see Andronico (1998), McGuinness (2002), and Breithaupt et al. (2003).

[39] It is not by chance that in Goethe one can find what we may call a 'proto-pragmatic maxim' like this: 'Indeed, strictly speaking, it is useless to attempt to express the nature of a thing abstractedly. Effects we can perceive, and a complete history of those effects would, in fact, sufficiently define the nature of the thing itself. We should try in vain to describe a man's character, but let his acts be collected and an idea of the character will be presented to us'. This is in the Preface of the *Theory of Colors* (Goethe 1840), which Wittgenstein knew very well (McGuinness 2012, pp. 456–458).

so gradually into those without it that it is not easy to say where the limit lies. Decisions without effort merge again into ideo-motor, and these into reflex acts' (PP, p. 1178). On the other hand, James' words highlight how the usual paradigmatic idea of voluntary action, according to which the subject elaborates and gets action off the ground through a specific decision and exercising willpower, is actually marginal, and does not correspond to most everyday cases of voluntary action. The PP chapter on the will, which, together with the chapter on the stream of thought, is surely one of the most consulted by Wittgenstein, is significant in this respect. James here opposes the idea that voluntary action is dictated by a perceptible stimulus going from the brain to the muscles and taking the shape of a 'feeling of innervation' (an idea sustained, among others, by Ernst Mach and Wilhelm Wundt), and affirms that normally it is enough for someone to have in mind the idea of the action she is about to perform and its perceivable effects, in order for the action itself to take place. The will, a mental and moral phenomenon, simply consists of paying attention to the idea: if there are no concurrent ideas in the mind, action follows, without the need for any particular effort. This is the commonest case of voluntary action, which James labels as ideo-motor action and considers the starting point also for explaining actions which involve an explicit consent (PP, p. 1135).

When there are more, contrasting ideas in the mind, a process of deliberation takes place, which terminates when one of the ideas prevails over the others. Only in very rare cases does this require, by the agent, the exertion of an effective effort with the aim of making one idea prevail. In these cases, voluntary action is not only deliberate: it entails a 'feeling of effort'. But the will remains on a mental level; the effort is essentially an effort of *attention*, and as soon as the subject is able to concentrate and keep only one idea fast in the mind, again, the motor action develops automatically, guided by cerebral and nervous mechanisms.

Other writings by James dating back to the years of the PP testify a constant attention to the themes of will and action not only in physiological and psychological terms. In 'Reflex Action and Theism',[40] for instance, James

---

[40] Originally published in 1881, then in WB.

distinguishes the three 'departments' of human nature, *feeling, conceiving, and willing*, and he gives priority to willing. In 'The Dilemma of Determinism'[41] a vision of freedom emerges which has little to do with theoretical aspects and much to do with the first person: freedom is lived, acted, or 'enacted', as Koopman (2014) notices. Yet, it is in 'The Will to Believe'[42] that Peirce points out James' inclination towards action. In this article, originally written for a conference, James affirms that there are truths which at least in part depend on our personal action, and that in these cases faith in a fact can help 'create' the fact itself—this is what happens with institutional facts, which exist in virtue of the mutual trust of citizens, or with religious truths, of which in particular the voluntary nature of belief constitutes a crucial element. More generally, James brings out the role of will and action in relation to the concepts of hypotheses and truth, in a perspective against which Peirce reacts very definitely:

> In 1896 William James published his Will to Believe, and later his Philosophical Conceptions and Practical Results, which pushed this method to such extremes as must tend to give us pause. The doctrine appears to assume that the end of man is action—a stoical axiom which, to the present writer at the age of sixty, does not recommend itself so forcibly as it did at thirty. (CP 5.3)

Shortly after the publication of 'The Will to Believe', Peirce expressed the same perplexities in a letter to James, emphasising that 'it is not mere action as brute exercise of strength that is the purpose of all', but rather what tends to generalization, regularization, and 'the actualization of the thought' (CP 8.250).

In turn, starting from that 1896 which saw the publication of 'The Will to Believe', James would focus on experience more than action, and introduce his radical empiricism.[43] The outcome of this shift of attention is well condensed in the title of a paragraph of 'The Pragmatist

---

[41] Originally published in 1884, then in WB.

[42] Published in 1896 as an article, it also gives the title to the collection of essays WB, which appeared the following year with a dedication to Peirce.

[43] He announces this in the Preface of WB.

Account of Truth and its Misunderstanders' (MT, pp. 101–102), in which the idea that pragmatism consists essentially of an appeal to action is stigmatized as a simple *misunderstanding*.

In the following years, Peirce would specify that pragmaticism could not identify *action*, but rather *evolution*, as the 'summum bonum' (CP 5.433).[44] In any case, as the words quoted above reveal, he himself had formerly emphasized the relevance of action—he had written for example: 'It is plain that intelligence does not consist in feeling in a certain way, but in acting in a certain way' (CP 6.286).[45] Besides, his attention to habit at any rate indicates the importance that *doing* continued to have in his thought. From this point of view, in his writings we can find a characterization of action aiming specifically at highlighting its belonging to a habit, to a general behaviour that on the one hand may dominate action by forcing it into an already shaped path, but on the other hand is itself learned and, to a certain extent, plastic and mouldable by exerting rationality. According to Kilpinen (2009), this is what constitutes the 'Copernican Revolution' that pragmatists apply to the concept of action: action is thought of as part of a habit, without by this adopting a Humean vision of habit as automatic repetition. In other words, habit does not deny the intentional nature of action, so much so that, while paraphrasing Kant, Kilpinen concludes that habit without intentionality is blind, and intentionality without habit is empty.[46]

In Kilpinen's interpretation, Peirce's idea of habit invalidates the possibility of a comparison with Wittgenstein's theme of following a rule: in the latter there is no chance of change; once the rule is learned, it is followed *blindly*. Conversely, I would like to argue that the dialectic between the linguistic game and rule *is* effectively comparable to the dialectic between action and habit. But before turning to this, it is necessary to focus on Wittgenstein's treatment of these themes.

---

[44] From 'What Pragmatism Is', 1905.

[45] From 'Mind and Matter', 1893.

[46] Action's belonging to habit, we may add, is not alien to James either, especially considering the relevance that the *education of the will* has for him. See Franzese (2008, Chap. 3) and Marchetti (2015b).

Action and Its Surroundings

Let us consider a couple of passages from OC dealing directly with action.

> Why do I not satisfy myself that I have two feet when I want to get up from a chair? There is no why. I simply don't. This is how I act. (OC, §148)
>
> Giving grounds, however, justifying the evidence, comes to an end;—but the end is not certain propositions' striking us immediately as true, i.e. it is not a kind of *seeing* on our part; it is our *acting*, which lies at the bottom of the language-game. (OC, §204)

With perhaps even more clarity than in the remarks belonging to the 'pragmatist week', Wittgenstein puts to the fore that action has primacy over knowledge and justification: indeed, it is itself the basic ground of justification. With the aim of investigating these basic grounds, Wittgenstein decides to consider human beings as primarily animals or primitive beings with no ratiocinating (OC, §475). It is at *this* level that he now intends to pursue the study of logic and language, a level at which the latter matters chiefly as 'primitive means for communication' (*ibid.*), because it is at this level that its main features are more evident. Similarly, during infancy, the child learns by doing things, and not by assimilating abstract knowledge. As he puts it in OC, §538, 'knowing only begins at a later level'.

In this sense, acting is foundational, and yet in a very peculiar way: it is a fundament which 'is there—like our life' (OC, §559), which is what it is not in virtue of the solidity of what sustains it—nothing, evidently, sustains it—but in virtue of the movement of what surrounds it: thanks to the fact that it is *acted*, practised, kept in use. Wittgenstein insists that acting comes *before* words; not only in the sense that in growing up, doing comes before knowing, but also in the sense that when we act we do not do so *on the basis* of the knowledge we have: when we act, we *show* that we hold some certainties.

This is not a trivial point. Indeed, if certainties are shown, one may think this means that they are *held*, before, during and after the action. The fact, in this case, it seems to me, is that what action shows is not so much the epistemic nature of certainties, but their practical nature: what

Chapter 4: Action and the Pragmatic Maxim 171

one can see in action is sureness, knowing-how, naturalness, the going-without-saying of movements. Rather, it is asking the *question* about certainty that can give rise to an epistemic outlook, and when this happens sureness also takes the form of a sort of awareness or of knowledge. When I stand up to walk, normally I do not ask myself whether or not my feet are still there, at the end of my legs; but if someone were to ask me if they were there, I would answer that they are and that I *know* that they are there. Did I know this before as well? In practical knowledge, is it always as if an epistemic knowledge were inscribed? Does knowing-how always have to be grounded in knowing-that?[47] *No*, Wittgenstein seems to reply: knowing-how is not necessarily rooted in knowing-that. On the contrary, once we look at the primitive in us, or at the child in us, or at the animal in us, we can see that sometimes it is the other way around: knowing-that is rooted in knowing-how and knowing-how is essentially acting.

A context in which Wittgenstein invites us to see the active and gestural nature of words, instead of their descriptive function, is certainly that of spontaneous utterances. Danièle Moyal-Sharrock (2000) and (2003) insists on the fact that Wittgenstein shows that, particularly in this context, some words and expressions belong to the same category of action, in such a way that language itself can be thought of as a real extension of behaviour and primitive language games; the classic example being groaning. Besides, according to Moyal-Sharrock (2003, p. 128), for the 'Third' Wittgenstein, logic itself belongs to the realm of instinct, and not of reason.[48] In her view, it is Wittgenstein's idea of belief that emerges from OC that shows his 'logical pragmatism'. Despite not referring directly to the pragmatist literature, Moyal-Sharrock (2000) appeals to a notion which we have seen is decisive especially in Peirce, that is, the idea that behaviour manifests belief, or, as Alexander Bain, the inspirer of the pragmatic maxim, put it, belief is what a person is ready to act upon.

---

[47] According to Coliva (2013), the pragmatic acceptation of a certainty, also and chiefly if it has a normative nature, requires that the *content* of the norm be *grasped*; in this sense, it is only because we have grasped its content, that a certainty can work as a practical platitude not subject to doubt.

[48] An idea we could perhaps compare to Peirce's concept of instinctive insight, CP 5.604. For other aspects, the idea Moyal-Sharrock gleans from Wittgenstein could be put side by side with James' description of rationality in 'The Sentiment of Rationality' (in WB).

Moyal-Sharrock surely points out a crucial aspect of the later Wittgenstein. Yet, this holds the opposite risk: the risk of failing to see the instrumental value of Wittgenstein's suggestion, and making him the advocate of a vision centred solely on the primacy of action. If words are *also* actions, they are not *only* actions; and actions themselves are steeped in words, conceptuality and meaning. Indeed, the aim of the exhortation to look at the praxes is to understand the meaning of words while breaking the enchantment of the usual image: that it is the sensation or the mental state with which we pronounce an expression, the 'place' of its meaning (OC, §601), and hence that the word *describes* the sensation.

As Schulte (1993) stresses—while working, it must be said, on the 1946–1949 manuscripts more than on OC, but reading them as the anticipation of the themes and the outlook of OC—if it is true that action is at the basis of concept (the reason why, according to Schulte, Wittgenstein cites Goethe), it is also true that the concept is a constitutive part of action. In Wittgenstein's words:

> A concept is not merely a way of thinking about something.
> It is not only a way of dividing up things, not only a point of view according to which they can be arranged. It is a constitutive part of our acting. (MS 137, p. 60b)[49]

According to Schulte, we would not even be able to understand the structure, the nature of an action, if we had not developed language games and concepts which make it accessible for us.

This point of view also seems interesting to me in relation to the pragmatist tradition: what is relevant is not only the fact that some words and expressions have something of the nature of actions but also and precisely the blurred contours between word and action, propositional and non-propositional, believing and acting. It is *this* terrain, the terrain of blurred contours, more than the terrain of the word as action *tout-court*, that both Wittgensteinian philosophy and pragmatist thought

---

[49] Quoted in Schulte (1993, pp. 22, 167).

invite us to consider.[50] For the pragmatists as well, the aim is to fight too rationalistic a vision of language and belief. However, by this, they do not wish to project an equally misleading picture of a dulled humanity, reduced to the level of instinct and pre-linguistic behaviour. Wittgenstein's emphasis on language as consisting of practices and games, and the Peircean vision of beliefs as habits, are 'alternative expressions of a common determination to resist the abstractness and overintellectualism of much traditional philosophy' (Bambrough 1981, p. 266). Yet, this does not mean that any of them (including James) would be at ease in a mere naturalizing perspective. The mix of voluntary, deliberate and automatic which James individuates in action, and Peirce's insistence on action's belonging to a habit, in this sense agree with Wittgenstein's non-unilateral way of conceiving action and linguistic behaviour.

As Goodman (2002, 78 ff.) highlighted, there is a strict affinity between James' description of actions which do not need any effort of attention and Wittgenstein's description of everyday action and know-how. Both also underline the impossibility of distinguishing clearly voluntary and involuntary actions.[51] As for OC, Richard Shusterman[52] noticed how Wittgenstein, partly following James, draws attention to the going-without-saying of action and its embodying a know-how shown in the fluidity of movements. According to Shusterman, although Wittgenstein generally does not consider bodily sensation a central factor in the determination of our concepts, in OC he acknowledges it an important role. Unfortunately Shusterman chooses a wrong example, but in order to sustain an interesting thesis. The wrong example comes from a note written by Wittgenstein in 1931, later a part of CV:

Music, with its few notes & rhythms, seems to some people a primitive art. But only its surface [its foreground] is simple, while the body which makes

---

[50] See Pihlström (2012).

[51] James' relevance is clear for example in BBB, pp. 150–151, PI §§611–631, LPP, pp. 157–158 and 202–204, RPP I, §§759 ff. See also Citron (2015a), pp. 20–22. Goodman's work is very detailed on these issues.

[52] Shusterman (2008, Chap. 4); see also Shusterman (2012a) and (2012b, Chap. 2), the latter are essentially the same.

possible the interpretation of this manifest content has all the infinite complexity that is suggested in the external forms of other arts which music conceals. In a certain sense it is the most sophisticated art of all. (CV, pp. 8–9)[53]

In Shusterman's interpretation, there is an opposition between foreground and background, and the latter corresponds to the body. If I understand him correctly, Shusterman thinks this '*Körper*' to be the body of the listener or of the music performer, and therefore in these lines he reads the acknowledgment of the relevance of sensations, movements, and bodily 'knowledge'. Yet, Wittgenstein uses the term *Körper*, it seems to me, in order to speak of the body *of music*, in opposition to its surface (Peter Winch's translation into English is, indeed, 'substance'), and the opposition is between the simplicity of the few sounds that are effectively heard and the complexity of everything which *makes* music—melody, harmony, composition, but also, I would like to add, the rich fabric of the entire culture which music expresses.

Nevertheless, the thesis for which Shusterman moulds the interpretation of this passage is interesting: the underlining in Wittgenstein's philosophy of the background as a load-bearing concept. The background will be the object of the next chapter, and here I shall limit myself to a few notes. In relation to action, James highlighted how action is part of everyday know-how, as if it were part of a flux which gives it sense and relieves the agent from the necessity to elaborate an act of decision for every single movement.[54] But here it is also possible to take one more step, which in a sense leads us closer to Peirce again. Namely, it is possible to highlight not only an action's belonging to the habit which constitutes its surrounding, but also the social, intersubjective, cultural, and

---

[53] From MS 110, p. 12. Quoted here with the translation used in Shusterman (2008, p. 126). Original text: 'Die Musik scheint manchem eine primitive Kunst zu sein mit ihren wenigen Tönen & Rythmen. Aber einfach ist nur ihre Oberfläche [ihr Vordergrund] während der Körper der die Deutung dieses manifesten Inhalts ermöglicht die ganze unendliche Komplexität besitzt die wir in dem Äußeren der anderen Künsten angedeutet finden & die die Musik verschweigt. Sie ist in gewissem Sinne raffinierteste aller Künste'.

[54] The recent perspectives of *enactivism* in philosophy of mind, an alternative to the cognitivist paradigm, can be read as a development of this kind of approach, a development also suggested by John Dewey; see Hutto and Myn (2013, pp. 14, 50), Steiner (2013), and Boncompagni (2013).

normative nature of habits themselves. Action, Wittgenstein says, belongs to the flux of life, in its complexity, a flux in which the actions of different human beings are variously combined and mixed together. For this reason, if we want to describe human behaviour, we need to go beyond the single action performed by a single person, and take into full account 'the whole hurly-burly', or 'the background [which] determines our judgment, our concepts, and our reactions' (RPP II, §629).[55]

An action's belonging to its surrounding does not necessarily imply that action has to *passively* be part of it. It clearly is not so in James, with his emphasis on the first person and on the individual's possibility to choose not only what *to do*, but, to a certain extent, also what *to believe*, and which habits to nurture.[56] It clearly is not so in Peirce either, with his insistence on the malleability of habits and their permeability to rational choice and self-control. Conversely, according to Kilpinen (2009), as I hinted, it is so in Wittgenstein: in his conception of following a rule, once the rule is learnt, it is followed *blindly*, and in this sense the dialectic between the action and rule, language game and form of life would be totally tipped in favour of the rule. Kilpinen correctly cites an expression by Wittgenstein, according to whom '[w]hen I follow the rule, I do not choose[:] I follow the rule *blindly*' (PI, §219). Yet, this affirmation, in my view, needs to be contrasted with other passages, also from OC, in which it is patent that the rule does not always or inevitably prevail over action and praxes. The possibility that the banks of the river be modified through time by the flux of the water (OC, §§96–99), although slowly and partially, shows that the 'blindness' of the rule-follower is not so complete. Indeed, Wittgenstein does not rule out the possibility of novelty, for example, in science and in other practices, nor the existence of jokes, metaphors, and more generally extensions in the uses of concepts outside their ordinary contexts (Putnam 2001). One could even say, with Colapietro (2011), that it is the rule's characteristic of being, to a certain extent, plastic, that constitutes one of the most interesting points of contact between

---

[55] Also in Z, §567; originally in MS 137, p. 54a, June 1948, then in TS 232, pp. 753–754.
[56] See Marchetti (2015b) on this.

pragmatism and Wittgenstein. Precisely in OC we find not only the metaphor of the river (we will come back to this) but also the explicit affirmation that by itself the rule is not sufficient to determine all the occurrences of the praxis:

> Not only rules, but also examples are needed for establishing a practice [*Praxis*]. Our rules leave loop-holes open, and the practice has to speak for itself. (OC, §139)

In other words, the not rigid, not predetermined, not blocked relationship between rule and action is part of an approach to normativity which is *shared* by Wittgenstein and the pragmatists.

If a relevant difference is to be found between the two approaches to action, therefore, it is not in the dialectic between practice and rule. Rather, a contrast that may be drawn between Wittgenstein and the pragmatists is perhaps that while the former seems to be interested in the *general* theme of action as a way for drawing the attention to the background of what we do for understanding what we say, the pragmatists are more focused on the instrumental value of *particular* (though sometimes potential) actions or habits in particular contexts, for their role in letting us understand particular meanings or beliefs.[57] Yet, to my eyes, in this case too, the contrast is not so marked. Indeed, it is true that Wittgenstein does not examine real specific cases of actions and practices, but he does refer to specific, sometimes fictitious, language games and contexts: one might even say that the use of examples of this kind is an integral part of his methods. Again, this is aimed at showing how actions and words are part of a multifarious background without which meanings would not be accessible; but this is also true of the pragmatist approach.

Hence, here we have the sense in which the issue of action is dealt with, by Wittgenstein and by the pragmatists, according to strategies which resonate positively with each other: action is part of a background, intended

---

[57] This was pointed out to me by an anonymous reviewer, who referred chiefly to Peirce.

both as a bodily know-how guiding our movements and as a normative and cultural context orienting behaviour. The underlining of this background and of its partial permeability marks a great distance from the traditional approaches, as well as from contemporary analytical approaches.

Concluding Remarks

This chapter, with the comparison between Peirce's and James' pragmatic maxim and Wittgenstein's way of dealing with similar issues in OC, and with the examination of the notion of action in the three thinkers, concludes the central part of the volume, dedicated to the pragmatic and pragmatist aspects of OC.

The analysis of the different formulations of the maxim by Peirce and James, and the highlighting of the crucial coexistence between perceptive and behavioural elements, has offered a starting point for an examination of the way in which Wittgenstein connects matters of knowledge and meaning with the issue of practical consequences. This theme, to my knowledge, has not emerged to date as an autonomous subject in the secondary literature on OC, although commentators do sometimes refer to pragmatism. Yet, precisely an in-depth analysis of what may legitimately be identified as the (not just) methodological heart of classical pragmatism, that is, the pragmatic maxim, enables us to see the same attention and the same worries in the later Wittgenstein of OC, albeit inflected according to a different vision. Thus, it has—I hope at least—been possible to notice that a quite significant set of remarks written by Wittgenstein in the second half of March 1951 rotate around the same concepts singled out by the pragmatists' maxim, hence motivating the appearance of the remark on pragmatism in OC, §422. By drawing on this analysis, it has also been possible to return to the issue of meaning as use, to compare it to the notion of meaning emerging in pragmatism, and finally to extend the examination to the broader theme of action. The theoretical caution which was part of the premise to this chapter helped to avoid approximate comparisons levering on the presence, in the later Wittgenstein, of a particular stress on action, practices, and praxes in order to instead investigate the effective way in which both the pragmatists and Wittgenstein used and characterized these concepts. The common emphasis on action's belonging to a habit, a background, a set of shared praxes, represents an attempt to go beyond the classical notion of action as the voluntary 'putting to use' of a rational plan, and it sheds doubts on the subject's alleged complete accessibility to intention and will, thus returning to these semantic areas their complexity, their web of cross references, their mixture with prejudices, automatisms, and common sense. In this sense, the idea of action implied in both approaches rejects the usual dichotomies—for instance, body/mind or fact/value—and suggests that it is in this very option that one of the most significant, and perhaps still not entirely acknowledged novelties of pragmatism and of Wittgenstein's philosophy lies.

Action's belonging to a background, which provided the conclusion to this reflection, will be the basis of an investigation in the following chapter which, partly departing from OC, will examine the issues of the fundament and objectivity.

Part III

Broadening the Perspective

Chapter 5: From Ground to Background

Preliminary Remarks

The consonances highlighted throughout this inquiry are gradually converging towards a thematic centre. Both from the point of view of knowledge and the point of view of action, broadly understood, these authors indicate the complex and elusive depth of the background as the place from which sense, meaning, coherence and rationality stem. It is in this depth, never completely open to view, because by definition it is behind, *back*, while at the same time inevitably always present, implied by what stands in front, that thinking and acting no longer (or perhaps not yet) belong to two separate reigns. The *background* is an alternative philosophical instrument with respect to the traditional one of the *ground*. While maintaining the practical and undisputed value of *terrain*, it forsakes the absolute solidity of a *foundation*. In this, it once again manifests the rejection of the apparently inescapable dichotomy between foundationalism and anti-foundationalism and offers a new description of the scenario. This perspective, though not explicitly endorsed by either Wittgenstein or the pragmatists, is, I think, one of the most fruitful outcomes of the present comparison.

The exploration of these issues continues in this chapter with the analysis of the Wittgensteinian notion of form of life, or way of life, as he preferred the German expression *Lebensform*[1] to be translated. In my view, this concept is intentionally kept vague by Wittgenstein, as it is *not* part of an investigation into the natural and cultural features of human beings; rather, as will become clearer, it is part of a technique for approaching from a grammatical point of view something which reveals itself precisely by remaining sufficiently out of focus. Once again, the examination will consider both Wittgenstein's published works and his manuscripts, to understand the context in which he introduces this concept and to see whether his way of employing it changes through time. A look at the secondary literature will help focalize on some interpretative debates, including those concerning relativism and Wittgenstein's alleged conservatism. By acknowledging the instrumental nature of this concept, it will be possible to develop a perhaps unusual reading of it, according to which the capability to catch sight of the *limits* of one's own form of life and the *difference* represented by other forms of life become a stimulus for self-reflection and change. On these bases, a looser comparison with pragmatism will be proposed, embracing wide-ranging concepts like those of objectivity, rationality and justification, which will be traced back to the change of perspective allowed by the shift from ground to background.

As mentioned in the introduction, this chapter and the next expand on the outcomes of the comparison drawn thus far, going beyond what can be found in OC and offering broader suggestions. Therefore, these chapters remain more tentative on a number of themes. They do not claim to put forth fully-fledged and complete interpretations, but more modestly hint towards (hopefully) interesting directions in which the investigation may be furthered in the future.

---

[1] Indeed, this is what appears in TS 226, pp. 10, 15, a partial translation of a pre-war version of PI, made by Rush Rhees and corrected by Wittgenstein. See also Gier (1980, p. 251), Fischer (1987, p. 40) and Garver (1994, p. 248). However, given the pervasiveness of 'form of life' in literature, I will use this expression too, while nevertheless keeping in mind Wittgenstein's suggestion.

Form of Life in Wittgenstein's Writings

Let me start from another affinity of expression between Peirce and Wittgenstein. In 'Some Consequences of Four Incapacities', after arguing against doubt as the starting point for thought, the former examines the 'four incapacities' mentioned in the title, which rotate around one core point: a pure, direct intuition, not mediated by signs or previous knowledge, is not possible. Consider this passage, already seen in part.

> [N]o present actual thought (which is a mere feeling) has any meaning, any intellectual value; for this lies not in what is actually thought, but in what this thought may be connected with in representation by subsequent thoughts... At no one instant in my state of mind is there cognition or representation, but in the relation of my states of mind at different instants there is. In short, the Immediate (and therefore in itself unsusceptible of mediation—the Unanalyzable, the Inexplicable, the Unintellectual) runs in a continuous stream through our lives.... (W 2, p. 227)[2]

Peirce rejects the idea that the immediate be directly accessible, affirming instead that the immediate belongs to a continuous flux. What one can perceive is not its singularity but its being part of the flux. Consider now the following remark by Wittgenstein, on the concept of the 'given'[3]:

> Instead of the unanalysable, specific, indefinable: the fact that we act in such-and-such ways, e.g. *punish* certain actions, *establish* the state of affair thus and so, *give* orders, render accounts, describe colours, take an interest in others' feelings. What has to be accepted, the given—it might be said—are facts of living. [variant: forms of life]. (RPP I, §630)

---

[2] This essay is not part of CCL, but it is in SW and CP (the quoted passage is in SW, pp. 236–237, CP 5.289), both of which were accessible to Wittgenstein.
[3] This vicinity was noted by Fabbrichesi (2002) and (2004).

This remark, quoted here as it appears in RPP, was written in MS 133 on 7 November 1946.[4] The context was a reflection on what we may call *qualia*, and more precisely on the specificity of colour sensations which, apparently at least, cannot be explained to others.[5] Although in Wittgenstein this is not linked to the theme of the flux of our thoughts, we are not so distant from the Peircean reflection on the immediate and the undefinable. During that period, Wittgenstein was reading and re-reading James' PP, a text clearly influenced by Peirce's account of the continuum of thought, although it differs from Peirce in precisely the value that James assigns to the 'specific' and the immediate.

The same themes can be found in Wittgenstein's lectures from the very same days. Although we may be tempted to say that there is something 'specific' in, for instance, colour experiences or experiences of hope and fear, it is impossible to define this specificity by mere concentration. 'The specific is something that has to be shown publicly', Wittgenstein observes here (LPP, p. 23). But what can be shown publicly are not private feelings or sensations: 'What can be shown publicly and are specific are certain phenomena of life' (*ibid*), which means certain *practices*. Wittgenstein's examples are the typical ones he uses in his writings: 'comparing colours, measuring time, comparing lengths, playing games'. More generally, what is specific and can be shown are 'thing[s] we humans do' (LPP, p. 24).[6]

The point, for Wittgenstein, is that the *primary* is not the immediate, but the flux of life (or the habit) to which the immediate belongs, and it is at *this* level that we must look if we are interested in grasping the 'specific' of human beings (Wittgenstein indeed contrasts the case with unknown tribes, beetles and even a Martian). The 'specific' of the lives of human beings is the way in which they act in activities like counting,

---

[4] Originally in MS 133, p. 28r, then in TS 229, p. 333. Another formulation of the same remark is in PPF, as we shall see shortly. See also LFM, p. 249.

[5] See RPP I, §§627–628.

[6] From the lecture of 8 November 1946. See also LPP, pp. 139–142 and 263–264. In the following lecture, Wittgenstein would hint at the 'good' in pragmatism: see *infra*, Chapter 6.

Chapter 5: From Ground to Background 185

expressing judgments, measuring, and the way in which they teach and learn these activities. As Bouveresse (1987, p. 589) observes, Wittgenstein's 'pragmatism' can be identified with the idea that concepts like thought, calculus, deduction and so on are determined by an agreement which is not based on incontrovertible experience (as empiricism would have it), nor on the data of a sort of 'ultra-experience' (as Platonism would have it), nor on simple definitions (as conventionalism would have it), but on forms of actions and life. *This* is what is primary and primitive. Yet, Wittgenstein does not aim to construct an anthropological theory about humankind. Primitive language games are 'poles of a description, not the ground-floor of a theory' (RPP I, §633). In brief, it is the form (forms) of life which constitutes that 'given', that background beyond which it is impossible to go, because to analyse it further, and try to divide it into simpler items, amounts to losing it as a significant phenomenon and not being able to see it anymore, owing, as it were, to an excess of focus.

Let us now consider more attentively Wittgenstein's use of this notion, as was actually quite common in the cultural context of the time.[7] A precursor of *Lebensform* is perhaps the expression '*Lebensgemeinschaft*', community of life, which Wittgenstein uses in RF, p. 139[8] to describe what united 'certain races of mankind' to the oak tree they venerated. But the first time *Lebensform* appears in his writings is in MS 115 (1936), a draft of the translation (and partial revision) of the *Brown Book* from English into German.[9] In BBB, pp. 134–135, one reads:

> Imagine a use of language (a culture) in which there was a common name for green and red on the one hand and yellow and blue on the other....

---

[7] See Janik and Toulmin (1996, p. 230), the introduction in Padilla Galvez and Gaffal (2011) and Hacker (2015, pp. 2–3). William James also used the expression 'forms of life', when dealing with animal forms of life; see PP, pp. 149, 941, WB, p. 72.

[8] From MS 110, p. 298, 1931.

[9] See also Biancini (2011). It must be said that when translating the text Wittgenstein probably did not work on the *Brown Book* as we now know it, but on another notebook dictated to Francis Skinner. See Pichler and Smith (2013, p. 311n3).

We could also easily imagine a language (and that means again a culture) in which there existed no common expression for light blue and dark blue...

In MS 115, pp. 237–239, the passage becomes:

Let us imagine a linguistic use (a culture) in which there is a common name for green and red, and one for blue and yellow.... Conversely, I could also think of a language (and this means again a form of life) which establishes a chasm between dark red and light red.[10]

Accordingly, the origins of the concept lie in Wittgenstein's rewriting 'culture' as a 'form of life', and it is indeed as such that it enters the stage in PI, where Wittgenstein would repeat: 'To imagine a language means to imagine a form of life' (PI, §19). What he was thinking of in 1936, hence, was culture, including the cultures of fictitious tribes, as his invitation to imagine people with different ways of speaking and living suggests; yet, he was perhaps not completely satisfied with the word 'culture', and introduced another expression.

One aspect he intended to include in his notion was probably the connection between language and actions, as a couple of other remarks written at the end of 1936 and in 1937 show. Besides underlining that the very expression 'language game' has the aim of 'bring[ing] into prominence the fact that the speaking of a language is a part of an activity or a form of life' (MS 142, pp. 19–20),[11] Wittgenstein highlights again that the foundation on which language grows 'consists in steady ways of living [*fester Lebensformen*], regular ways of acting' (MS 114, p. 74v).[12] This characterization also seems implicit in PI, §241, which places the *Übereinstimmung*, the agreement among human speakers, precisely on the terrain of the form of life:

---

[10] Original text: 'Stellen wir uns einen Sprachgebrauch vor (eine Kultur), in welchem es einen gemeinsamen Namen für grün und rot, und einen für blau und gelb gibt.... Umgekehrt könnte ich mir auch eine Sprache (und das heißt wieder eine Lebensform // Form des Lebens) denken, die zwischen Dunkelrot und Hellrot eine Kluft befestigt. Etc.'

[11] This passage, which presents some variants and underwent corrections, is a draft of PI, §23.

[12] Later in CE, p. 397.

'So you are saying that human agreement decides what is true and what is false'—What is true or false is what human beings *say*; and it is in their *language* that human beings agree. This is agreement not in opinions, but rather in form of life.[13]

In two other remarks, Wittgenstein also combines forms of life with forms of language, *Sprachformen*, connecting the theme with that of understanding, and making examples concerning giving and obeying orders, greeting, and following a rule.[14]

In all the passages mentioned up to now,[15] dating from 1936 to the definitive version of part I of PI, ca. 1945 (save for the first quote examined in relation to Peirce, which is later), Wittgenstein seems to use the notion of form/forms of life in quite an elastic way. Indeed, the affinity with the notion of culture can be interpreted both in a general sense, for which the form of life corresponds to the entire culture of a given society or population, and in a particular way, for which within an overall way of living there are peculiar forms of life, consisting of a mixture of speaking and acting, like greeting, giving and following orders, and so on (Witherspoon 2003, p. 228). The *subject* Wittgenstein refers to as possessing (a) form(s) of life is alternatively an entire population or a group of people.

In later writings, while the elasticity of the concept is preserved, the subject is sometimes identified as humankind in general, and compared to real or imaginary examples of other forms of life (animal forms of life, tribes and 'alien' forms of life). In PPF, §1, after asking himself if it is possible to imagine a dog that *hopes*, Wittgenstein states (famously) that 'only those who have mastered the use of a language' can hope, because 'the manifestations of hope are modifications of this complicated form of life'.[16] Still in PPF, elaborating on the remark we saw at the beginning

---

[13] From MS 160, pp. 26r–26v (1938).

[14] See MS 165, p. 110; RFM, p. 413, from MS 124, p. 150 and MS 127, p. 92 (1944).

[15] Another, quite puzzling remark can be found in MS 127, p. 128 (1944), where Wittgenstein states that 'even the devil in hell has a form of life' (auch der Teufel in der Hölle hat eine Form des Lebens); see Hacker (2015, pp. 14–15).

[16] From MS 137, p. 115a (1948), where instead of *Lebensform* Wittgenstein uses *Lebensmuster* or the variant *Muster*, pattern, model or prototype. See also LW I, §365.

of this paragraph, Wittgenstein connects the idea of forms of life as 'the given' to mathematics, noticing that certainty in mathematics is based on the *fact* that mathematicians agree, and repeats: 'what has to be accepted, the given, is—one might say—*forms of life*' (PPF, §345).[17]

Certainty *and uncertainty* are also the topics of the last two remarks on forms of life, now in OC and LW.

After distinguishing between the 'comfortable certainty' expressed by the words 'I know', and 'the certainty that is still struggling', Wittgenstein affirms in OC, §§357–359[18] that he wants to consider the former as a form of life. By this, he explains, he means something 'animal', lying beyond justification (that is: neither justified nor unjustified), and *not* something irrational, 'akin to hastiness or superficiality'. He was not very satisfied with this note, as he affirmed that it was 'badly expressed' and also probably 'badly thought', but the themes are roughly the same as those examined in the previous chapter. What is new is the explicit association between (animal or comfortable) certainty and form of life.

Wittgenstein's last remark on forms of life, written one month later than the one just seen and only a couple of weeks before his death, has often escaped the notice of commentators interested in this topic, perhaps because of the unusual English translation (not 'form of life' but 'way of living' in LW II, p. 95[19]). Wittgenstein is here concerned with the 'imponderable evidence' governing our life with others and our understanding of what goes on in others' minds. Although we are generally quite confident that we know what other people think or feel, it would be very hard to explain our ability to read others' faces or to guess their mood from their gestures and behaviour. This imponderability goes hand in hand with the impossibility of being absolutely certain of the others' feelings and thoughts. Reflecting on these themes, Wittgenstein wonders what we would do if it were possible to substitute

---

[17] From MS 144, p. 102. For the connection with mathematics see the previous remarks in PPF, §§341–344, and the following, §§347–350.

[18] From MS 175, p. 55v (15 March 1951). Animality is also connected to forms of life in a remark on pretence and instinctive action in MS 137, p. 59a (1948).

[19] Possibly, this translation matches *better* Wittgenstein's intentions; see note 1 in this chapter.

our usual language games based on 'imponderable evidence' with a mechanical system having similar consequences, like a 'lie detector', redefining a lie as 'that which causes a deflection on the lie detector'. He asks:

> So the question is: Would we change our way of living [*Lebensform*] if this or that were provided for us?—And how could I answer that? (*ibid.*[20])

Albeit the former is concerned with certainty and the latter with uncertainty, both remarks show that Wittgenstein seems to be interested in highlighting the way of living of the 'human animal' in general. A similar outlook can be found in the notes from PPF briefly examined above. Whether he is inviting us to imagine a form of life in which mathematical certainty or the 'imponderable evidence' regulating our relationships with the others does not hold, or whether he is describing the difference between forms of life possessing and not possessing a verbal language, the aim is one and the same: to show 'things we humans do', as he put it in LPP. The aim is to explore what is *primitive* in us, in those ways of life constituting the background against which words and actions acquire meaning.

Yet, this does not amount to offering a fully-fledged naturalist account of how human beings are. Wittgenstein's outlook, as I see it, remains *grammatical*. He is interested in clarifying the meanings of our concepts and of their relevant connection, often with an eye on an ethical understanding of ourselves and our limits, but without claiming to explain the emergence and the functioning of our concepts by finding causes in nature.

To sum up, while on the one hand Wittgenstein's oscillation between the singular and the plural form of the expression '*Lebensform(en)*' is substantially irrelevant, on the other hand one can read an evolution in his thought[21], as he initially (usually) describes the way of life of

---

[20] From MS 176, p. 51v (15 April 1951). This remark comes from a particular section of MS 176, not published in OC but in LW. Indeed, it represents a sort of thematic parenthesis, in which Wittgenstein deals with the issue of certainty and uncertainty from the point of view of the knowledge of the other. Were one to reinsert this section in OC, it would be placed between §523 and §524.

[21] This is the reading proposed in Boncompagni (2015).

particular groups or populations, and later tends to deal with how human beings behave in general. Yet, throughout this development, Wittgenstein does not build a theory of forms of life: rather, he employs this notion as a methodological tool for a grammatical investigation.

Secondary Literature: Relativism and Other Issues

I hope this reading, focused on the non-univocal way in which Wittgenstein uses the notion of forms of life, can help unravel some theoretical discussions characterizing the secondary literature, in which interpretations at times emphasize one aspect and at times another, without considering that different views may be present in Wittgenstein's writings. By working on this idea, I recently proposed seeing the different interpretative positions as being arranged along two perpendicular axes: the monistic versus pluralistic and the empirical versus transcendental axes, suggesting that by crossing the two axes four main positions might be identified (Boncompagni 2015). I do not wish to bring this figure back up here, nor describe in detail the large and still growing literature existing on this subject: to do so would require a complex *excursus* which is not so relevant for the present inquiry.[22] Yet, some of the themes that have emerged in the literature do bear some suggestions that may be worth touching on, as they are connected to existing debates in pragmatism. I am referring in particular to the intertwined issues of relativism, conventionalism and conservatism.

The debate on Wittgenstein and relativism is itself huge and complicated. In particular, what is often recalled by both advocates and adversaries of relativism are some remarks in OC highlighting how our *Weltbild* constitutes a system and how the truth and falsity of empirical propositions depend on the frame of reference within which they work. 'Our knowledge forms an enormous system—Wittgenstein says for instance—And only

---

[22] See the special issue of the *Nordic Wittgenstein Review* (Donatelli and Moyal-Sharrock 2015) for other surveys of the existent views, as well as for the most recent voices.

within this system has a particular bit the value we give it' (OC, §410).[23] Needless to say, *Weltbild* and form of life are intrinsically connected, as the former can be read as the cultural expression (in a wide sense) of the latter. Therefore, the debate on forms of life overlaps with the debate on OC, chiefly those parts of OC regarding the encounters and clashes between different *Weltbilder*.[24]

On the basis of OC, many interpreters have explicitly endorsed the idea that Wittgenstein was a relativist; some of them have been identified with this position, though sometimes they have rejected this label; but supporters of the opposite position also abound.[25] The *querelle* between Richard Rorty and Hilary Putnam is an exemplary case.[26]

Let me mention just a few recent interpreters. According to Coliva (2010a, pp. 188 ff., and 2010b), despite being anti-foundationalist, Wittgenstein was *not* relativist, neither in factual terms (he did not affirm the *actual* existence of radically alternative epistemic systems) nor in virtual terms (he did not affirm the *potential* existence of radically alternative epistemic systems).[27] In her view, the point is that the imaginary forms of life that Wittgenstein repeatedly invites the reader of OC to imagine are not, in a strict sense, conceivable. Epistemic relativism requires us to understand these alternative forms of life and *Weltbilder*, but we simply cannot (Coliva 2010a, p. 197). If we *do* understand the other *Weltbild*, the latter is not radically alternative to our own; if it *is* radically alternative, we cannot understand it. The outcome of Wittgenstein's reflection on imaginary tribes and communities, for Coliva, is that the mere *metaphysical possibility* of their existence, which is the only aspect under which we can still think about them, makes us aware of the ungroundedness of our own *Weltbild*. Hence, Wittgenstein is an anti-foundationalist, but not a relativist.

---

[23] See also OC §§83 and 105.
[24] For an analysis of Wittgenstein's notion of world-pictures see Hamilton (2014, Chap. 7).
[25] See Baghramian (2004, 74 ff.), Kusch (2013) and (2016).
[26] See Rorty (1979) and Putnam (1992b, Chap. 8).
[27] The distinction between factual and virtual relativism is in Marconi (1987, pp. 122 ff.).

Coliva's position is opposed by Martin Kusch (2013), who contests the cogency of her argumentations and affirms instead, in Kusch (2016), that it is a mistake to count OC as a whole as either relativistic or anti-relativistic. In his view, however, 'there is a space' in OC for a form of epistemic relativism, as Wittgenstein is interested in sensitizing us to the various forms our responses can assume towards other people who challenge our most firmly established certainties: he is *not* putting forth a theoretical-rational argument in order to defeat relativism. Tripodi (2013) too criticizes Coliva, affirming in particular that many remarks by Wittgenstein on religious belief show precisely an epistemic relativist position. Indeed, for instance, although believers may have reasons for believing in the Last Judgment[28] which are not accessible to non-believers, if the latter are sufficiently sensitive, they would be able to understand these reasons to a certain extent, without needing to believe them. This shows that two alternative epistemic systems, both correct from their own standpoint, can exist side by side without being irremediably incomprehensible to one another.

Clearly, there are different ideas of relativism at work in the debate, and different attitudes towards it, so it is hard to attain a coherent general account. For instance, Tripodi's remark on the partial comprehension of the reasons of the believer by the non-believer could also suggest a *non*-relativistic position: it all depends on the preliminary definitions. Also among sympathizers of pragmatism there are very diverse positions regarding what relativism is and if and how it should be endorsed.[29]

A well-known approach often associated with Wittgenstein's when the latter's alleged relativism is defended, but which could also be associated with Wittgenstein for some non-relativistic aspects, or even for some transcendental tones, is that of Peter Winch.[30] Precisely like

---

[28] Wittgenstein explicitly connects belief in the Last Judgment to forms of life: 'Why shouldn't one form of life culminate in an utterance of belief in a Last Judgement ?', LC, p. 58.

[29] Besides the already mentioned Rorty (1979) and Putnam (1992b), see Bernstein (1983), Margolis (2007) and Fine (2007).

[30] A non-relativistic reading is proposed in Christensen (2011b), Hertzberg (2009), Pleasants (2000); transcendental aspects are highlighted in Hertzberg (1980). For a balanced relativistic

Wittgenstein, at times Winch applies the concept of form of life to parts of the culture of a people—for example, when he deals with science or art (Winch 1990)—and at others to different cultures, and human culture as a whole (Winch 1964). According to Winch (1964), deep as they may be, cultural differences will progressively soften as one backtracks one's research towards the common roots of human cultures, which rotate around fundamental aspects like birth, death and sexual relations. As Christensen (2011b) suggests, these aspects are at the core of the deepest human interests and worries. On the one hand, they concern every social group, and on the other hand they are incorporated in diverse ways by diverse communities, thereby constituting both the terrain of similarity and the terrain of difference, of understanding and of misunderstanding.

This is perhaps an unusual reading of Winch: he is typically listed among relativists, and also among conventionalists. In sustaining that by 'forms of life' Wittgenstein referred to 'an intelligible human life', Witherspoon (2003, p. 223), for instance, attributes to Winch (and to Carnap and Kripke) a conventionalist reading of Wittgenstein, without seeing that there is 'another' Winch, particularly interesting for those, like himself, who intended to investigate the connection between form of life and intelligibility.

Conventionalism, in turn, is something on which interpretations are not univocal, and some clarification seems necessary. If what is meant by 'conventions' is arbitrary agreements, conventionalism is rather distant from the Wittgensteinian perspective, in which agreement occurs in language, *that is*, in forms of life (PI, §241). But if conventions are thought of as complex institutional and historical forms, rooted in education, scientific practices, community and social life, then agreement does occur in conventions (OC, §298); yet, one must bear in mind that the concept has been radically re-described.

As I see it, the importance of Wittgenstein's investigation lies in the reflection suggested on the possibility of fruitful and authentic encounters

---

reading, as well as for a brief survey of the different positions in the literature on Winch, see Durante (2016).

between different *Weltbilder*, meant as expressions of forms of life. Apparently, the situation is as follows: If a framework defines a system, and the elements belonging to the system can only be understood when they are read from within the framework, then either language games and practices are intelligible using the standard defined by the framework—and in this case the interlocutors already share a general scheme; or if the frameworks are authentically different, the interpreter will attempt to apply her own framework to understand the other, and therefore will *lose* the other. Yet, this dichotomic alternative is only apparent. What will happen, and what effectively normally happens, is that while attempting to let the other speak but at the same time trying to understand him using *her own* language, the interpreter will be induced, albeit slightly, to modify her point of view, extending her way of life to conceptually make room for the others' way of life. This is not a theoretical or a notional exercise, nor actually an unusual phenomenon: suffice it to think of educational contexts in which children progressively enlarge their conceptual framework; or of what happens (at least sometimes) during real encounters between foreign communities, or in processes of territorial integration, or simply in learning a new language. What is merely theoretical is the aforementioned dichotomic alternative between the (useless) understanding only occurring within a framework and the impossibility of a 'true' understanding of the radical otherness. It goes without saying that there are degrees and shades, and that complete integration is (fortunately) impossible: the necessary deviation or gaps characterizing any encounter are what makes it interesting. This kind of enlargement of one's form of life is what Winch describes in relation to the concept of intelligibility in anthropology when he says:

> [W]e must somehow bring S's conception of intelligibility (b) into (intelligible!) relation with our own conception of intelligibility (a). That is, we have to create a new unity for the concept of intelligibility, having a certain relation to our old one and perhaps requiring a considerable realignment of our categories.... [W]e are seeking a way of looking at things which goes beyond our previous way in that it has in some way taken account of and incorporated the other way that members of S have of looking at things. Seriously to study another way of life is necessarily to seek to extend our own.... (Winch 1964, pp. 317–318)

When Winch appeals to phenomena like birth, death and sexual relations, he is not simply anchoring the encounter to common objective features of human forms of life. What he is suggesting, following Wittgenstein, is that in these domains the salient and significant aspects of the lives of the others in their communities are disclosed before our eyes: these are the domains in which the most essential practices of sense come to light. If we are to approach the meaningfulness of the life of the other in this way, we slowly come to see 'the familiar in the unfamiliar' (Hertzberg 1980, p. 164), in such a way that we realize that even in disagreement there can be shared meanings, because both ways of thinking and acting embody similar deep interests and concerns (Hertzberg 2009). The humanity of humans is indeed shaped by this intertwinement of factual (anthropological) and linguistic, action and word, which gives substance to meaning and, therefore, to understanding (Cavell 1976, p. 240).

Seen from this perspective, the theme of difference places itself on an ethical more than a cognitive level. What is relevant is not the epistemological indifference which voids the otherness of the other community, but the listening attitude and attention to the other, enabling one to find oneself and one's 'real need' at the same time, to use a passage often quoted by Stanley Cavell.[31] Hence, Wittgenstein can be said to be aiming at orienting not much to the quite traditional theme of tolerance, but to a form of respect in front of the heterogeneous, which manifests itself in the naturalness of reactions of surprise and wonder. As Zerilli (2001), following Cavell, observes, Wittgenstein constantly invites us to imagine the other using common sense concepts in completely unfamiliar ways. His purpose in this, far from suggesting that we stop at our forms of life and simply assert that we cannot escape from them, is to call for imagination and new judgments: it is 'here, where I cannot convince you and must simply face up to your point of view, that I may actually be able to see something new' (Zerilli 2001, p. 40).[32]

---

[31] PI, §108. See Cavell (1979, p. 83) and (1989, pp. 41–42).
[32] This reading seems confirmed by Cavell (2006).

According to Zerilli, the pragmatist reading of Wittgenstein, especially Rorty's version, fails to see this point clearly and instead suppresses the very question, using the notion of form of life as a sort of 'conversation stopper'. Similarly, Law (1988) had observed that while in Wittgenstein there is space for imagination and a sensitivity to what is unusual, strange and difficult, pragmatists like Rorty pose a sharp distinction between 'easy' and 'impossible' interpretations: either we can easily understand the other because we already share a form of life, or we simply cannot. I am not interested here in assessing whether Zerilli and Law are right or wrong regarding Rorty. Yet, as we shall see shortly, in classical pragmatism there *is* indeed space for imagination, and even if some pragmatist legacies of Wittgenstein may fail to develop this point, Wittgenstein and pragmatism do share a similar perspective.

A widespread view has it that the remarks in OC on persuasion and conversion justify a conservative interpretation of Wittgenstein's thought.[33] When the other's difference is so radical that the application of even minimal criteria of rationality becomes impossible, according to these remarks one has to abandon argumentation and shift to persuasion and conversion. Is this not surrendering to a conservative attitude, for which comparisons and exchanges of view between different communities are impossible and, in the end, each culture cannot but remain self-confined? Let us consider the OC notes that allegedly support this view more closely.

In OC, §92, Wittgenstein invites us to imagine a king brought up in the belief that the world came into existence when he himself was born. Having always been told so and never having had reasons to suspect otherwise, this belief is part of the king's *Weltbild*. Wittgenstein asks:

> And if Moore and this king were to meet and discuss, could Moore really prove his belief to be the right one? I do not say that Moore could not convert the king to his view, but it would be a conversion of a special kind; the king would be brought to look at the world in a different way.

---

[33] See Marcuse (1964, Chap. 7), Nyíri (1982), Haack (1982), and Gellner (1992).

The 'special kind' of conversion Wittgenstein thinks about, as he specifies in the lines that follow, may have to do with *simplicity* or *symmetry*: these sometimes induce people to adopt a new point of view, or another *Weltbild*. This is a form of persuasion (OC, §262).

In OC, §§609–612 the concepts of conversion and persuasion are evoked again. This time, Wittgenstein describes people who instead of being guided by physics consult an oracle. 'If we call this "wrong"—he asks—aren't we using our language-game as a base from which to *combat* theirs?' In cases like this, where there are two principles which cannot be reconciled, each disputer would declare the other wrong, fool, or heretic, and use *slogans* to support their view. He adds:

> I said I would 'combat' the other man,—but wouldn't I give him *reasons* [*Grunde*]? Certainly; but how far do they go? At the end of reasons comes *persuasion*. (Think what happens when missionaries convert natives.) (OC, §612)

What is often overlooked by those who consider Wittgenstein as a conservative thinker and read in the concept of form of life a description of a sort of cage unsusceptible to changes, is that persuasion and conversion *are* possible, and *de facto,* they do occur (Gill 1974). In a sense, as Franken (2015) convincingly argues, persuasion is even more common and more fundamental than giving reasons: it lies at the level of primitive practices, at the level of ungrounded ways of acting, and our ordinary life is constantly imbued in these practices, so much so that we are often unaware of how apparently contingent new practices can become new grounds. These processes do not necessarily imply violence or coercion—although of course, one must not hide these aspects. Persuasion works at the same level as education, or re-education (Perissinotto 2016a), does. We are actually often interested in and willing to be trained in new grounding practices. What happens when we are persuaded or converted to another way of seeing is that we come to see our own *Weltbild* and our way of living as one possibility among others. As Durante (2016, p. 115) says with respect to Winch, successful persuasion 'let[s] other people see how their way of thinking may not be the only one around, and how their world-picture is not, as they previously thought, unique'. Moreover, these processes often produce new ways of seeing in the persuader, and not only in the persuaded. The aesthetic element which can contribute to the phenomena of persuasion should not be neglected either: a new point of view can convince us on the basis of its simplicity or symmetry, before which—Wittgenstein seems to observe—it is as if the person spontaneously embraced the new perspective, finding it naturally and evidently convincing.

This aspect takes us back to James, who offered a similar description of *rationality* itself.[34] A conception, he claimed, is accepted as rational simply if it bears the subjective signs of *ease, peace and rest*. If the conception appears to us as self-sufficient, not in need of any further justifications, capable of stimulating action and satisfying our aesthetic needs, we will accept it. It is this ease, this 'comfortable certainty' (OC, §357) as Wittgenstein would put it, that constitutes rationality, and our aesthetic, as well as practical needs, are the pivot of our acceptance, of our being persuaded.

Regarding these issues seen from a political and social point of view, it is clear that Wittgenstein was not particularly attracted by the idea of change. His fascination with Russia, for instance, had probably more to do with an archaic and romantic ideal of a sober life, than with Bolshevik militancy.[35] His musical taste also testified an aversion towards cultural novelties and the tendencies of his times. Yet it is not in these kinds of cultural and social changes that Wittgenstein seems interested in his work. In OC, change is thematized in connection with the intelligibility of the other and the limits of intelligibility that can push the confrontation to a non-argumentative level. Wittgenstein's remarks concerning persuasion and conversion are partly dubitative and also critical, for instance when he highlights that our attitude towards the other whom we consider wrong will materialize in the use of 'slogans'. But the fact that we may be *inclined* to declare the other

---

[34] In 'The Sentiment of Rationality', WB, p. 57.

[35] Yet, see the criticism he levelled at Ramsey, according to which his friend was a 'bourgeois' thinker, more interested in how this state could be organized than in the fact that this state is not the only one possible: MS 112, p. 70v (CV, p. 17), 1931.

Chapter 5: From Ground to Background 199

'heretic', to insult him, and to treat his reasons as foolishness and idiocy, does not *justify* our conduct. Wittgenstein merely acknowledges that this is what may happen. Sometimes, indeed, the responses to foreign forms of life may vary, as they are subject to degrees, practices, time and habit. By simply considering what kind of attitude we would be inclined to adopt, we can already become aware of the limits of our form of life, or of the contours of our *Weltbild*. This can lead to a critical self-examination, thanks to which our usually tacit background certainties come to light. Even if they take the shape of slogans, at least we are now able to *see* them, thereby discovering one of the axes around which our life rotates (OC, §152),[36] perpetuated by our practices. At the same time, we discover its compatibility or incompatibility with other conceptual frameworks and other praxes. By putting us back in contact with our 'real need', this exercise may sometimes provoke an interior conflict and the realization of a lack of harmony with our form of life intended in its cultural dimension. Accepting the form of life as 'the given' does not amount to accepting institutions and social practices as they are and adapting to them, but being able to see and feel the human condition with its tensions on one's skin—to feel the natural, biological or vertical dimension of the form of life, which sometimes is in contraposition with the cultural, ethnological or horizontal dimension, to use Cavell's categories.[37]

While on the one hand, Wittgenstein was probably not so favourable to political transformation, and certainly hostile to the idea of progress, he was constantly striving towards a personal transformation, a transformation consisting chiefly of changing his and our point of view, of turning over and paying attention to unusual aspects, or aspects so usual and obvious that they had escaped our awareness. Far from being residual or extreme, the practices of conversion and persuasion are indeed an integral part of Wittgenstein's philosophical methods.[38]

---

[36] On this topic see Bax (2011, p. 132).

[37] See again Cavell (1979, p. 83) and (1989, pp. 41–42). See also CV, p. 27.

[38] I shall come back to this, seen from the point of view of Wittgenstein's method and of ethics, in the next chapter, Section 'Beyond Method'.

Seen in this light, the concept of form of life manifests its instrumental nature. Through this notion, Wittgenstein does not simply describe, nor explain of course, the features of a culture or of human nature like a sociologist, an ethnologist or a scientist could do. Rather, he invites the reader to look towards the place of birth of what has significance for human beings. Attributing to Wittgenstein versions of relativism or of conservatism, as well as their opposites, overlooks the methodological and hortative aspect of the concept of form of life. In fact, Wittgenstein himself shows disinterest in relativism and anti-relativism as philosophical positions. During a conversation in 1945, for example, he criticized Platonic anti-relativism, which aimed to define the essence of 'the good' because otherwise relativism would destroy the 'imperative' in morality (Rhees 1965, p. 23); yet at the same time he explained that affirming the existence of different ethical systems does not amount to affirming that each of them is right from its own standpoint: this position is meaningless, Wittgenstein added, because it is redundant, just like saying that 'each judges as he does'.[39]

I shall come back to Wittgenstein's attitude towards ethics in Chapter 6. In the next paragraph, instead, Wittgenstein's notion of forms of life will be compared to pragmatism, in an attempt to clarify what both perspectives suggest concerning objectivity.

A Human Objectivity

By highlighting the fabric of human practices which is the environment of language games, the concept of forms of life abandons traditional foundations and produces a shift in the terrain where justification, rationality and objectivity find their place. As Strawson (1985, p. 78) puts it:

> the great point is that there is ... no need for anything beyond or behind it all to constitute a philosophical explanation of it.... [T]he suggestion is

---

[39] The same attitude is expressed in Citron (2015a, pp. 30, 52). On these notes see Christensen (2011a, p. 812).

that we can just rest with, or take as primitive, the great natural fact that we do form speech-communities, agree in linguistic practice, and so on.

Thoughts and actions take their sureness from the practical background which surrounds them, the background of a 'community bound together by science and education' (OC §298). Hence, certainty does not derive from every single person being certain. The 'we' is not a sum of 'I's trying to find an agreement on something, rather, the agreement is antecedent to the convergence of opinions because it is an agreement on the meaning of words, or even more radically on the conditions of possibility of meanings. McDowell (1998, p. 253) calls it a 'capacity for a meeting of minds': the communitarian character of linguistic practices derives from the possibility to share meanings. It is precisely thanks to the immanence of the 'we' in the practices of meaning that Wittgenstein finds an equilibrium between what McDowell (1998, p. 242) describes as two opposed theoretical disasters: the reduction of understanding to interpreting, and its reduction to behaving.

> Wittgenstein's problem is to steer a course between a Scylla and a Charybdis. Scylla is the idea that understanding is always interpretation. This idea is disastrous because embracing it confronts us with a dilemma . . . : the choice between the paradox that there is no substance to meaning, on the one hand, and the fantastic mythology of the super-rigid machine, on the other. We can avoid Scylla by stressing that, say, calling something 'green' can be like crying 'Help!' when one is drowning—simply how one has learned to react to this situation. But then we risk steering on to Charybdis—the picture of a basic level where there are no norms; if we embrace that . . . , then we cannot prevent meaning from coming to seem an illusion. The point [of Wittgenstein] is that the key to find the indispensable middle course is the idea of a custom or practice.

Some neo-pragmatist readings of Wittgenstein perhaps have not grasped the equidistance between Scylla and Charybdis that this perspective pursues. According to Lynne Rudder Baker (1984), for instance, Putnam interprets Wittgenstein's form of life as consisting of a series of empirical regularities (falling victim to Charybdis, one might argue), while Rorty interprets it as the outcome of arbitrary decisions on vocabulary (falling victim to Scylla). Rudder Baker's position appears somewhat forced,[40] but as we have seen in part, others hold the same view: Zerilli (2001) made a similar point regarding Rorty (though saving Putnam), and so did Law (1988). More recently, after placing pragmatism, together with Wittgenstein and Strawsonian naturalism, in the family of the 'hinge epistemologies' which offer a novel account of our basic certainties and justification, Coliva (2015, 121 ff.) affirms that pragmatism (or at least 'certain pragmatist positions') is not able to defend the *rationality* of this view, as it simply asserts that we can rely on hinges because, for our practical needs, they work. In my view, this vision of pragmatism is too narrow. Although the risk remains that some pragmatism-inspired *interpretations* of Wittgenstein flow into a form of empirical naturalism or into a sort of self-imprisoned hermeneutics, to a certain extent, in classical pragmatism it is possible to see, even if within a different framework, the search for the same course and equilibrium that Wittgenstein pursued. In particular, for pragmatists too the belonging of actions and words to practices and communities involves a normative dimension, which is what distinguishes following rules from mere empirical regularity.

In Peirce, the concept of community assumes great relevance from the outset, as it plays a role in shaping both the idea of the 'I' and the idea of 'reality'. It does so, by making people aware of their fallibility. Reflecting on the period in which a child learns to use language, Peirce observes:

> It must be about this time that he begins to find that what these people about him say is the very best evidence of fact. So much so, that testimony is even a stronger mark of fact than the *facts themselves*, or rather than what must now be thought of as the *appearances* themselves. . . . A child hears it said that the stove is hot. But it is not, he says; and, indeed, that central body is not touching it, and only what that touches is hot or cold. But he

---

[40] Especially in the case of Putnam, whose 1979 volume Rudder Baker considers; but see also Putnam (2000).

touches it, and finds the testimony confirmed in a striking way. Thus, he becomes aware of ignorance, and it is necessary to suppose a *self* in which this ignorance can inhere. (W 2, p. 202)[41]

Similarly, in a related essay he states that 'the real' is an idea that we must have conceived for the first time when we discovered that there was an 'unreal' and corrected ourselves, adding:

> The real, then, is that which, sooner or later, information and reasoning would finally result in, and which is therefore independent of the vagaries of me and you. Thus, the very origin of the conception of reality shows that this conception essentially involves the notion of a COMMUNITY, without definite limits, and capable of a definite increase of knowledge. (W 2, p. 239)[42]

Like in Wittgenstein, reality is to be found in the linguistic practices of the community, and like in Wittgenstein community is the pivot of a new approach that dethrones the criterion of immediate intuition and the first-person perspective from their privileged position, thereby suggesting an altogether new notion of rationality. Indeed, the 'primitiveness' of ways of acting and thinking does not imply their irrationality: on the contrary, they themselves shape the conditions for rationality to emerge.[43] And it is here that the normative dimension emerges as well, again manifesting itself as immanent in the processes of the creation and sharing of meanings. To use Calcaterra's words, 'attention to the instances and meanings validated by the community... leads on the one hand to confirm the inescapability of the intersubjective dimension and therefore, somehow, to acknowledge its role as a load-bearing structure, as an "objective fact" of human reality'; on the other hand, this same attention leads to 'recognizing its specifically *normative* significance, that

---

[41] Also in CP 5.233, from 'Questions Concerning Certain Faculties Claimed for Men' (1868).
[42] Also in CP 5.311, from 'Some Consequences of Four Incapacities' (1868). See also W 2, p. 271 (or CP 5.356).
[43] See Gill (1974). See also Coliva (2015, Chap. 4).

is, to considering "sociality" as the parameter of the meaning that the notion of rationality itself comes to assume' (Calcaterra 2003a, p. 62).[44]

Yet, we are not authorized to push the analogy between the two thinkers much further. The difference between the two, as I see it, does not lie in the alleged incapacity of the pragmatists to defend an extended version of epistemic rationality, as Coliva would perhaps assert. Rather, the point is that the communitarian epistemological practice that Peirce has in mind is primarily the practice of scientific inquiry, and in this respect, he also sanctions the regulative and ideal convergence of practices towards a perspective point. The historical element, as well as the social element, are not foreign to Wittgenstein, but the progressive and convergent direction of these elements *is* foreign to him. Moreover, the role of science as a model for the optimal functioning of sociality in the search for truth is distant from his view, though, as we have been able to see, he does not negate the relevance of science in our form of life. Finally, the importance that Peirce attributes to interpretative processes, while insufficient—in my view, because of the conceptual thickness that characterizes his approach—to push the American thinker towards the sea monster that McDowell connected to interpretation, *is* instead sufficient to differentiate his position from Wittgenstein's, who was always careful to avoid the perils of infinite regress that, as he had it, the idea of interpretation conveys.[45]

In any case, both thinkers assign a foundational role to communitarian practices with respect to the idea of reality and the idea of the self, criticizing the myth of the given and the myth of the Cartesian subject. For both, normativity, which inevitably pertains to practices, hints towards a new approach to rationality, which in Peirce is connected to scientific reasoning and in Wittgenstein to the meaningfulness of forms of life. In both cases, this includes a bond between facts and values which marks a distance from traditional philosophy (and, I would like to add, from most analytic philosophy as well). The intertwinement between facts and values is also clear if one considers the *sentimental* aspect of rationality.

---

[44] My emphasis. On similar issues see also Calcaterra (2015).
[45] See for instance Z, §§229–230 and Fabbrichesi (2002, pp. 114–115, 122 ff.).

Peirce himself underlines the normativity of sentiments[46] and the strict relationship they have with rationality: indeed, the promotion of our aesthetic and sentimental attitudes often assumes the form of public argumentations that are typically rational. While what emerges in this perspective is the normative—and in this sense rational—nature of sentiments, in James' perspective what emerges is the affective and sentimental—and in this sense value-related—nature of rationality. More precisely, James, as partly already seen, retains that the rationality of a certain conception is detected by subjective signs like ease, the sufficiency of the present moment and the absence of the need for justification (WB, p. 64). In judging something rational, we are primarily guided by practical and aesthetic considerations, and not only by logical requisites or the correspondence to alleged features of reality.

On both the aesthetic and practical aspects, the later Wittgenstein manifests a similar view. The former often have a relevant role when it comes to letting oneself be persuaded by a *Weltbild*: there is a kind of aesthetic satisfaction in abandoning oneself to symmetry, proportion, to the reasonable harmony of a vision of the world. Our thinking is attracted by simplicity, as it is naturally *convincing*: where there is a simple answer, '*that's* how it must be' (OC, §92). As for the practical aspects, Wittgenstein too underlines that sureness consists of being satisfied or content with how things are: 'We are satisfied that the earth is round', he writes for example, and 'My *life* consists in my being content to accept many things' (OC, §§299, 344). Satisfaction and being content, similarly to James' sense of 'ease, peace, rest', signal the absence of any exigency or further reasons or grounds. Our *Weltbild* is not arbitrary (it is not chosen deliberately), yet neither is it justified or grounded in the traditional sense. By accepting certain things without feeling the need to justify them, we are not irrational or irresponsible (Johanson 1994): on the contrary, our reasonableness consists of realizing that seeking a ground for everything makes no sense. What constitutes the background of justification can be neither justified nor put

---

[46] See 'Philosophy and the Conduct of Life' (CP 1.616–648) and the analysis proposed by Calcaterra (2003b).

in doubt—not in ordinary circumstances, at least. Mathematics and logic, for instance, belong to the framework of rationality, and what revising it would amount to, we are not even able to fully understand. More generally, normativity cannot be described in terms of empirical regularities. As Putnam (2000, p. 229) affirms, in a criticism of Quine:

> The trouble with talk of 'naturalizing' epistemology is that many of our key notions—the notion of understanding something, the notion of something's making sense, the notion of something's being capable of being confirmed, or infirmed, or discovered to be true, or discovered to be false, or even the notion of something's being capable of being stated—are normative notions, and it has never been clear what it means to naturalize a normative or partly normative notion.

In this sense, objectivity—that form of human objectivity which the notion of forms of life invites us to grasp—is imbued with normativity, because it is itself the terrain of agreement and of that entanglement between facts and values which shapes rationality.

Only by conceiving objectivity in a very strict and canonical sense can one see the human-related aspect of cognitive practices as a threat or a fall into Protagoreanism. Conversely, the relativity of points of view is perfectly compatible with objectivity, both in the pragmatist and Wittgensteinian perspectives.[47] This is even more so in ethics. To use Christensen's (2011a, p. 812) words, 'we can identify different ethical attitudes and still hold on to the idea that each of them involves a claim to objectivity—in fact, they all do, because *this is what makes them ethical*' (my emphasis). Interpreting the belonging of language games to forms of life as a limit to their claim to objectivity is, therefore, misleading. Rather, the opposite move becomes plausible: considering social bounds and emotive aspects relevant and vital for our very identities, thereby widening the meaning of objectivity. With Crary (2003), one might say that the 'semantically hygienic' conception according to which the knowledge contact with the world is attained only when we

---

[47] See Bambrough (1981); Brice (2014, p. 13).

Chapter 5: From Ground to Background 207

are, so to speak, 'purified' from the practical and emotive elements, is a *polemical target* for Wittgenstein. Our philosophical understanding of objectivity, Wittgenstein and James seem to suggest, can be widened, and the same can be said of the concept of rationality. Seen in this light, when Wittgenstein describes the encounter between cultures using words like 'persuasion' and 'conversion', he is not saying that these methods are irrational, but is offering a broader conception of rationality, which is not in conflict with, but includes sensibility.[48]

These ideas of objectivity and rationality can support what Scheman (2011, p. 107) has called an epistemology of *largesse*, as an alternative to the epistemology of parsimony: a vision according to which the partiality of any point of view is not seen as a defect to be corrected but as one of the voices contributing to objectivity, where the latter is pursued by allowing different voices to be heard, rather than depriving them of their particular and idiosyncratic aspects. The awareness of our dependence on others in any epistemic activity has the ethical consequence of promoting the search for a more and more shared terrain, a terrain necessarily (almost transcendentally) constituted by solidarity and trust. In the end, this is something very similar to that sociality which both Peirce and Wittgenstein identified with the source of sense, and to that plurality which James considered pervasive not only in ideas but also in empirical reality.[49]

Similarly to McDowell, Scheman finds in Wittgenstein the possibility of an intermediate path between two dangers: the danger of ice and the danger of excessively rough ground. In other words, on the one hand, there is the danger of a form of idealism aiming at absolute objectivity; and on the other hand, there is the opposite danger of a complete adherence to the existent social practices, collapsing into the acceptance of the *status quo*. In her view, this intermediate path requires the

---

[48] See Crary (2005); in this case, even broader than Coliva's (2015) already *extended* rationality.

[49] Scheman's view has, I think, interesting affinities with pragmatism. It calls to mind not only Rorty's appeal to solidarity intended as the expanding of the 'we' (though there are relevant differences from this perspective; see Rorty 1898, Chap. 9), but also the vision imagined by Bernstein (2010, Chap. 5) on the basis of some ideas proposed by Brandom (2004) and Wellmer (2004).

adoption of a critical attitude towards one's own *Weltbild*. The epistemology of largesse, applied not only to the confrontation between *Weltbilder*, but also to the confrontation between different ways of belonging to the same form of life, unmasks the only apparently uniform nature of social groups and unveils the fabric of differences which compose it, with their asymmetries, hierarchies and often with their practices of violence and oppression.

In order for this critical outlook to be possible, the voices of those occupying marginal places in the community must be heard and understood. The *silence* characterizing *Weltbild* certainties, their 'going without saying', here manifests its negative side: common sense *rules* by remaining implicit, and *rules out* other voices by silencing them.[50] 'Knowledge of other cultures makes one aware of one's world-picture', observes Hamilton (2014, p. 141), and '"unspoken presuppositions", once spoken, become open to criticism and doubt'. For this reason, seeing the *Weltbild* and making it explicit goes hand in hand with being able to listen to those who speak from the sidelines. Thanks to the other, one becomes aware, perhaps for the first time, of an axis of rotation of one's life, and can adopt a disenchanted outlook towards oneself (Bax 2011, Chap. 5). According to Scheman, language is *not* a universal medium enabling the understanding of any perspective from the outset. Rather, any discourse is inevitably partial, and by acknowledging this partiality, we are invited to participate actively in widening understanding.

> [T]he epistemic resources of variously marginal subject positions provide the ground for a critique of 'what we do' that rejects both the possibility of transcending human practice and the fatalism of being determined by it, but ... those resources are not available to someone who is unwilling or unable to stand on that ground. (Scheman 2011, p. 153)

Scheman's 'shifting' ground, as she calls it, is not completely stable: it is composed of different materials and layers, like the terminal moraine (this is her metaphor) which forms at the edges of a glacier. Yet, the moraine *is* a

---

[50] See Medina (2004) and (2006).

terrain on which it is possible to walk, provided there is sufficient attention to its shifting parts. The difficulty seeing them, the difficulty hearing the marginal voices, is also the difficulty to see the prejudices and hinges of our own *Weltbild*. And this is just another aspect of the more general difficulty to thematize the background at the origin of our ideas of sense and objectivity.

Background and Foreground

When Wittgenstein says that, like our life, our language games are there without a ground (OC, §559), he is not saying that we speak and act unreasonably. We may speak or act without a ground, but not without a background. What we say or do is rooted in habits, institutions, rules, education[51]—in a word, in a *Lebensform*. Objectivity resides in this 'we' which, by remaining in the background, gives sense to our actions and words.[52]

Wittgenstein uses the word *Hintergrund* and related terms both in the notes of OC and in other writings. In the early 1930s, the background is that against which words and sentences gain meaning, and that against which understanding and expression are possible (BT, p. 116; CV, p. 16[53]). In PI, the background is also described as something deep and not easily accessible, where sense has its roots:

> What do I believe in when I believe that man has a soul? What do I believe in when I believe that this substance contains two carbon rings? In both cases, there is a picture in the foreground, but the sense lies far in the background; that is, the application of the picture is not easy to survey. (PI, §422)[54]

---

[51] See for instance LFM, pp. 203–204, RPP II, §§707–708 (also in Z, §§387–388); see also Emmett (1990, p. 223).
[52] See the example of the joke in CV, p. 78 (from MS 137, p. 136b, 1948).
[53] Respectively from MS 109, p. 185 (1930) and MS 112, p. 1v (1931).
[54] From MS 116, p. 283, ca. 1944. See also MS 130, p. 48.

In slightly later remarks, Wittgenstein uses this word to highlight the multifarious and complicated pattern of our actions, practices, and ultimately of life, variously intertwined with concepts. 'We judge an action according to its background within human life,' he observes, and the background is a bustle so varied and complex that we would not be able to copy it, albeit we are able to recognize it in general terms (RPP II, §§. 624–625).[55] As noticed earlier, through the concept of the background Wittgenstein wants to give voice to 'the whole hurly-burly' determining 'our judgments, concepts, and reactions' (RPP II, §629).[56] Finally, in OC the background is described as an inherited *Weltbild* against which we distinguish between truth and falsity (OC, §94),[57] and, in a more limited example, as what we need in order to understand the working of words in particular contexts (OC, §461).[58]

Trying to keep together all these uses of the term, I think one could say that, for Wittgenstein, the background concerns *sense*, on the planes of both words and actions, and it highlights precisely the interconnection between the two: we understand a word or a sentence only by connecting it with its contexts of use and hence the practices surrounding it, and we understand an action by connecting it with the conceptual, linguistic and cultural meaningfulness which hosts it.

In the philosophical debate, the concept of the background is chiefly linked to the name of John Searle. He used the notion first as an instrument for a linguistic analysis, aimed at opposing the idea that there can be a literal meaning cut off from contextual assumptions (Searle 1979); later he broadened its application to the issue of

---

[55] From MS 137, p. 54a, 1948.

[56] In the manuscript (MS 137, p. 54b), there are some other sentences between the two latter remarks that I have just mentioned, including: '*Der Hintergrund des Lebens ist gleichsam pointiliert*', the background of life is so to speak 'pointilled'. The term is quite difficult to translate, but I guess Wittgenstein is referring to pointillism. Elsewhere he refers to impressionism; see PI, §368 (from MS 162b, p. 49v, 1939–1940) and MS 135, p. 186, 1947.

[57] From MS 174, p. 21v., 1950.

[58] From MS 176, p. 32r, 1951. Other interesting passages can be found in CE, pp. 406–407 (from MS 159, pp. 10v, 12r–12v, ca. 1938); RFM, pp. 304 and 437 (from MS 164, p. 5, 1941–1944, and MS 124, p. 199, ca. 1944); RPP I, p. 101, also in Z, §530 (from MS 130, p. 161, 1946). Regarding OC, see also §162 (MS 174, p. 35r, 1950) and §350 (MS 175, p. 52v, 1951).

intentionality in general, connecting it to the notion of know-how (Searle 1983); and he eventually extended the analysis to the sphere of social phenomena (Searle 1995, 2010). But his approach, especially in the later works, is quite distant from Wittgenstein's. Indeed, Searle assimilates the background to a neuro-physiological category, affirming that background capacities are causally sensitive to the constitutive rules of social institutions. This makes one think of a mechanism which, starting from social rules, shapes habits and background capacities through complex processes which concretize in neuro-physiological features of the brain, and in turn these operate causally on behaviour, producing individual and social actions. As Margolis (2012b)[59] has observed, Searle's argument is based on two disputable assumptions: that consciousness derives from basic physical facts, and that the social dimension derives from individual intentionality. There is a (double) reductionism here, which overlooks the genuine theoretical shift allowed by the concept of the background. In fact, the concept of the background offers an alternative route avoiding both the mind/body and the individual/social dualisms, and it is in this sense that Wittgenstein himself seems to use it.

I already mentioned that one of the branches of the debate on OC concerns its foundational vs anti-foundational readings. As Hamilton (2014, pp. 98–102) suggests, Wittgenstein talks of 'foundations without foundationalism'—and without anti-foundationalism too, one might add. The concept of the background is also helpful in this context. Indeed, the defenders of both views seem to be obliged to acknowledge that there is a distance from the canonical philosophical notions of foundationalism and anti-foundationalism. For instance, Conway (1989), who defends a foundationalist interpretation against conventionalist and relativistic readings, underlines that Wittgenstein has moved the analysis from the foundations of objective reality and of the transcendental subject to the idea of justification. Stroll (1994 and 2004) speaks of a 'rupturalist', non-traditional foundationalism; Moyal-Sharrock (2003 and 2007, pp. 78–79) speaks of a form of pragmatism

---

[59] For another critical comment on Searle's notion of background see Moyal-Sharrock (2013b).

with foundations, specifying that these foundations are not metaphysical and that coherence is also part of Wittgenstein's picture of certainties. Conversely, M. Williams (2005) defends the hypothesis of a non-foundationalist Wittgenstein but underlines the centrality of justification as an activity carried on in a certain context and according to certain praxes. The conceptual shift from ground to background makes the inconsistency of this debate explicit: the background represents neither the foundation nor the absence of foundations, but the human, practical and cultural nature of the fabric from which meanings stem.[60] The concept of justification is often singled out in this context, but again it seems in need of a reformulation. *Weltbild* certainties are neither grounded nor ungrounded, and similarly, they are neither justified nor unjustified (OC, §§175, 192, 559, 563). The point is that justification itself is a practice, variously interwoven with the other practices of our form of life.

In pragmatism, too, the opposition to absolute foundations is accompanied by the awareness of the inevitability of background certainties or beliefs, and the mind/body distinction and the individual/social dialectic do not assume the form of a dualism. In a sense, the very origins of the concept of the background can be traced back to James. The Husserlian phenomenological tradition itself, the point of departure for both Searle's reflection (with the mediation of a slightly misread Wittgenstein[61]) and the reflection of another thinker often associated with the concept of the background, Hubert Dreyfus[62] (with the mediation of Heidegger and Merleau-Ponty), as well as for the more recent enactivist approach,[63] is indebted to James in this respect.

---

[60] See Bax (2013) and Calcaterra (2003a).

[61] Searle partly acknowledges the distance in Searle (2011). The vicinity is instead underlined by Goodman (2002, p. 21).

[62] See for instance Dreyfus (1982), especially the introduction; Dreyfus (1992), (2002); and the opening chapter of Radman (2012).

[63] The approach was inaugurated by Varela, Thompson, and Rosch (1991). For some recent developments in connection with the theme of the background, see Radman (2012). For an introduction to enactivism in connection with Wittgenstein, see Boncompagni (2013). As some

Chapter 5: From Ground to Background 213

Two aspects of James' work seem particularly relevant for this theme. First, in the PP chapter on the stream of thought, he underlines the blurredness of our ideas, and how they merge into each other. In describing the continuity of thought, he affirms that the metaphor of the stream aims to suggest that the drops and waves composing the flux are always surrounded by other water, so that every idea in the mind is always in a relationship of continuity with its surrounding environment of ideas, thanks to the fringe that connects and mixes it up with other ideas. In the stream of thought, there are not only distinct ideas or entities but also feelings of a tendency that keep ideas joined to each other. The relevance of this conception is clear if one considers that it is in this context that James announces one of the purposes of his work.

> ... '[T]endencies' are not only descriptions from without, but ... they are among the *objects* of the stream, which is thus aware of them from within, and must be described as in very large measure constituted of feelings of tendency, often so vague that we are unable to name them at all. It is in short, the re-instatement of the vague to its proper place in our mental life which I am so anxious to press on the attention. (PP, p. 246)

It is very natural to compare this 're-instatement of the vague to its proper place' to Wittgenstein's desire to 'grab imprecision conceptually', instead of 'reducing imprecision to precision'.[64] The difficulty lies in consigning vagueness as it is—vague—to reflection. James is concerned here with mental life, but, I think, his objective is general because the call to anti-reductionism is a constant element of his work. Moreover, he offers a very general application of the concept of fringe, affirming for instance that 'the word "real" itself is, in short, a fringe' (PP, p. 947), because it is not in virtue of a direct perception but thanks to the connections that concepts have with each other that we believe that

---

interpreters have noticed, John Dewey also anticipated many themes of the contemporary debate: see Shusterman (2012a) or (2012b), Steiner (2013), Madzia (2013), and Gallagher (2014).

[64] 'Schärfe ist Schärfe, Unschärfe ist Unschärfe. Unschärfe will ich nicht auf Schärfe zurückführen; sondern sie als Unschärfe begrifflich fassen', MS 137, p. 64b, 1948. See also PI, §71 as well as PPF, §356, on indefiniteness.

parts of reality far from us in time and space are real. James speaks of a fringe, halo and horizon, but the affinity with the notion of background is quite evident. Both James and Wittgenstein feel the need to re-establish the vagueness of the contours of concepts and ideas and their relations of familiarity and vicinity with other concepts and ideas (Fairbanks 1966, 335 ff.). Although Wittgenstein would criticize some aspects of James' vision, the relevance of vagueness and its link with a typical difficulty of *expression* have a strong resonance on Wittgenstein's approach.

A second element tracing the theme of the background back to James is his reflection on the basis of rationality, in 'The Sentiment of Rationality'. While speculating on the possibility of finding a unified system which could explain everything, and supposing that a universal concept be found which 'made the concrete chaos rational', James asks: 'Can that which is the ground of rationality in all else be itself properly called rational?' (WB, p. 62). It would seem so, he goes on, but after a quick reasoning, he observes:

> Unfortunately, this first answer will not hold. Our mind is so wedded to the process of seeing an *other* beside every item of its experience, that when the notion of an absolute datum is presented to it, it goes through its usual procedure and remains pointing at the void beyond, as if in that lay further matter for contemplation. (WB, p. 63)

Oscillating between the 'datum' and non-entity, the mind seems to find no peace, until the philosopher has to acknowledge: 'The bottom of being is left logically opaque to us, as something which we simply come upon and find, and about which (if we wish to act) we should pause and wonder as little as possible' (WB, p. 64). There is no sense in searching for an ultimate answer, because belief, rooted as it is in the practical and emotive sphere of man, is itself the (back)ground of action. In the end, it is the practical exigency to act, both in the philosopher and in the 'boor', that prevails. Yet, this does not mean that rationality is abandoned: it means that the sentimental and practical aspects of rationality are taken into account, so that, given different conceptions of the world, each one satisfying the 'logical demand' and consistent with the facts, 'that one

Chapter 5: From Ground to Background 215

which awakens the active impulses, or satisfies other aesthetic demands better than the other, will be accounted the more rational conception, and will deservedly prevail' (WB, p. 66).

This amounts to nothing more, but nothing less either, than recognizing 'how entirely the intellect is made up of practical interests' (WB, p. 72): it is not renouncing rationality, but investigating what it really comprises.

With his remarks on the 'datum', James can obviously be associated with Wittgenstein and Peirce, for whom, too, there is no sense in looking for an ultimate 'given', and the analysis must start from vital practices, from 'men and their conversation' (CP 8.112),[65] as Peirce puts it, but as Wittgenstein might have put it as well. The search for the ultimate foundation is one of the obstacles that 'block the way of inquiry', a cardinal sin in Peirce's philosophical system. One form that this sin assumes, he says,

> consists in maintaining that this, that, or the other element of science is basic, ultimate, independent of aught else, and utterly inexplicable—not so much from any defect in our knowing as because there is nothing beneath it to know (CP 1.139).[66]

Considering something inexplicable, he continues, is 'no explanation at all' and ultimately it is 'a conclusion which no reasoning can ever justify or excuse' (*ibid.*).

One could object—with reason, I think—that, in Wittgenstein, there is neither the need for explanations nor more generally the perspective of an unlimited semiosis for which any inference or interpretation can give rise to a potentially infinite process of inferences or interpretations. In this sense, it would be wrong to identify in these themes a similarity between Wittgenstein and pragmatism. Yet, this objection can be counterbalanced by considering two points. First, in Wittgenstein too there is a neat

---

[65] From a review by Peirce of J. Royce's 'The World and the Individual', ca. 1900.
[66] From 'The First Rule of Logic', 1898.

opposition to the idea that it is possible to find an ultimate ground resting on itself:

> 'You can't go on having one thing resting on another; in the end there must be something resting on itself'. (The *a priori*) Something firm in itself.
> I propose to drop this mode of speech as it leads to puzzlements (CE, p. 407).[67]

The cardinal sin that Peirce saw in blocking the way of inquiry is identified by Wittgenstein in ways of thinking that create puzzles; but, so to say, the sinner in this case is the same. It is the idea that something must be firm in itself because 'there is nothing beneath', that is, because 'you can't go on having one thing resting on another'. Moreover, if it is true that, in Peirce, everything is a sign and points to something else, and that signs are linked to one another in potentially infinite processes, it is also true that the chain of interpretants comes to an end in the final logical interpretant, which is a habit of action.[68] What associates Peirce and Wittgenstein, differentiating the former from an advocate of a sort of hermeneutic anti-foundationalist and the latter from a sort of a behaviourist foundationalist, is precisely the shift towards an idea of the background, which removes at once both traditional foundationalism and anti-foundationalism.

In this light, the Peircean—but also the Jamesian—reflections on common sense play the same role as Wittgenstein's remarks on the *Weltbild*. As Broyles (1965, p. 87) observes,

> [o]n his [Peirce's] view these common sense beliefs provide the background which makes the very practice of giving reasons possible. It is this backdrop of the familiar, the expected, of 'the way things are' that determines when reasons are required as well as what sorts of things shall count as reasons at all.

---

[67] From MS 159, pp. 12r–12v, ca. 1938.
[68] See CP 5.491, from 'A Survey of Pragmaticism', 1907.

Another description that, like this one, fits perfectly well with Wittgenstein too, is the following by Richard Bernstein (2010, pp. 33–34):

> In opposition to Cartesianism and to what Hans-Georg Gadamer calls the 'Enlightenment prejudice against prejudice', Peirce insists that all inquiry, including scientific and philosophical inquiry, begins with tacit prejudices and prejudgments.... [W]e never escape from having tacit background prejudgments that we do not question.... In this sense we can speak of a foundation from which any inquiry begins. Peirce... is an anti-foundationalist when foundationalism is understood as the doctrine that claims that there are basic or incorrigible truths that are not subject to revision. But he is not denying—indeed, he is *affirming*—that all knowing has a foundation in the sense that there are tacitly held beliefs, which we don't doubt and take to be the bedrock of truth.

This description has the additional merit of shedding light on another crucial element that both approaches underline: the fact that background beliefs and certainties are tacit, or only rarely expressed, and often difficult even to identify. To use Peirce's words once again, 'It is the belief men *betray* and not that which they *parade* which has to be studied' (CP 5.444).[69]

That background certainties go *sans dire* implies a difficult challenge for this kind of inquiry. Putting the background to the fore means trying to focus on what by definition *cannot* be focused on. Only if we do not look at it directly does the background remain a background: if we concentrate our gaze on it, it disappears, or worse blocks the inquiry in the immobility of a schema or lifeless description. The background fools the observer. What can perhaps be attempted is to train our peripheral gaze, by exercising its capacity to glimpse the limits of the visual field without fixing itself on the scene. We cannot have the whole picture or the whole background, but we may be able to see some details that, if chosen with a happy criterion, suggest what the surroundings may be like. This is the job of someone who draws 'sketches of landscapes', as Wittgenstein described himself in the preface of PI, upon realizing, in a

---

[69] Footnote, from 'Six Characters of Common-Sensism'.

crucial moment for his work, that it was pointless to force his thoughts along a single track. This kind of perspective may appear very distant from pragmatism, and on the whole, it certainly is. Yet, as we shall see in the next chapter, an anti-theoretical strand is also present in Peirce and (especially) in James.

Concluding Remarks

With the aim of exploring the most profound convergences between Wittgenstein and the pragmatists' approach, this chapter began by analysing the Wittgensteinian notion of form of life. For him this is a conceptual tool, initially used to indicate the particular cultural form of groups of people, and later, more often, to point out the intertwinement between ways of living and language that makes meaning possible. Yet, far from offering a naturalistic description or explanation of human cultural life, Wittgenstein seems to privilege the methodological employment of this notion, and through this, he tries to bring the philosophical outlook back to the every day and to what usually remains in the background and goes unnoticed.

Secondary literature on this concept was taken into account by focusing on some issues that have often been connected to this theme, like relativism and conservatism. This led to the acknowledgement that the attribution of various 'isms' to Wittgenstein is of no use if one intends to see what is distinctively new in his approach, and something similar was singled out for pragmatism. More precisely, the way in which Wittgenstein, Peirce, and James deal with the 'we' and the bond between the human practices of sense and the concepts of objectivity, reasonableness and rationality emerged as the sign of a consonant attitude. The contingent yet not arbitrary, grounding yet not absolute nature of the terrain on which linguistic practices grow, always interwoven with the praxes of social life and education, for both Wittgenstein and the pragmatists takes the shape of an unusual image for philosophy, that of the background, that which is constantly behind or beyond the contours of the subject under scrutiny. The philosopher who has chosen to investigate the background of form of life, aware of the impossibility of keeping what she ideally aims to see in the line of fire, recovers her humanity in the very limits of the epistemic enterprise, and recovers an instrumental and methodological value in the concepts which have helped the inquiry. Concepts like form of life or background can be seen, in this sense, as 'methodological *a priori*'[70] with a heuristic and ethical value. Giving attention to forms of life, one's own and other people's, means training the peripheral gaze to the perception of our limits and the practical and cultural matrix at their origins. At the same time and in virtue of this training, it means looking at the other with an understanding intention, while imagining uses, motives, reasons, actions, practices and meanings, against *another background.*

---

[70] See Andronico (2008, p. 45), Witherspoon (2003, p. 230).

Chapter 6: Between Method and *Weltanschauung*

Preliminary Remarks

The heuristic and ethical value of philosophical concepts stressed in Chapter 5 is now the starting point for the last step in this comparative work. By examining the methodological aspects of the philosophies of Wittgenstein and pragmatism, it will be possible to return with more awareness to the distinction between pragmatism as a method, which Wittgenstein sometimes seemed to approach, and pragmatism as a *Weltanschauung*, towards which he tended to appear hostile. Yet of course, things are not so clear-cut: a way of doing philosophy always implies, if not a *Weltanschauung*, a way of seeing, a point of view, a perspective, and the connections between the two poles of method and world view need to be examined as well.

I will begin with the only undoubtedly *positive* remark Wittgenstein expressed on pragmatism, concerning the purpose of descriptions. This will offer the chance to treat Wittgenstein's idea (and ideal) of description more fully, which he typically proposed as an alternative to explanation. The link between description and *the ordinary* is a relevant feature not only of Wittgenstein's approach but also, in a sense, of Peirce's: indeed, the latter often investigates the basic operations of thought, and in this sense both thinkers look for techniques that enable us to see what usually escapes the attention because it is always right before our eyes. Conversely, the link between descriptive methods and the theme of *importance* is a common feature of Wittgenstein and James, and this will help to enlarge the analysis towards the ethical and hortative motivation behind methodological choices. An anti-theoretical attitude towards ethics actually characterizes all three thinkers, although with different nuances that I will try to highlight. Going back, after this detour, to the distinction *and* the connection between method and *Weltanschauung*, it will emerge that Wittgenstein himself sees a relationship between his main method of synoptic presentation and a world view, but progressively loosens this bond while also widening his techniques of investigation and writing. Finally, it will be possible to re-examine Wittgenstein's remark on pragmatism in OC, §422 ('Here I am being thwarted by a kind of *Weltanschauung*'), and to identify those aspects of pragmatism which he probably felt to be more disturbing.

'The good in pragmatism'

As mentioned in the first chapter, Wittgenstein's only positive observation on pragmatism is in one of his lectures on philosophical psychology (LPP). The notes by Peter Geach, Kanti Shah, and A.C. Jackson agree in their account of this lesson, dating back to November 1946. The general topic is description, and Wittgenstein proposes an example concerning the description of a child who is learning to count, in this way also linking the discussion to the topic of following a rule. At a certain stage, an observer would say that the child has learned to count, and therefore *can count*; but how is such a judgment, or such a description, possible, given that the observer can only see the child counting up to, say, 100 (or any other limited number)? As a student points out during Wittgenstein's lecture: 'If the child has counted 100, the problem still arises whether it *can count* to 100' (LPP, p. 26). Wittgenstein agrees that there is a problem here and focuses the attention on 'description'. According to Geach's notes, he says:

Chapter 6: Between Method and *Weltanschauung* 223

Wittgenstein: This is quite true. Well, is saying what a child can do a description?
Kreisel: One might ask what you want the description for.
Wittgenstein: Yes; this is the good in pragmatism. What is the description for? (LPP, p. 26–27)

As I take it, the 'good' in pragmatism is identified by Wittgenstein in shifting the question from the general concept of 'description' to the purposes and the uses of the specific description at issue. This is confirmed by Shah's and Jackson's notes, according to which Wittgenstein connected pragmatism with asking: 'What do you do with a description', and in the case under discussion with asking: 'When, under what circumstances, to achieve what, would you say "He can count"?'. Shah reports that he went so far as to affirm: 'It may be said we are pragmatists. But there is much truth in it [pragmatism]' (LPP, pp. 145, 266).[1]

In order to understand whether a description is correct, says Wittgenstein, and more generally, in order to understand a description, it is essential to ask ourselves how we use it, for what purpose, in which circumstances. Wittgenstein emphasizes the instrumental nature of description on other occasions too, and in my view, this is relevant for counterbalancing the sometimes idealized picture that emerges when he opposes description to explanation. Indeed, he repeatedly affirms that philosophy should not offer explanations and that description is its main method (PI, §109), thereby risking idealizing the latter, as if it were possible to adopt a non-perspectival point of view and offer a complete and neutral account of what there is. While this model may have been present in the early and perhaps in the 'phenomenological' Wittgenstein, it certainly disappears later. 'What we call "*descriptions*"', he states in PI, §291, 'are instruments for particular uses', and the activity of philosophy rotates around particular uses or purposes. Philosophy does not look for weird and unusual phenomena, nor new discoveries, but 'marshal[s] recollections for a particular purpose' (PI, §127), it looks at what is already known and describes it with the aim of noticing aspects that had remained, so to say, 'hidden before our eyes'.

---

[1] See also RPP I, §§625, 635–636.

When it investigates language uses, the point of philosophy is to see the *Dienst*, the service that a certain way of using words accomplishes, in such a way that, in order to see the ordinary, it is also necessary to distinguish the effective, peculiar, and instrumental employment of words.

The ordinariness of what is described, and the instrumentality of the description, then: this double aspect, which Wittgenstein invites us to consider, prevents him from adopting an idealized model of description as mirroring what there is.

Both features are also relevant in a pragmatist perspective. As regards instrumentality, the connection is obvious. Peirce underlines precisely this aspect in 'How to Make Our Ideas Clear'. In order to understand if we have a clear idea of something, he explains, we need to ask ourselves what is the use of thinking of that idea or concept and thinking of it in those terms. He makes the example of the concept of force, while affirming: 'According to our rule, we must begin by asking what is the immediate use of thinking about force; and the answer is, that we thus account for changes of motion' (W 3, p. 268).[2] Indeed, 'it is absurd to say that thought has any meaning unrelated to its only function' (W 3, p. 266),[3] a function to be defined, for the Peirce writing in 1878, with reference to its perceivable effects. More generally, as extensively seen in Chapter 4, through the pragmatic maxim the meaning of a concept is connected to its practical and potential bearings, not so differently from what happens according to Wittgenstein's indication that the meaning of a word is generally to be found in its use. It is interesting that Wittgenstein identified the 'good' and even the 'truth' in pragmatism precisely in this call to the instrumentality of descriptions, and hence in its methodological side.[4] Occasionally he even 'used' this pragmatic plea against Ramsey, rebuking his friend's tendency to rely on meaning as a sort of feeling (there is perhaps also an indirect criticism of James here):

---

[2] Also in CP 5.404.
[3] Also in CP 5.401.
[4] On Peircean pragmatism as a method see Tiercelin (2016, p. 184).

Wittgenstein said often that Ramsey used to say, in discussion, 'I seem to mean something by it'... This was almost like speaking of how it *looked* to him. At any rate, it is not a way of deciding whether the expression you contemplate does mean anything or not. And Wittgenstein's move was always to ask, 'Well, what do you *do* with it?' To find what it means, consider its application. (Citron 2015a, pp. 54–55)[5]

The other aspect of Wittgenstein's descriptive methods, that is, the ordinariness of what is described, also finds its matching part in pragmatism. As is well known, Wittgenstein repeatedly observes that his remarks concern 'very general facts of nature' (PI, §142), and that if these platitudes were put under the shape of theses, 'everyone would agree to them' (PI, §128).[6]

On the pragmatist side, Peirce too highlights that 'certain facts escape us because they are so pervading and ubiquitous' (CP 1.159)[7] or because 'they permeate our whole lives, just as a man who never takes off his blue spectacles soon ceases to see the blue tinge' (CP 1.241).[8] And for Peirce too attention to this everyday aspects is central to the task of philosophy:

> ... by Philosophy I mean that department of Positive Science, or Science of Fact, which does not busy itself with gathering facts, but merely with learning what can be learned from that experience which presses in upon every one of us daily and hourly. (CP 5.120)[9]

In both Wittgenstein and Peirce the everyday as the subject of philosophy includes the grammatical or logical hinges of our way of living, and the difficulty lies in being able to see them in the obvious.

---

[5] The same theme was highlighted in Chap. 4, Section 'Meaning and Understanding', and I will come back to it also in Section 'Science and Philosophy'.
[6] See also PPF, sec. xii and RPP I, §46.
[7] From 'Fallibilism Continuity and Evolution', prob. 1897.
[8] From 'A Detailed Classification of the Sciences', 1902.
[9] From 'The Three Kinds of Goodness', fifth of the Harvard Lectures on Pragmatism, 1903.

The philosopher is indeed someone who flies over a familiar landscape, trying to detect a pattern, a form, a grammar which is 'revealing of the human'.[10] As has been noticed, both Wittgenstein and Peirce make use of the metaphor of the landscape (Colapietro 2011). The former affirms that his job consists of showing his students 'details of an immense landscape' (CV, p. 56),[11] and speaks of the necessity 'to travel criss-cross in every direction over a wide field of thought' to draw 'a number of sketches of landscapes... in the course of these long and meandering journeys' (PI, Preface). Similarly, Peirce addresses the reader with these words:

> I invite you to journey with me over a land of thought which is already more or less known to you. It is a land where I have sojourned long, and I wish to point out objects for you yourself to see, some of which, I am pretty sure, have hitherto escaped your attention.[12]

For both, philosophy is a guide for this 'field of thought' (Wittgenstein) or 'land of thought' (Peirce), which subtracts the (already Cartesian) task of clarity from the exigency of constituting a foundation, and takes it back to the ordinary, also entrusting it with a new assignment: to show that if they do not have any practical bearing, problems and dilemmas are idle and inconsistent, and can simply be dropped. Here, both Peirce and James are in harmony with Wittgenstein, who does not propose 'a new set of answers to the once-and-future set of philosophical problems' (Jolley 1998, p. 55), but works to dissolve puzzles and show how often alleged problems are false problems due to misuses of language. As Peirce states, pragmatism at the end simply 'shows that supposed problems are not real problems' (CP 8.259)[13]; and as James reiterates, the pragmatic method aims at setting seemingly interminable metaphysical disputes by

---

[10] Here I adopt an expression of Lars Hertzberg spoken during the conference 'In Wittgenstein's Footsteps', Reykjavik, September 2012.
[11] From MS 133, p. 82 (1946); see also CV, p. 78, from MS 137, p. 141a (1949).
[12] Peirce's MS 598, pp. 1–2, cited in Colapietro (2011, p. 7).
[13] From a letter to James, 1897.

tracing the practical consequences of each position, and by declaring them idle when no differences in consequences can be traced (P, p. 28).[14]

Attention to the everyday as an alternative to explanation assumes quite a radical tone in Wittgenstein, coming to mean a general opposition to theses and theories, which is not always easy to pursue.[15] Only in some cases does this drastic attitude find a back-up in the pragmatists. On the one hand, in fact, they too underline the methodological nature of their inquiries (Madelrieux 2012): Peirce explicitly asserts that pragmatism 'is, in itself, no doctrine of metaphysics, no attempt to determine any truth of things [, but ...] merely a method of ascertaining the meanings of hard words and of abstract concepts' (CP 5.464),[16] and James that 'it is a method only' (P, p. 31). Yet, on the other hand, they do not deny, but rather they sometimes emphasize the bond between that method and a whole world view, as will be clearer shortly.

Wittgenstein was probably attracted by the non-theoretical aspect that emerged at times, also involuntarily, in James. While associating him with Goethe, for instance, he once remarked:

> Goethe's theory of the constitution of the colours of the spectrum has not proved to be an unsatisfactory theory, rather it really isn't a theory at all. Nothing can be predicted with it. It is, rather, a vague schematic outline of the sort we find in James's psychology. Nor is there any *experimentum crucis* which could decide for or against the theory. (RC I, §70)[17]

If the guilt of both Goethe and James lies in their intention to construct a theory, their merit is that sometimes they show awareness of the need to let phenomena speak for themselves, without adding a theoretical schema to them. In VRE, in the ethical writings, but also in PP, what was most interesting for Wittgenstein was probably the richness of James' examples and his attention towards the variety and variability of

---

[14] On these themes see Goodman (2002, pp. 163–164, 174).
[15] See RPP I, §723.
[16] From 'Pragmatism', 1907.
[17] From MS 173, pp. 28v–29r, 1950. See also RC III, §125, from MS 176, p. 17v, 1950.

phenomena, and certainly not the theoretical or scientific intentions that sometimes surface. The 'good' of pragmatism, in this sense, is its attention to the concreteness of experiences and phenomena, with their contexts, motives, and purposes: the kind of attention that the methodological side of pragmatism helps to put into practice.

Beyond Method

If method was essentially the 'good' in pragmatism, what Wittgenstein appreciated of James probably went beyond this. Even in his *failed* attempts to do science, James showed something of interest for him, and this something was not *only* a method. In trying to be scientific, Wittgenstein says of James, he was only trying to 'extricate himself from the cobwebs of metaphysics' and in his attempts to walk, he could only 'wriggle': but this was actually *interesting* for Wittgenstein.[18]

James' is not a scientific activity, but it is an activity which, in its incessant effort to extricate itself from metaphysical webs, is the expression of 'a real human being', of James *the man*, with his weaknesses and his virtues. 'This is what makes him a good philosopher' (Rhees 1984, p. 106), Wittgenstein remarked: James let his whole nature show through his philosophy.

He did so self-consciously and deliberately. 'Pretend what we may,' he said, 'the whole man within us is at work when we form our philosophical opinions' (WB, p. 77). The history of philosophy itself was for James largely a history of *temperaments* and how they had fought, prevailed, and failed through time (P, p. 11). In philosophy, intended as an activity, the most intimate nature of a person finds expression. In James' philosophy, in his way of interpreting and embodying pragmatism, indeed, the relevance of meanings and conceptions lies in the practical effects they produce on individuals, in the difference they make 'to you and me' (P, p. 30), and to our way of living. In this sense, the personal and ethical dimension of James' thought is not simply one aspect of it: it is its core, and only by

---

[18] See MS 165, pp. 150–151 (1941–1944), quoted and translated in Hilmy (1987, pp. 196–197).

taking it fully into account can one understand the more technical parts of his work, including his problematic notion of truth (Marchetti 2015a, Chap. 4).

This existential thickness is particularly manifest when James deals with issues in the ethical context, and it is here that his non-theoretical or even anti-theoretical stance also emerges. 'The Moral Philosopher and the Moral Life'[19] is emblematic in this respect. In the real world, says James, there will always be conflicting needs and exigencies, and it is not possible to devise an ethical system telling us in advance what choices are to be made in each and every situation. The only guide for choices involving ethics can be to aim at the progressive widening of the benefits for the community, but this minimal requirement will always need to be interpreted and adapted to the singular cases. No system can be definitive. To make a moral choice is not simply to exercise an option, but to contribute to shaping one's personality and creating a portion of the shared reality itself.[20] In this sense, James' reflection depicts human beings not so much as they are, or as they should be, but as they *might* be, conceiving ethics as a reflection on self-cultivation and self-transformation, and essentially as a work on one's potentialities (Marchetti 2015a, Chap. 3). Similarly, when concerned with understanding the other, James sees the other's point of view as potentially expressive of a whole way of being; when encounters take place, what is at stake is the capacity to see with someone else's eyes, to see the 'point' of their lives, what matters to them.[21]

I read a convergence here with the Wittgensteinian use of the notion of forms of life. Intended as a methodological tool, as I tried to show in the previous chapter, this concept helps us to focus not only on the way we live but also on the way we and others *might* live. This ethics of attention, suggested by both James and Wittgenstein, aims to train the capacity at the same time to see details, and to grasp the overall sense, the 'point' in the lives

---

[19] In WB, pp. 57–89. Putnam (1992a) interpreted this text as an anticipation of Wittgenstein's private language argument.
[20] See Putnam, A.R. and Putnam, H. (1992).
[21] See 'On a Certain Blindness in Human Beings', in TT, pp. 229 ff.

of people. The intimate connection between philosophical reflection and life, especially life with others, indeed characterizes both thinkers, and in my view, it is chiefly this aspect, which goes far beyond the methodological side of pragmatism, that Wittgenstein liked in James. As Goodman (2002, p. 172) writes, in James, Wittgenstein found

> a philosopher whose humanity was a part of his philosophical investigations; someone who worked with a sense that the problems of philosophy were not merely technical quandaries but problems of and for human beings[;]

a philosopher, to use Putnam's (1992a, p. 30) words, interested in cases of 'real hunger', whose work, 'whatever its shortcomings, provides substantial food for thought—and not just for thought, but for life'.

In Wittgenstein too the ethical value of the notion of form of life has the sense of denying theory an effective role in our lives, instead underlining, for instance, the primitiveness of the helping behaviour we display when faced with someone who is suffering, as well as the importance of sharing a way of living (Putnam 1995). Moreover, in Wittgenstein too ethics is declined in the first person. Not—of course—in the sense that the subject autonomously decides what is ethical, but in the sense that ethics has to do with the subject's overall attitude or stance (*Einstellung*) towards the world. I think that this is already present in Wittgenstein's LE and the writings of the same period (if not even before, in TLP, though in a transcendental form). An example is the affirmation that 'an ethical sentence is a personal action' (MS 183, p. 76).[22] The personal nature of ethics (and religion) does not imply privateness, but the complete and non-theoretical involvement of the person. 'If I could explain the essence of the ethical only by means of a theory—he observed during a conversation annotated in Waismann (1979, p. 117)—then what is ethical would be of no value whatsoever'. That is why in this domain it is 'essential' (*ibid.*) to speak in the first person, as he did in the conclusion of LE (LE, p. 44).

Speaking in the first person means expressing a personal attitude, taking a position; when necessary, it may mean changing one's own life.

---

[22] Dated 1931. Quoted in Christensen (2011a, p. 810).

It is not a matter of argumentation or theorization: theories are of no use, and what is needed is rather examples, exhortation, persuasion or conversion. It is now possible to more fully understand the ethical sense of Wittgenstein's often misread remarks on persuasion. In accepting that the other cannot be convinced through rational argumentation, there is not resignation but respect (which does not imply an unconditional acceptance of the other's position): respect for a difference that can be so radical as to appear to us unreasonable, out of place and unreachable. Yet, the path of persuasion remains open.

This is especially true for philosophy. Wittgenstein's descriptive method is essentially a method of persuasion—and here the distance from a traditional conception of description is particularly open to view. As we partially saw in Chapter 5, as a technique aimed at letting one see other aspects of a situation, persuasion is an integral part of Wittgenstein's way of working, and as we hinted in Chapter 1 there is a consonance here with William James.[23] In a 1938 lecture on aesthetics, Wittgenstein explains:

> Those sentences have the form of persuasion in particular which say 'This is really this'. [This means] there are certain differences which you have been persuaded to neglect....
> I very often draw your attention to certain differences... If someone says: 'There is not a difference', and I say: 'There is a difference' I am persuading, I am saying 'I don't want you to look at it like that.'
> ...I am in a sense making propaganda for one style of thinking as opposed to another (LC, pp. 27–28).[24]

It is by showing the fly the way out of the bottle, converting it to a new perspective, that his philosophy achieves its objective (PI, §309). This may require resistances and habits to be overcome. As he pointed out during a conversation with Rush Rhees:

---

[23] See Perissinotto (2016a, p. 166) for a parallel between Wittgenstein and James on conversion.

[24] See also LFM, p. 103 and Citron (2015a, pp. 39, 62). On 'aspect-seeing' as a method see Floyd (2010) and Agam-Segal (2015).

> For me to write or teach philosophy is futile unless it brings in those who read or hear and discuss with me a deep change in their way of thinking.... It is hard to change one's way of thinking when this goes deep—one's own way of thinking about 'intelligibility', for instance; it is hard ... not because it's hard to understand, but because you don't want to give up the ways you've always gone. (Citron 2015a, pp. 60–61)

Persuasion goes deeper than theory, and in this sense in particular ethics is a matter of personal attitude and ways of doing, which cannot be approached by rational argumentation.

While these aspects find full consonance in James, things are a little more complicated in the case of Peirce. For the latter, as for James and Wittgenstein, ethics is not a theory; but on the other hand, he does not share their perspective of the first person nor that of the intimate bond between philosophy, ethics, and life.

This seems in need of some clarification. If it is not a theory, then neither is it practical (in the sense of personal), what *is* ethics for Peirce? Let us consider 'Philosophy and the Conduct of Life'[25], the first of the Cambridge Lectures of 1898. In order to understand its tone, it must be remembered that it was James who offered Peirce the chance to give these lectures. Concerned about the preliminary ideas that his friend showed him, centred on mathematical and logical issues, James suggested that Peirce instead talk about 'vitally important topics'. James' suggestion took something for granted that Peirce could not admit: that philosophy should deal with practical life. Peirce declares his intentions at the very beginning of the first lecture, by outlining the opposition between Plato, according to whom the study of dialectics and virtuous life are inextricably connected, and Aristotle, pioneer of the scientific spirit, who neatly separated moral from theoretical studies. So, Peirce announces:

> Now, Gentlemen, it behooves me, at the outset of this course, to confess to you that in this respect I stand before you an Aristotelian and a scientific man, condemning with the whole strength of conviction the Hellenic tendency to mingle philosophy and practice. (CP 1.618)

---

[25] In RLT, pp. 105–122; EP II, pp. 27–41; and CP 1.616–648.

In two senses philosophy and practice should be kept separate. First: in order to be rigorously scientific, science must leave aside anything that has a practical utility. 'Pure science has nothing at all to do with *action*,' says Peirce. 'Nothing is *vital* for science', because the scientist knows that the propositions he accepts are to be considered opinions, and not beliefs: 'The scientific man is not in the least wedded to his conclusions. He risks nothing upon them' (CP 1.635). On the other hand, he continues, when we are concerned with vital matters, the situation is different: we need to *act*, and we inevitably base our actions on the principle of *belief*. For this reason, science has nothing to say regarding practical issues, let alone regarding vital crises and matters of vital importance. These, Peirce concludes, 'must be left to sentiment, that is, to instinct' (CP 1.637).[26]

In other words, in the domain of theoretical knowledge, be it philosophical or scientific, practical issues risk being a source of confusion and distraction for the researcher. For this reason, practical utilities 'should be *put out of sight* by the investigator'. Indeed, '[t]he point of view of utility is always a narrow point of view', and 'the two masters, *theory* and *practice*, you cannot serve': the scientist will be able to pursue his objectives only by putting aside human desires, 'all the more so the higher and holier those desires may be' (CP 1.640–642).

From this point of view, Peirce's appeal is, after all, quite a traditional appeal to an ideal of pure and disinterested research, which pursues truth while leaving any practical application of its results out of consideration.[27] But this plea also means—and here is the second sense according to Peirce in which philosophy and practice must be kept separate—that it is not the job of philosophy (nor of science) to provide people with an ethical theory telling them how to behave. Nothing could be worse, in moral life, than following a philosophical theory, because moral and practical life are guided by beliefs and instincts which belong to the evolutionary and historical heritage of human nature. Here it is worth quoting again this passage:

---

[26] The early Wittgenstein seemed to share this view: 'We feel that even if *all possible* scientific questions be answered, the problems of life have still not been touched at all. . . .' TLP 6.52.

[27] But see Bergman (2010) for a broader contextualization of Peirce's attitude.

... [T]he man who would allow his religious life to be wounded by any sudden acceptance of a philosophy of religion or who would precipitately change his code of morals at the dictate of a philosophy of ethics—who would, let us say, hastily practice incest—is a man whom we should consider unwise. The regnant system of sexual rules is an instinctive or sentimental induction summarizing the experience of all our race. (CP 1.633)

Although Peirce derives this idea from the necessity to keep philosophy and practice separate, it is an idea that both James and Wittgenstein share with him. Yet, for them,[28] this very conclusion, that is, the impossibility of considering ethics a theory, derives from different premises: not from the separateness, but from the *closeness* of philosophy to practical life. Closeness not in the sense of obedience, as if philosophy prescribed rules that have to be put into practice, but in the sense of what one might call *embodiment*. An *Einstellung*, a general attitude towards the world and other people, is already incorporated in the way one lives. There is a deep difference here between the two pragmatists, and Wittgenstein would most likely side with James. The difference emerges with most clarity where James describes the pragmatist attitude as 'turn[ing] away from abstractions ... fixed principles, closed systems', and 'appealing to particulars, ... emphasising practical aspects' (P, pp. 31–32): indeed, these lines are probably at the origins of Peirce's decision to distance himself from James by coining the new word 'pragmaticism'.[29]

The connection between rejecting ethical theories and feeling an intimate bond between philosophy and concrete life which we find in James and Wittgenstein has a long tradition, and in the context of American thought it is certainly one of the main features of transcendentalism, particularly of Henry David Thoreau and Ralph Waldo Emerson. The familiarity James had with these thinkers does not need to be underlined. Wittgenstein too has been associated with this perspective, most notably by

---

[28] And for Dewey as well; see his *The Quest for Certainty* (Dewey 1929).
[29] On the difference of attitude between Peirce and James see Hookway (2012, Chap. 10).

the influential interpretation of Stanley Cavell.[30] One may wonder therefore, if Wittgenstein knew these thinkers, and it is worth dedicating a short digression to this.

The name of Emerson appears twice in Wittgenstein's writings. In November 1914 he writes in his notebook, adding no comments: 'I am reading now Emerson's essays. Perhaps they will have a good influence on me' (MS 102, p. 16v).[31] The second note is from October 1931. After a remark on the difficulty of describing the shape of an object when the latter is depicted so as to look like another object, he remembers:

> My sister Gretl once read a passage from an essay by Emerson in which he describes his friend, a philosopher (I forgot the name); from this description she thought she could gather that this man must have been similar to me. I thought to myself: What sport of nature!—What sport of nature where a beetle looks like a leaf but then it is a real beetle & not the leaf of an artificial flower. (MTD, p. 121)[32]

The philosopher described by Emerson is most likely Thoreau, as Isle Somavilla suggests, referring to Emerson's funeral address for his friend in 1862.[33] In it, Thoreau is pictured as solitary, maverick, poor by choice, an eremite, stoic, and nature lover. It is not clear whether Wittgenstein's sister is referring to this description, or to a mere physical description. Be what it may, Wittgenstein does not remember the name of the philosopher, and he reacts with surprise. Whether or not he read Thoreau, and whether or not he finished reading Emerson, it seems that he was not so struck by these thinkers, and so no direct influences can be traced. Independently from this, it is difficult to deny that there are convergences in their views. Regarding Emerson, as is well known, Cavell, again, has underlined the vicinity between the two thinkers in particular with respect to ordinary language.[34] Regarding Thoreau, Wittgenstein was surely in tune with

---

[30] See Cavell (1979, p. 463), (1992, p. 92) and (2005, pp. 199–201).
[31] It is a coded note, not in NB.
[32] From MS 183, p. 113.
[33] Emerson (1862). See MTD, p. 121 footnote d.
[34] See in particular Cavell (1989), but also West (1989) for other aspects.

him on many aspects: the emphasis on morality and a sober life, the call for simplicity and nature, the need to build one's own little house (Wittgenstein had a small one in Norway) are examples. According to Jolley (1994), the two deal with human nature in a very similar way, and they both work towards a return to a sort of *Weltanschauung* of the ordinary, the world view that would result from the consideration of the essential elements and needs characterizing the life of a human being. In Jolley's interpretation, seeing the ordinary *as ordinary* would amount to having a natural *Weltanschauung*, but since we have lost it, it is necessary to re-gain it (1994, p. 10), and this is what Wittgenstein is after (I have some doubts on this, as it seems to me that Wittgenstein constantly tries to avoid all-encompassing systems and world views, though without thereby denying their relevance in the life of human beings).

This short digression on transcendentalism, therefore, once again pushes the investigation back to a core question: what does Wittgenstein mean by *Weltanschauung*?

Synoptic Presentation and *Weltanschauung*

Wittgenstein's preoccupation with world views and the relationship between philosophical methods and world views is not only a theme in OC. On the contrary, it seems to be a constant concern in his work.

In a passage from PI, he refers to one of his own fundamental methods and connects it precisely to a *Weltanschauung*, though adding a question mark. He begins by noticing that one of the main problems in philosophical understanding is the lack of an *overview* on the uses of our words, or the lack of the capacity to see them, as it were, from above [*übersehen*], and he observes:

> Our grammar is deficient in synopticality [*Übersichtlichkeit*]. A synoptic presentation [*übersichtliche Darstellung*] produces precisely that kind of understanding which consists in 'seeing connections'. Hence the importance of finding and inventing *intermediate links*.

Chapter 6: Between Method and *Weltanschauung*

The concept of synoptic presentation is of fundamental significance for us. It characterizes the way we represent things, how we look at matters. (Is this a *Weltanschauung*?). (PI, §122)[35]

For a better understanding, as usual, it is worthwhile to search for the textual origins of this remark. In this case, it dates back to 1931. Before examining the original note, I would like to add that Wittgenstein had reflected on this theme even earlier. In TLP 6.371 he wrote that 'at the basis of the whole modern view of the world [*Weltanschauung*] lies the illusion that the so-called laws of nature are the explanations of natural phenomena'.[36] And in a letter from his sister Hermine, dated 1915, one can read this curious remark:

> Since your last leave, I have registered in me a word I previously could not understand, '*Weltanschauung*'. Since then, I smell a *Weltanschauung* everywhere, and I could also fear to become similar to you, because I believe that this is the reason for your 'taking everything as tragic', as I used to say, am I wrong? Yet given that I do not have a precise *Weltanschauung*, that of the others certainly cannot irritate me so much. (McGuinness et al. 1996, p. 26)

It seems that, for the young Wittgenstein there is something 'irritating' in a vision of the world, although it is not easy to understand whether what irritates is having one's own or perceiving the others' *Weltanschauung* (or perhaps both).

It is likely that Wittgenstein's use of this concept in later years was influenced by the way in which Oswald Spengler dealt with it in *Der Untergang des Abendlandes (The Decline of the West)*, rather a relevant work for the development of Wittgenstein's thought. Indeed, as we shall see, the name of Spengler appears in the early formulations of the quoted remark from PI. According to Spengler, every society has its own identity and is animated by its own style of thought, its

---

[35] Modified translation. In his lectures in English, Wittgenstein uses the adjective 'synoptic', and not 'perspicuous' or 'surveyable'; cf. LCM, pp. 50, 107, 114. See also Dias Fortes (2015).

[36] Originally in MS 103, p. 7r, 1916 (NB, p. 72).

Weltanschauung. Yet, he also thought all civilizations share a common deep structure, composed of the same elements, in such a way that each of them finds correspondence in the others. By studying the relationships among the different parts of the different cultures, it is possible to search for their deep structure, and this can also lead to the discovery of the characteristics of ancient and vanished civilizations, in the same way as palaeontology can reconstruct, from a few fragments of a skeleton, the original features of a once living being (Spengler 1933, p. 113). The method of synoptic presentation, at least in its initial formulation, adopts a similar perspective: the search for intermediate elements or links is similar to the search for lost fragments of the skeletons of ancient living beings (Peterman 1992, pp. 61 ff.). In this sense, it is possible to trace back to Spengler the very idea of a synoptic vision, and Spengler's own view, in turn, can be traced back to Goethe's idea of morphology, which is referred to in the subtitle of Spengler's work (*'Umrisse einer Morphologie der Weltgeschichte'*) as well as in many passages in the text. The same Goethean-Spenglerian elements are at the heart of Wittgenstein's method as developed at the beginning of the 1930s, rotating around synoptic presentation and family resemblances.[37] Therefore, it is not a surprise to see that, just like Spengler, Wittgenstein associated his method with a *Weltanschauung*.

Let me turn now to the origins and development of the PI, §122 remark in Wittgenstein's manuscripts.[38]

The first formulation is in MS 110, p. 257 (1931), and the same words are in RF, p. 133, TS 211, TS 212, and in TS 213 or BT, from which I quote:

> The concept of synoptic presentation is of fundamental significance for us. It designates our form of representation, the way we look at things. (A kind of '*Weltanschauung*', as is apparently typical of our time. Spengler.)

---

[37] Another concept prefigured by Spengler (see for instance Spengler 1933, p. 202), as well as by James, as mentioned earlier (see Section 'Outlines for a Comparison' in Chapter 3).

[38] Dias Fortes (2015) also proposes a reconstruction of the development of this remark.

Chapter 6: Between Method and *Weltanschauung* 239

Synoptic presentation provides just that kind of understanding that consists in our 'seeing connections'. Hence the importance of finding connecting links. (BT, pp. 307–308)[39]

In the intermediate versions between the first (in BT) and the last (in PI), some particulars change, which can be summarized as follows. First, Wittgenstein introduces a '*vielleicht*' ('perhaps') and eliminates the reference to 'our time': 'synoptic presentation', one reads in a note from 1936, 'is perhaps a kind of *Weltanschauung*'.[40] Second, the 'perhaps' is substituted by a 'similar to' and the reference to Spengler is suppressed (synoptic presentation is 'similar to a *Weltanschauung*').[41] Third, Wittgenstein adds the verb 'to invent' (*erfinden*), so that it becomes important not only 'to find', but also 'to invent intermediate links'.[42] Finally, a question mark appears: Wittgenstein does not assert that synoptic presentation is a kind of, or similar to, a *Weltanschauung*, but he asks himself whether or not it is one, and he leaves the question open.[43]

What can one deduce from these changes? By eliminating references to his time and to Spengler, Wittgenstein distances his own notion of *Weltanschauung* from Spengler's. Moreover, as he develops his method, he does not assert that synoptic presentation *is* a kind of *Weltanschauung*, but merely asks himself whether it is. In any case, he remains worried about this possibility, as the open question shows. In other words, he seems to be aware of the fact that a philosophical method *can* imply, or at least can favour, to a certain extent, a whole world view.

If one interprets the OC remark on pragmatism in the light of this reflection, Wittgenstein's concern appears even clearer. Because of

---

[39] Modified translation.
[40] MS 142, p. 17 (1936), also in TS 220, p. 81 (1937–1938).
[41] 'Ähnlich einer "*Weltanschauung*"' in TS 238, p. 8 and TS 239, p. 82, both 1942–1943 revisions of some parts of TS 220.
[42] Again in TS 239, p. 82 (1942–1943), 'Daher die Wichtigkeit des Findens und des Erfindens von Zwischengliedern'.
[43] TS 227, p. 88, corresponding to PI final version (ca. 1945).

the methods he uses, so akin to pragmatism, his worry is that the investigations he is pursuing may imply the overall pragmatist *Weltanschauung*, which he felt to be an obstacle in his work.

Before turning more directly to this, I would like to spend a few words on two interpretations of the OC, §422 passage, put forth some time ago by Joachim Schulte and very recently by Cheryl Misak. Starting from the latter, Misak (2016, p. 279) affirms that what prevented Wittgenstein from embracing pragmatism was its *weltanschaulicher* character, but also that his own view *was* a kind of *Weltanschauung* (she answers Yes to Wittgenstein's question in PI, §122). In this sense, she deems that it was actually Wittgenstein's own *Weltanschauung* forbidding him to accept or to advance theories, that thwarted him on his way towards embracing pragmatism, and that his stance was, in fact, 'a kind of pragmatist theory that tells us to look at our practices if we want to understand our philosophical concepts'. While I agree with Misak in identifying the *weltanschaulicher* aspect of pragmatism as what disturbed Wittgenstein, in my view, her attribution of a theory and a *Weltanschauung* to Wittgenstein is too straightforward, and risks overlooking differences. Indeed, Wittgenstein's awareness that methods are somewhat connected to world views is not an acknowledgement that methods *are* world views, but more modestly that there is not a neat separation between investigation techniques and ways of seeing things. Secondly, the indication to 'look at our practices if we want to understand our philosophical concepts'—granted that this sums up Wittgenstein's view—can only in a very loose sense be labelled a 'theory'. Conversely, a *Weltanschauung* can only in a very strong sense be labelled a 'theory'—it is in fact much more, it is a *system* of theories. In sum, I take it that Wittgenstein's worry in OC was not unmotivated, and was not simply dictated by a sort of self-admonition to avoid theories.

Concerning Schulte's (1999, pp. 303–304) comment on OC, §422, after convincingly observing that the remark simply asserts that what Wittgenstein is saying *looks like*, rather than *being*, pragmatism, and that it is the vicinity with that *Weltanschauung* that annoys him, he analyses the context of the remark, and in particular, what precedes it:

I am in England.—Everything around me tells me so; wherever and however I let my thoughts turn, they confirm this for me at once.—But might I not be shaken if things such as I don't dream of at present were to happen? (OC, §421)

According to Schulte, OC, §422 is a reaction against the hypothesis that 'things such as I don't dream of at present were to happen', and what Wittgenstein was about to say (what 'sounded like pragmatism') was something like: why should I 'rack my brain' for such a remote possibility, when I know perfectly well that it is totally useless to reflect on that? As Schulte takes it, although natural, this reaction might have appeared to Wittgenstein as incorporating a pragmatist stance, the reason for which he then affirmed that the pragmatist world view was thwarting him.

As I see it, limiting the analysis of the context of OC to the immediately preceding remark only allows for a partial reading.[44] Even in doing so, Schulte's interpretation does not seem to be completely justified, in that he needs to imagine an intermediate passage between OC, §421 and §422, having to do with the uselessness of thinking about most unlikely situations. In short, again, while I agree with Schulte in seeing the *weltanschaulicher* aspect of pragmatism as the problem, to me his interpretation seems to go too far.

It is much more natural, as well as supported by the textual analysis developed in Chapter 4, to argue that Wittgenstein simply noticed the similarity between his remarks and the pragmatic maxim, and worried about his being too akin to the pragmatist vision of the world. The method under focus now is not synoptic presentation, but looking at the practical consequences in order to understand meanings. This offers the opportunity to make a

---

[44] What strikes me in OC, §421, moreover, is another aspect: Wittgenstein speaks of letting thoughts go around, which permits us to imagine that he might have been thinking about James' *stream of thought*, and that through James he might have arrived at pragmatism. Indeed, the expression he uses, 'Gedanken schweifen lassen', is quite similar to 'meinen Blick schweifen lassen', that he uses in a 1944 remark which closes with these words: '(Stream of thought). James' (MS 129, p. 114; cf. Z, §203).

clarification I have kept implicit up to now, on the plurality of methods and techniques used by Wittgenstein.[45] While Wittgenstein was anchored to synoptic presentation at the beginning of the 1930s, he gradually adopts other conceptual instruments and interprets synopticality itself in broader terms. While synoptic presentation initially aimed at a certain orderliness, it later comes to mean the capacity to see particulars and differences, to get glimpses of aspects of everyday scenes. Similarly, the conceptual and practical tools also come to include particular writing and teaching techniques. This plurality of methods and instruments is perhaps what prevents Wittgenstein from adopting a *Weltanschauung*. In this sense, the monochromatic character that his remarks risk assuming in OC may have contributed to his perception that he was coming close to a *Weltanschauung*.

It is now time to deal more directly with the question that has been lingering over us since the beginning of this chapter: is pragmatism a *Weltanschauung*? More specifically, was it a *Weltanschauung* in the intentions of its founders, and what kind of connection is there, if any, between its methodological and systematic aspects? Finally, what was there in the pragmatist vision of the world that Wittgenstein felt with most annoyance?

As mentioned, both Peirce and James identified pragmatism primarily with a method and not with a philosophic system.[46] In a remark which, one might say, 'sounds like Wittgenstein', Peirce even affirmed that 'pragmatism is not a *Weltanschauung* but is a method of reflection having for its purpose to render ideas clear' (CP 5.13, ca. 1906). Yet, he elsewhere specified, while speaking of the tasks of philosophy and chiefly of that part of philosophy which is metaphysics: 'Its principal utility, although by no means its only utility, is to furnish a *Weltanschauung*, or conception of the universe, as a basis for the special sciences' (EP 2, pp. 146–147).[47] Then, though pragmatism is identified with a method, more generally philosophy has among its tasks that of providing

---

[45] See Perissinotto (1991, p. 222) and Conant (2011).
[46] See for instance CP 5.464 for Peirce and P, p. 31 for James.
[47] From 'On Phenomenology', 1903.

a *Weltanschauung*. As far as pragmatism is a philosophy (and this is not obvious, at least for Peirce[48]), one of its tasks will be to offer a vision of the world.

James too connects the main function of philosophy to world views, but he does so in his own style, that is, by calling attention to the personal aspect of the issue. In a passage already quoted, he uses the expression 'world-formula', whose meaning, I assume, is quite close to *Weltanschauung*: 'The whole function of philosophy,' he says, 'ought to be to find out what definite difference it will make to you and me, at definite instants of our life, if this world-formula or that world-formula be the true one' (P, p. 30). James had no particular sympathy for theories, but he considered conceptions or visions of the world important since they express a point of view. He did not like *some* world views: those '"classic", clean, cut and dried, "noble", fixed, "eternal"' ones, which for him 'violate the character with which life concretely comes and the expression which it bears of being, or at least of involving, a muddle and a struggle, with an "ever not quite" to all our formulas, and novelty and possibility forever leaking' (Perry 1935 II, p. 700). Yet, he did not disdain adherence to a *Weltanschauung* in general, and sometimes he talked of his own perspective as a *Weltanschauung*:

> For many years past my mind has been growing into a certain type of *weltanschauung* [sic]. Rightly or wrongly, I have got to the point where I can hardly see things in any other pattern.... I give the name of 'radical empiricism' to my *weltanschauung*. (ERE, p. 22)

Therefore, whereas Wittgenstein attempts to keep himself distant from world views, though not denying that matters of a method may have implications on this level, Peirce and James acknowledge that offering a *Weltanschauung* is one of the jobs of philosophy. James, in particular, defends the *weltanschaulicher* character of his own vision, intended not as a closed system but as a general attitude towards the world.

---

[48] See CP 5.464 (1907).

If one considers *only* what the pragmatists explicitly said about the subject, the connection that Wittgenstein establishes between pragmatism and a world view appears to be only partially justified. But by considering what this current of thought came to mean in Wittgenstein's time, and hence going beyond Peirce and James' words, the connection is not only justified but to a certain extent even obvious. In Wittgenstein's eyes, this kind of perspective bore deep distortions. In order to focus on these aspects, it is worth lingering for a while on an issue which was of prime importance for Wittgenstein: the distinction between logical or grammatical on the one hand, and empirical or experiential on the other. I shall approach it by examining one of the best-known images of OC, that of the riverbed of thoughts.

The River and the Riverbed

In Boncompagni (2012b) I argued that the image of the *riverbed of thoughts* (*Flussbett der Gedanken*) can (also) be read as a Wittgensteinian comment on James' image of the *stream of thought*, a comment insisting precisely on that distinction between grammatical and empirical that James, according to Wittgenstein, overlooks. Let me recall the contents of the OC passages. In them, Wittgenstein invites us to imagine that some empirical proposition for some reason were 'hardened' and worked like fixed channels that regulate the flux of ordinary empirical propositions, those remaining fluid. But in his metaphor, the relationship between hardened and fluid proposition can change through time: hard propositions can become fluid and fluid ones can become hard (OC, §96). This does not amount to saying that the two kinds are mixed together:

> The mythology may change back into a state of flux, the river-bed of thoughts may shift. But I distinguish between the movement of the waters on the river-bed and the shift of the bed itself; though there is not a sharp division of the one from the other. (OC, §97)

Although it is true that the same proposition can at one time be fluid, and hence subject to the test of experience, and at another time be hard and so itself a rule for testing, it would be wrong, in Wittgenstein's view, to conclude that logic is an empirical science (OC, §98). In other words, although the bank of the river is constituted by different layers of different materials, and some parts of it can alter easily while other parts only imperceptibly (OC, §99), the bank remains a bank: there is a distinction between the bank and the riverbed on the one side, and the waters in the river on the other side.

As will be remembered, here Wittgenstein is working on the nature of those apparently empirical propositions that, being constitutive of a *Weltbild*, play a regulative-normative role. Contributing to the definition of standards, these propositions are not subject to ordinary empirical control. The image of the riverbed of thoughts describes the relationship between hinges and empirical propositions as *relatively* changeable, but it safeguards the distinction between the two. The image also suggests that the bed itself is composed of different parts and layers, some of which are more subject to changes, while others are steady and almost immobile.

Needless to say, the image of the river in philosophy has illustrious ancestors. Without disturbing Heraclitus and before arriving at James, I would like to hint at one thinker who, as far as I know, has never been associated with Wittgenstein, but who uses a very similar metaphor to discuss the relationship between logical and empirical, Emile Boutroux. In *De la contingence des lois de la nature* (1874) he wrote:

> Logic, however, would prove false to science instead of serving it, if, after artificially completing for the benefit of the human mind the crystallisation outlined by experience, and giving to the generic form a rigidity of contours which nature did not impose upon it, it then claimed to set up this abstraction as an absolute truth, a creative principle of the reality which gave it birth. Laws are the channel along which rushes the stream of facts: these latter have hollowed it out, although they follow its track. And so the imperative character of the formulas of logic, although practically justified, is but an appearance. In reality, objective logical relations do not

precede things: they spring from them. They might vary, if things themselves happened to vary, so far as their fundamental differences and resemblances are concerned. (Boutroux 1916, p. 45)[49]

Boutroux's description is more unbalanced towards the contingent nature of logic than Wittgenstein's, as the title of his work suggests. He was well known among the pragmatists,[50] and he and James cultivated a short friendship in the last two years of James' life. The introduction of James' thought to France was partly due to him, and James, in turn, attributed to him the authorship of some pragmatist ideas and focused on the notion of contingency in a brief note written for 'Nation' when Boutroux visited Harvard, in 1910 (EPH, pp. 166–171).[51]

Wittgenstein's metaphor, though acknowledging the changeability of the riverbed, is focused on the *distinction* between the riverbed and the flowing waters, and it is for the lack of this distinction that he reproaches James (as well as Ramsey and Russell). A couple of remarks Wittgenstein wrote in 1944 makes this clear, enabling his riverbed metaphor to be interpreted, I think, as a partial criticism of James. Indeed, after mentioning the latter's stream of thought, he states: 'The mistake in his picture is that *a priori* and *a posteriori*, grammatical and experiential, are confused, not distinguished' (MS 165, p. 25).[52]

This distinction is a constant topic in Wittgenstein's work, and, besides OC, LPP and RPP are also full of remarks around this theme,

---

[49] It is not my intention to suggest that Wittgenstein (or James) found inspiration in Boutroux, but simply to underline how this metaphor—as often happens—was part of a *Zeitgeist* before belonging to individual thinkers.

[50] Menand (2001, p. 279). Another pragmatist that used a similar image is John Dewey: 'Experience is no stream, even though the stream of feelings and ideas that flows upon its surface is the part which philosophers love to traverse. Experience includes the enduring banks of natural constitution and acquired habit as well as the stream' (Dewey 1925, p. 7). I owe this quote to Larry Hickman (private conversation).

[51] See also Boutroux (1911), written shortly after James' death, and Russell's critical review of it (Russell 1912).

[52] See also MS 129, p. 107. For a fuller analysis see Boncompagni (2012b).

sometimes linked to James' psychology. For instance, Wittgenstein considers the Jamesian idea that before speaking one has already thought the meaning, and observes: 'If it's a psychological statement it's a hypothesis: but James wishes to say something essential about thinking' (LPP, p. 245). James' fault, in Wittgenstein's eyes, is that on the one hand, he establishes a necessary connection between understanding or intending to say something and some internal phenomena, like the feeling of understanding, or the feeling of having a thought; while on the other hand, he affirms that this necessary connection is empirically ascertainable.[53] In Wittgenstein's view, the kind of necessity that has to do with meanings and grammar cannot be verified through experience. Rather, it belongs to the grammatical-anthropological background governing the relationships among the concepts of our language (Steiner 2012). For this reason, James's way of speaking of psychological phenomena and more generally of thought, in his view, is inaccurate. Conversely, the image of the stream of thought, once reinterpreted so that the distinction between the banks and the water is put under focus, is a good image: Wittgenstein saves the metaphor by reinterpreting it, but rejects James' description.

Is Wittgenstein's criticism justifed? From James' point of view, the continuity between logical and empirical is not a defect, but a precise claim. Curiously, the image of a river *with its banks* is used by James too, but as an example of a case in which two factors cannot be separated. While dealing with the 'sensible core of reality' and the presence of human and non-human elements in it, he writes:

> Does the river make its banks, or do the banks make the river? Does a man walk with his right leg or with his left leg more essentially? Just as impossible may it be to separate the real from the human factors in the growth of our cognitive experience. (P, p. 120)

---

[53] PE also contains interesting notes on this topic. See for instance PE, p. 276.

Like Boutroux, James uses the image to emphasize the banks' permeability to change and the reciprocal influence of the river and the riverbed. Also when concerned with the features of mental life, James seems aware of the implications of the stream metaphor, which he develops by pointing out, among the main characteristics of thought, its being 'always changing' and 'sensibly continuous' (P, p. 220). He also takes advantage of the virtues of the metaphor in the description of attention and effort:

> The stream of our thought is like a river. On the whole easy simple flowing predominates in it, the drift of things is with the pull of gravity, and effortless attention is the rule. But at intervals an obstruction, a set-back, a log-jam occurs, stops the current, creates an eddy, and makes things temporarily move the other way. If a real river could feel, it would feel these eddies and set-backs as places of effort. (P, p. 427)

In other parts of PP he highlights precisely those elements that, like riverbanks, force the water to follow a certain direction and obey certain rules. In the chapter on habit, for instance, the image of the flux of water is used to explain what happens in the brain when some persistent currents shape paths or channels; these channels, he also observed, can change through time thanks to the plasticity of the brain (PP, pp. 111 ff.).[54] But it is mostly in the last chapter of PP, 'Necessary truths and the effects of experience', that the issue of the laws of thought and of logic comes to the fore.

James approaches the problem from the point of view of the conformation of the brain and asks himself whether necessary truths, which, as 'universally admitted' (PP, p. 1215), are due to the biological structure of the mind, must be explained by referring to experience or not. Evolutionary empiricists say yes, 'apriorists' say no. James takes it that while single judgments, such as the judgment that fire burns, can be caused by the phenomena with which we come into contact,

---

[54] Peirce too uses the image of the flux in connection to habits: 'The stream of water that wears a bed for itself is forming a habit', from 'A Survey of Pragmaticism', CP 5.492.

the categories of knowing and judging must be accounted for differently. There are ideal relationships between objects of thought that cannot be explained by the mere reproduction of empirical events. Mathematics and logic belong to this field, for instance, and are characterized by the operation of comparison. Comparison is a *'house-born'* operation, due to our mental structure: experience has nothing to do with it (PP, pp. 1237 ff.). In a way that can call to mind Wittgenstein's insistence on the difference between conceptual and phenomenal, James affirms that we know the difference between white and black, as well as the result of a mathematical sum, without the need to consult experience: '*What I mean* by black differs from *what I mean* by white,' he explains, '*what we mean* by one plus one *is* two', because 'we are masters of our meanings' (PP, pp. 1239, 1249).[55] Hence, while propositions expressing spatial or temporal relations are *empirical* propositions, those expressing the results of comparison are *rational* propositions (PP, pp. 1239–1240).

In this context, then, James seems to distinguish sharply between empirical and rational (what Wittgenstein calls logical or grammatical). Yet, he does so from within a scientific and naturalistic point of view, according to which what is responsible for our rational operations of comparison is the biological structure of the brain, which can evolve thanks to Darwinian spontaneous variations. Therefore, if James is not an 'evolutionary empiricist' like Spencer and does not retain that logical relations can be explained solely through experience, so that he cannot be charged with a form of psychologism in this respect (Klein 2016), he nevertheless interprets the very distinction between empirical and logical from a naturalistic point of view, that is, he ultimately refers to the structure of the brain. In this perspective, logical relations established through conceptual comparisons are possible thanks to spontaneous variations which favour the survival of those individuals in whom, casually, the cerebral mechanisms happen to be most suited to reality; only once confirmed by experience can logical relations be deemed 'true', and in this sense they must

---

[55] On the Jamesian conception of meaning see Myers (1986, p. 285).

be considered *empirical hypotheses*.[56] In other words, an experience is dealt with at two levels: the ordinary one, and the level, so to speak, of the experience of the species, and at this second level logic *is* effectively influenced by experience. The difference James draws between being master of our meanings and knowing something experientially is drawn internally from a naturalistic and scientific perspective.[57]

Wittgenstein could not share James' naturalistic and scientific framework, at least with respect to philosophical investigations. He identified the origins of this framework in the lack of distinction between grammatical and empirical that characterized, *in his view*, James' conception of the stream of thought. More deeply, then, Wittgenstein's criticism was directed against the lack of distinction between philosophy and science that he felt in the pragmatist *Weltanschauung*.

Science and Philosophy

The divergences between Wittgenstein and the pragmatists on science and philosophy are strictly connected to their respective ways of conceiving the role of knowledge in the life of individuals and society. Indeed, the vicinity between science and philosophy, defended by the pragmatists and opposed by Wittgenstein, is reflected in the case of pragmatism in a world view in which science has a key role in the improvement of social life; in the case of Wittgenstein, in an approach for which philosophy, custodian of grammar, to a certain extent requires the philosopher not to belong to any community (Z, §455).

Nevertheless, it is not correct to characterize the pragmatists' position in too simplistic a way, as a perspective simply centred on the continuity between science and philosophy in a naturalistic or even empiricist vein. In fact, on the one hand, their vision is not unreflective, as they show full awareness of the problematic aspects of the relationship between science

---

[56] See Crosby and Viney (1992, p. 111).
[57] But see the different interpretation offered by Flanagan (1997).

and philosophy; on the other hand, James and Peirce hold approaches that, though belonging to a common horizon, also present important differences.

Starting from James, Wittgenstein's main target, it is necessary from the outset to point out that, in his view, conceptual boundaries are more complex than it seems, and that the 'science versus philosophy' binomial is only apparent. Other disciplines—psychology and metaphysics—need to be added to the picture, as well as other perspectives that by their nature lie on tricky confines: experimental psychology in the first place; but also a phenomenological or proto-phenomenological vision of which James could be considered a precursor (Wilshire 1968; Edie 1987); and finally an anthropological reflection that, perhaps not so investigated widely in the literature, could still find fresh stimuli and nuances in James (Franzese 2008, Chap. 2).

Regarding those aspects which were particularly problematic for Wittgenstein, it must be said that at least at the beginning of his career James thought of psychology in physiological-scientific terms, by which I mean in terms that allowed for a significant overlap between the study of the mind and the study of the brain. In 1867, aged 24, he wrote to his father that what he wanted to study was 'the border ground of physiology and psychology, overlapping both' (Perry 1935 I, p. 254). In the opening of PP, he very clearly stated that he had 'kept close to the point of view of natural science throughout the book' (PP, p. 6), and that 'the psychologist is forced to be something of a nerve-physiologist' (PP, p. 18). But in later years, his trust in the possibility of scientific psychology in a strict sense mitigates. In the 'Epilogue' of PBC, written in 1892, he confesses that 'the natural-science assumptions with which we started are provisional and revisable things', that 'the only possible path to understand [the relations of the known and the knower] lies through metaphysical subtlety', and that 'this is no science, it is only the hope of a science' (PBC, pp. 399, 401). Psychology is therefore considered a scientific discipline but at the same time it cannot be kept separate from metaphysics. This point of view, which is not a starting point but an achievement for James, is coherent with the idea that science, on the whole, is not independent of our interests. Since metaphysics is the place in which interests find expression in the shape of general beliefs and visions of things,[58] science, for James, is inevitably and *positively* characterized by the presence of metaphysics. He writes, for instance:

> The popular notion that 'Science' is forced on the mind ab extra, and that our interests have nothing to do with its constructions, is utterly absurd. The craving to believe that the things of the world belong to kinds which are related by inward rationality together, is the parent of Science as well as of sentimental philosophy; and the original investigator always preserves a healthy sense of how plastic the materials are in his hands. (PP, p. 1260)

Far from putting science on a pedestal, James had often relativized its merits with respect to other forms of knowledge, giving value to sentiment and the continuum connecting the latter to rationality. 'Science', he warned, '... must be constantly reminded that her purposes are not the only purposes, and that the order of uniform causation which she has use for, and is therefore right in postulating, may be enveloped in a wider order, on which she has no claims at all' (PP, p. 1179).

Therefore, if Wittgenstein retained that James, more than doing science, was trying to 'extricate himself from the cobwebs of metaphysics',[59] James might have responded that he was *pursuing* the entwinement between science, psychology, and metaphysics, as this was part of an anti-dichotomist approach that consciously bears a point of view on the world.

This does not neutralize Wittgenstein's criticism, but makes it shift to the terrain of the relationship between philosophy and metaphysics, a slippery terrain as the two thinkers assign different meanings to these words, especially to 'metaphysics'. The positive connotation and the possibility to somewhat overlap with philosophy present in James finds no correspondence in Wittgenstein. Whereas the former gives it a clarificatory task, affirming that 'rightly understood', it 'means only the search for *clearness* where common people do not even suspect that there is any lack of it',[60] and that it consists of 'nothing but an unusually obstinate

---

[58] See the first chapter of WB.
[59] According to the already cited passage from MS 165, pp. 150–151.
[60] From a letter to the positivist psychologist Ribot, quoted in Edie (1987, p. ix) and Perry (1938, p. 58).

effort to think clearly' (PP, p. 148); Wittgenstein affirms that it is the result of the *lack* of clarity, and that to strive for conceptual clarity is instead the job of philosophy. When a conceptual problem is dealt with by treating it like a factual problem, or in other words when the differences between the conceptual and the factual are not clear, according to Wittgenstein, we are in the field of metaphysics.[61]

James' anti-dichotomist commitment somehow requires a metaphysical commitment, which, after manifesting itself in PP as the will to keep philosophy and experimental psychology together, and in P as the conviction that the pragmatist method could make science and metaphysics 'work absolutely hand in hand' (P, p. 31), would finally find a general outcome in radical empiricism, not by chance presented by James as a *Weltanschauung*. It is exactly this kind of work, in which the pragmatist project, as Goodman (2002, p. 166) observes, is 'allied with empiricism and the sciences', that Wittgenstein rejects. And it is a kind of work that for James represents a genuine challenge. By always trying to trespass over boundaries, not only between science and philosophy but also between academic and popular science, and to transgress over divides separating academic disciplines, as Bordogna (2008) suggests, he openly aimed to negotiate new spaces and more generally a new configuration of knowledge, both in universities and social life.

Wittgenstein also addressed a similar criticism to Ramsey[62] and to Russell. In 1936, when recalling the way in which he himself had talked of logic in past years, though rejecting some of his previous opinions (I omit this part in the quote that follows), Wittgenstein observes:

---

[61] See RPP I, §949, also in Z, §458 (from MS 134, p. 153).

[62] Interestingly, Wittgenstein associated Ramsey with a materialist *Weltanschauung*, as shown in letters exchanged between G.E. Moore and Sydney Waterlow: 'I quite agree with what you say about Ramsey,' writes Moore to his friend. 'I think [Ramsey's] *Weltanschauung*, without objective values, is very depressive. Wittgenstein finds this too: he calls Ramsey a "materialist"; and what he means by this is something very antipathetic to him.' The letter, dated 1931, is quoted in Paul (2012, p. 117). As mentioned, Wittgenstein also described Ramsey as a 'bourgeois thinker', see CV, p. 17 (from MS 112, p. 70v, 1931).

Logic seemed the archetype of order. I always wanted to say (against Ramsey): logic cannot be empirical science.... It was correct, that our considerations must not be scientific ones. (MS 152, pp. 94–95)[63]

Ramsey indeed had sustained that logic *could* be considered part of natural science, where the latter was intended as including 'psychology and all the problems of the relations between man and his environment' (Paul 2012, p. 116). In 1941, Wittgenstein again reproaches Ramsey for mingling empirical science and philosophy. After acknowledging that his friend was right when he said that 'in philosophy one should be neither "woolly" nor scholastic' (a clear reference to Ramsey's paper 'Philosophy', in which the latter talked of 'woolliness' and accused him of being scholastic[64]), he adds: 'But yet I don't believe that he has seen how this should be done; for the solution is not: being scientific' (MS 163, p. 57v). Finally, a few years later he states: 'Not empiricism and yet realism in philosophy, this is the hardest thing. (Against Ramsey)' (RFM, p. 325).[65]

Many traits of Ramsey's thought can be seen indeed as manifestations of an empiricist attitude. His appeal to causes and effects in investigating meaning is an example. In Wittgenstein's eyes, the search for causes in this domain, which is the domain of reasons, language, and grammar, is deeply mistaken in that it immediately conflates what is empirical and what is logical, giving rise to confusions of thought and suggesting that philosophy might or even should adopt the same explanatory methods as science. One aspect that this search assumes in Ramsey (again, in Wittgenstein's eyes) is the acknowledgment of philosophical significance to the feelings connected to meaning and intention. We have partially already seen this.[66] Wittgenstein took it that for Ramsey if I feel that I mean something when thinking or uttering a sentence, then the concepts

---

[63] The last sentence reappears in PI, §109.
[64] See Ramsey (1990, p. 7).
[65] From MS 164, p. 67 (ca. 1943–1944); see also MS 129, p. 128.
[66] See Sections 'Meaning and Understanding' (Chap. 4) and 'The good in pragmatism' (this chapter).

expressed have meaning. By introducing an experiential criterion for meaning, this move mingles the logical or grammatical and the empirical levels. The same outlook is at work in James' psychology, as he accepts experiential and hence empirical elements into the field of conceptual inquiry (Hutchinson and Read 2013, p. 163).

Related remarks can be found in CE. As suggested in the editorial note that appeared when these remarks were published, they were most likely stimulated by Russell's paper 'The Limits of Empiricism' (1936).[67] In it, Russell proposed to extend the notion of experience beyond what 'pure empiricism' intends by it, and asserted that we also perceive by intuition relations, like the relation between cause and effect. 'The underlying idea is this—commented Wittgenstein—Knowing this state of affairs is a state of mind[.] ... That such a state should interest us at all in a logical investigation is certainly remarkable' (CE, p. 391). Indeed, it should *not*, according to Wittgenstein. A conceptual or logical investigation has nothing to gain from an (alleged) empirical inquiry into knowledge or intuition intended as states of mind. More generally, again in commenting Russell, he later wrote: 'The limit of the empirical—is *concept-formation [Begriffbildung]*' (RFM, p. 237).[68] In his view, then, experience alone cannot satisfactorily explain the conceptual, and Russell, James, and Ramsey's inclination to confuse the two levels must be rejected.

Yet Wittgenstein, in the last of the quoted passages on Ramsey, while rejecting empiricism, accepts realism. What does he mean by it? Perhaps a kind of naturalism?

According to Goodman (2002, p. 71), despite maintaining the distinction between concepts and experiences, the later Wittgenstein was going in not so distant a direction from a sort of Jamesian empiricism when he acknowledged the contingency of language and underlined the importance of the natural history of humankind. It is this kind of direction that, as Goodman has it, one can perceive in Wittgenstein's observations, according to which his main objective is to supply 'remarks on the natural history of human beings' (PI, §415). More properly, as Goodman acknowledges,

---

[67] Russell (1936). The editorial note is now in CE, 370. See Perissinotto (2016b).
[68] From MS 125, p. 41v (1941).

these words can call to mind a form of naturalism rather than empiricism; but some qualifications are needed in the case of naturalism too. Indeed, Wittgenstein himself would explain a few years later that he was doing neither natural science nor natural history. In a remark belonging to RPP, he starts precisely from what in his approach may seem to point towards a form of naturalism and may support the claim that he is doing natural science. If we say that the formation of concepts [*Begriffbildung*] is grounded in facts of nature—he writes—then why not admit simply that the description of how we shape our concepts is part of natural science? To put it differently, why not leave the interest in grammar and focus the inquiry on what grammar is grounded in, that is, on nature? His reply is clear:

> Indeed the correspondence between our grammar and general (seldom mentioned) facts of nature does concern us. But our interest does not fall back on these possible causes. We are not pursuing a natural science; our aim is not to predict anything. Nor natural history either, for we invent facts of natural history for our own purposes. (RPP I, §46)[69]

The 'general facts of nature' Wittgenstein is concerned with are not necessarily existent, past, or future facts of nature, but *real or imaginary* facts of natural history, because the core of his investigations is not what exists, but the grammar of concepts. Only insofar as the inquiry into grammar can be aided by paying attention to the connections between grammar and natural facts, do natural facts enter the field of what is observed. Yet they enter, so to speak, through a back door, as instruments to help philosophy with clarification. Moreover, natural facts include not only biological characteristics of human life, but also cultural and historical facts[70] (again, real or imaginary), and these contribute even more to a perspective in which description concerns the variability of phenomena and what is relevant is the breadth of the spectrum of what is described.

---

[69] From MS 130, p. 72 (1946). See also PPF, sec. xii and RF III, §9.
[70] See RPP II, §§678, 706–708.

Seen from this point of view, Wittgenstein's approach is not only far from empiricism, but also from naturalism (unless one categorizes the latter in a very peculiar way[71]). In what sense, then, does it accept realism? Wittgenstein's must be a form of realism that includes both the existent and imaginary. This means that it is a realism about the 'hold' of concepts, their coherence, the way in which they hang together and the way in which they are grounded in the hinges of our life, including our basic certainties about 'very general facts of nature'.[72] In my view, this is not far from what Cora Diamonds intends when she speaks of the 'realistic spirit'. In this very same sense, a work of fiction like a novel can be realistic too, if it holds up, it shows attention to details, its characters are credible, its plot develops in an understandable way and so on.[73] Realism in this sense also means giving up the search for the 'reality' of philosophers, and, as Laugier (2013, p. 96) puts it, by bringing words back to the ordinary, coming 'closer to the real'. To say it with Wittgenstein, 'to study language apart from the sort of importance it has in the circumstances in which it is learned, the sort of importance it has in living, is to take a false view of it' (Citron 2015a, pp. 17–18).

I think this helps better specify to what degree there is a methodological convergence between Wittgenstein and pragmatism, and to what degree there is a distance. If both put instruments and techniques to work to highlight uses, usefulness, and practical consequences as (some) criteria for the determination of meaning, the pragmatists feel these instruments to be distinct but contiguous to those of science, while Wittgenstein feels a categorical difference.

For the pragmatists, the smoothing of the science–philosophy distinction is part of a general view, and the adoption of similar methodological instruments by the scientist and the philosopher not only makes a

---

[71] *More* peculiar, I think, than is envisioned in Strawson (1985). On Wittgenstein and naturalism see Tripodi (2009) and Hamilton (2014, pp. 286–291).

[72] See the first part of Moyal-Sharrock (2013b).

[73] Starting from Wittgenstein's remark on 'not empiricism yet realism', Diamond's seminal work (Diamond 1991) criticizes Ramsey for not being realistic. An interesting response is provided by Methven (2015), who claims that Ramsey *was* indeed committed to a realistic spirit throughout his whole (brief) work.

dialogue possible, but sometimes fosters an effective overlap in a very complex middle ground. Yet, although they hold science in high regard, also due to personal professional experiences as scientists that were significant for both Peirce and James, neither of them shows a *scientistic* attitude. On the contrary, both are aware that science is only one of the possible forms of knowledge and that it would be blatantly wrong to retain it free from influences, preconceptions, and world views. James, as already seen, continuously underlines how much science is imbued with interests and perspectives and how it is only one of the possible ways in which human beings cognitively approach what surrounds them. Peirce, for his part, precisely by denying that science has to do with 'vitally important topics', relativizes its relevance in regulating the life of people, and is well aware of the inevitable presence of prejudices and preconceptions in it:

> [E]xperience shows that the experientialists are just as metaphysical as any other philosophers, with this difference, however, that their pre-conceived ideas not being recognized by them as such, are much more insidious and much more apt to fly in the face of all the facts of observation. (CP 7.485)[74]

Hence, if the pragmatists show respect for scientists and consider science as a model for inquiry in general, they do not thereby idealize it or subtract it from the evaluation of philosophy. Rather, what they emphasize is its fallibility and revisionability: it is in its limits that science shows its usefulness, displaying its nature as an instrument and not as an end in itself.

Wittgenstein's reading of pragmatism probably does not grasp the relevance and the complexity of this at once positive and cautious perspective towards science. His insistence on a categorical difference, together with his personal way of often being counterpoised to the cultural world around him especially when this was inclined to exalt the role of science, sometimes lead him towards an anti-scientific attitude

---

[74] From 'Habit', 1898 (also in RLT, pp. 218–241). Here Peirce is criticizing Mach, but his reasoning applies, I think, equally well to scientists in general.

which went hand in hand with his hostility towards the idea of progress.[75] The drafts for a foreword that he wrote at the end of 1930 are explicit.[76]

> This book is written for those who are in sympathy with the spirit in which it is written. This is not, I believe, the spirit of the main current of European and American civilization.... Our civilization is characterized by the word 'progress'.... Typically it constructs....
> I am not interested in constructing a building, so much as in having a perspicuous view of the foundations of possible buildings.
> So I am not aiming at the same target as the scientists and my way of thinking is different from theirs. (CV, pp. 6–7)

This text has been interpreted, rightly I think, as a reaction against the project of the Vienna Circle (Hilmy 1987, 307 ff.)[77]; it can also be interpreted in a wider way as a reaction against a scientific conception of the world and what it embodies. And *nota bene*, Wittgenstein mentions not only science and progress but also European *and American* civilization.

His aversion to science as the standard-bearer of the idea of progress would become even stronger in later years, when he wrote about the age of science and technology not excluding that it may be 'the beginning of the end of humanity', and about the objective of seeking scientific knowledge not excluding that it may be 'a trap' for humankind (CV, p. 56).[78] In the same circumstance, he referred to 'the idea that the truth will ultimately be known' saying that it could be simply a delusion. Although nothing authorizes us to hypothesize that he was thinking of the Peircean ideal, it is clear that what Wittgenstein was expressing was deeply different from the attitude with which the pragmatists looked to

---

[75] On this topic see Sanfélix Vidarte (2001) and (2011), Hensley (2012).
[76] Rhees used these notes for the Foreword of PR. The quoted passages come from MS 109, p. 204, November 1930.
[77] On pragmatism and the Vienna Circle see also Chauviré (2003, pp. 94–96), Ferrari (2015), Uebel (2015), and Klein (2016).
[78] From MS 133, p. 90 (1947). See also Citron (2015a, p. 36).

the future, an attitude in which trust in the self-corrective capacities of scientific inquiry plays a crucial role (Schulte 1999). Even more generally, the pragmatist (in this case mostly Deweyan) insistence on social hope and the figure of the philosopher as an intellectual actively involved in the promotion of democracy finds no correspondence in Wittgenstein, who conversely retains that the philosopher has the duty to adopt a 'view from the distance' on society (Sanfélix Vidarte 2001). This does not amount to saying that philosophers cannot and, to a certain extent, must not exercise a critical outlook on the form of life to which they belong, or that their work does not impact on the self-perception and perhaps the self-transformation of individuals (including themselves) and communities. On the contrary, the hortative and self-transformative aspect of philosophy is perhaps, with respect to the vast theme of social change, the only point of contact between the two approaches.

Concluding Remarks

At the beginning of this chapter, the examination of Wittgenstein's only positive remark on pragmatism, centred on the purpose of descriptions, allowed the contrast he draws between philosophical descriptions and scientific explanations to be seen in an unusual light. Indeed, Wittgenstein's goal is not description intended as a passive and neutral registration of objective facts, free of interpretations and personal or cultural colouring. In a sense, things work the opposite way: description cannot but be guided by a certain way of seeing things, because it is guided by the use one makes of it. Description is instrumental and aspectual. Moreover, in Wittgenstein description is usually addressed to the everyday, with the aim of showing its unnoticed facets. These two features—ordinariness and instrumentality—help to display the vicinity between Wittgenstein and the pragmatists in terms of methods. Convergences also manifest themselves in Wittgenstein's anti-theoretical attitude to ethics, with James' propensity—rooted in American transcendentalism—towards an application of the philosophical outlook in the first person, and Peirce's opposition—motivated by other presuppositions and exigencies—against ethical theories, finding an echo in Wittgenstein's inclination to see ethics as something essentially personal and deeply non-theoretical.

While, therefore, in terms of method and attitude some affinities between Wittgenstein and pragmatism have appeared patent, the comparison has required an extension of the examination, in order to see if the methods themselves embody or imply general world views. In fact, this seemed to be Wittgenstein's main preoccupation in OC, §422. In previous years, the connection between a method and *Weltanschauung* was the subject of a specific reflection on his part, in relation to his technique of synoptic presentation. His remarks on this developed through time, and while in the end, he does not see a method as a direct expression of the *Weltanschauung* of its time, he nonetheless acknowledges that there *may* be reciprocal influences between the two levels. To sum up, this is the preoccupation behind OC, §422: the possibility that adopting, in his later remarks, a method so akin to that of the pragmatic maxim, a whole *Weltanschauung* towards which he felt no sympathies, could get in the way of his work. In spite of Peirce and James' own reflections on these themes, Wittgenstein saw pragmatism as a world view characterized by the exaltation of growth, progress, and science, unable to distinguish between science and philosophy, or to keep a distance between conceptual or grammatical investigations and empirical research. Precisely on these latter subjects, the pragmatists did effectively have a different view and claimed that an alliance between philosophy and science was not only possible but desirable.

Conclusion: 'I'll teach you differences'

In summing up the chief outcomes of this research, attention will be placed not only on the main similarities but also the biggest differences between Wittgenstein and classical pragmatism as expressed by Peirce and James. If the aim of this study is to fill a gap in the literature—indeed while Wittgenstein's latest writings are described as pragmatist, there is nevertheless quite a paradoxical gap in analyses as to how this alleged pragmatism could be characterized—the reasons why Wittgenstein's later thought also *departs* from pragmatism need to be considered too. Fundamentally, this amounts to respecting what Wittgenstein himself indicated as perhaps the most interesting aspect of his work, the aim to 'teach differences' that, citing a passage from Shakespeare's *King Lear*, he once thought of putting as a telling epigraph in PI. In fact, when answering a question on Hegel, in 1948, he explained to Drury:

> Hegel seems to me to be always wanting to say that things which look different are really the same. Whereas my interest is in showing that

things that look the same are really different. I was thinking of using as a motto for my book a quotation from *King Lear*: 'I'll teach you differences'. (Rhees 1984, p. 175)[1]

Therefore, in looking for differences in things that look the same, let me recapitulate what has been set out thus far.

Wittgenstein's return to philosophy in 1929 happened in a particular intellectual season, in which part of the debate was focused on issues connected to pragmatism. The colleagues with whom he was in contact—chiefly, Russell, Moore, and Ramsey—had worked extensively on these themes and mainly on the problems of the Jamesian conception of truth. Although Wittgenstein already knew James' VRE, it is by virtue of the debate on truth that pragmatism made its appearance in his writings. Wittgenstein's remarks indeed partly convey the commonest criticisms associated with the Jamesian approach, together with a series of reflections on related issues—hypotheses, probability, the instrumental nature of propositions, and induction—stimulated by his conversations with Ramsey and, via Ramsey, by his (likely) reading of some Peirce. During the 1930s, Wittgenstein distanced himself quite sharply from pragmatism. Though acknowledging that often the value of a sentence lies in its instrumentality and hence in its usefulness, he explicitly rejects the equation 'truth = usefulness', because it does not take into account all those contexts in which the truth of a sentence or the correctness of a prediction is not decided by a sort of advantage. In the following years, in which Wittgenstein worked on the concept of use, he seems to be more inclined to recognize a connection between truth and usefulness, deriving from the connection between usefulness and use. In mathematics, for instance, it is the fact that numbers and calculations accomplish a certain service, therefore proving to be useful, or more appropriately *used*, that allows the link between truth and usefulness. More generally, what is acknowledged is not the link between usefulness and truth, but that between use and meaning. In Wittgenstein's view, affirming that people do what is useful or advantageous is misleading; rather, what people do and the way in which they do it shows the meaning

---

[1] The quotation is from act I, scene IV of the drama.

and the sense they give to concepts such as 'useful', 'advantageous', and innumerable others. Owing to the central importance of practice, attention to the effective use and contexts of words assumes a high methodological value, and from this perspective, the methodological side of pragmatism in relation to meaning resonates in the later Wittgenstein, as emerges with most clarity in LPP. In a sense, one might say that the pragmatist technique and its insistence on the purposes of descriptions already constitutes an implicit critique against the indiscriminate attribution of general virtues to the category of usefulness. In other words, here we have a manifestation of that tension between method and *Weltanschauung* that would emerge in OC, §422. What Wittgenstein refuses is the general application of the concept of usefulness as a key to understanding everything. The same can be said of the category of purpose:

> I think it might be regarded as a basic law of natural history that wherever something in nature 'has a function', 'serves a purpose' [*Zweck*], the same thing can also be found in circumstances where it serves no purpose and is even 'dysfunctional' [*unzweckdienlich*] (CV, p. 72).[2]

If this is, roughly, Wittgenstein's general attitude towards pragmatism before OC, in his later writings, themes and ways of reasoning appear that show more significant affinities with the work of Peirce and James. These very affinities, once put in relation to Wittgenstein's general stance towards pragmatism, generate the concerns expressed in OC, §422.

The first theme on which a convergence is clearly detectable is doubt, to which the anti-Cartesianism characterizing both Wittgenstein and Peirce contributes by drawing a common argumentative strategy, grounded in the rejection of doubt as the first move in philosophical reflection and the parallel acknowledgement of the primacy of certainty or belief as the environment which makes doubt itself possible. Both highlight that doubt needs reasons, and that reasons cannot be feigned: either they are rooted in a context, in a practice, or they do not have a foothold and are already

---

[2] From MS 137, p. 49b, 1948. But notice that the pragmatists too underline that there are many aspects in human life that cannot be explained by usefulness or similar notions alone; an example is James in WB, p. 143.

situated outside the sphere of sense. Yet, the fact that Wittgenstein chiefly emphasizes certainty or sureness while Peirce is more interested in belief suggests that their convergence is not devoid of elements of difference. Indeed, the latter places his inquiry into the relationship between the individual (or the community) and belief on an epistemic level, or at least on a semiotic level, in which the subject is primarily a knowing subject or an interpreter; while the former places his investigation into the relationship between the individual (or the community) and certainty on the level of vital practices, in which the subject is primarily an agent or an expression of the form of life to which it belongs. The comparisons that have been proposed in the literature between Wittgenstein's notion of hinges and some Peircean conceptual instruments sometimes seem to suffer from the failure to consider this discrepancy. Hence, a parallel between Wittgenstein's hinges and Peirce's indubitables needs to consider that, in the end, indubitables are hypothetical beliefs. Similarly, only by interpreting Wittgenstein in an epistemic framework can the comparison with Peircean regulative assumptions or guiding principles of inference work. But an in-depth analysis of these issues shows that the epistemic readings of Wittgenstein fail to catch what is distinctive in his approach, namely, the reshaping of certainty in terms of the non-epistemic or perhaps pre-epistemic sureness characterizing practical action and know-how.

The enlargement of the examination to the wider theme of common sense confirms this kind of reading. It also enables a comparison with the ideas of William James, who builds on Peirce's critical common-sensism and interprets it within a perspective linked on the one hand to evolutionism, for which common sense is seen as a device favouring adaptation and the survival of the species, and on the other hand, to the reflection on language and Kantian categories, which are somewhat naturalized and historicized. By reading Wittgenstein in parallel with the pragmatists, many common features emerge. Among these, the relevance of the vagueness of common sense beliefs or certainties, their pervasiveness, the fact that we are usually not even aware of them, the systematic and holistic nature of common sense but also its stratified and composite aspect, and the very gradual way in which it can change. In order to account for these characteristics, but also perhaps to distance himself from the traditional way of conceiving common sense, in OC

Wittgenstein uses the expression *Weltbild*, conveying an idea of the 'all-embracingness' of common sense, instead of the image of a set of singular pieces of knowledge. These common elements notwithstanding, the way in which the pragmatists and the Viennese philosopher deal with these themes also presents dissimilarities, confirming the preceding analysis on doubt and certainty. Indeed, in the end, for James (and for Peirce as well) common sense consists of hypotheses or discoveries of remote ancestors that have proved useful for survival, and as hypotheses and discoveries they have an epistemic nature and can be put in doubt when other exigencies appear, requiring other methods and solutions. Wittgenstein too admits that a *Weltbild* can change; yet not in the same sense, as in this case, there is no uniformity between *Weltbild* and empirical-scientific knowledge: the former is the grammatical framework *inhabited* by the latter. With even more sharpness, Wittgenstein denies the continuity between philosophical (grammatical) inquiry and scientific (empirical) inquiry, whereas for the pragmatists the possibility of a concrete dialogue among these three stages, as James calls them—common sense, science and critical philosophy—is a strong point.

The connection between certainty or belief and action, underlined in both approaches, leads to the central issue of acting, often evoked but rarely analysed in the secondary literature on OC. Both perspectives show a way of dealing with action which, on the one hand, may only rarely put it under direct scrutiny, but, on the other hand, when it does, it accounts for action in a profoundly different way from traditional views. Action is not the putting to use of a voluntary choice according to a plan, but rather a fragment of a flux from which it can only artificially be separated. Action is part of a habit, background, or form of life, and only within its environment is it possible to account for it fully and meaningfully, because it is its environment that gives it meaning, not only with reference to its scope but also more generally to its sense. This, quite an elementary consideration, once seen in its generality and its consequences, can prevent the classical problem of the relationship between mind and body (put differently, between thought and action), as well as the problem of the relationship between facts and values (or between the empirical effects of actions and the values guiding decisions), instead placing attention on the complexity and ethical and existential thickness of the theme of action. This constant call also assumes a methodological and heuristic value in both Wittgenstein and the pragmatists, mirrored in the indication to look at the practical, experiential and behavioural consequences of a concept in order to understand its meaning.

This leads to the core of the alleged 'pragmatism' of OC: Wittgenstein's remarks on knowledge, certainty and consequences, so pervasive in these notes, strongly resemble Peirce and James' pragmatic maxim. Perhaps too strongly, in Wittgenstein's perception, and indeed as soon as he realizes this he carefully distances himself from the pragmatist *Weltanschauung*, by saying that it thwarts his movements of thought. Now, the Wittgensteinian version of the pragmatic maxim, as one may call it, does not overlap with the original version, because the terms at issue are partly different. Namely, Wittgenstein here usually does not talk of meaning but of certainty or sureness. Moreover, he rejects the connection between this method and the world view that it seems to imply, a connection that the pragmatists do not always deny—in fact, sometimes they openly pursue it. In this light, OC, §422 makes perfect sense. The affinity with the pragmatist method of inquiry, in Wittgenstein's eyes, bears the risk of following a unilateral diet and abandoning the attention to differences, nuances, variations and counter-examples that should guide philosophical reflection. For this reason, OC, §422 signals both a vicinity and distance.

The comparison offers interesting cues for more general considerations. The major issue on which the two approaches suggest a similar outlook is that of the foundation or ground, a reflection which involves other broad themes such as objectivity, relativism, rationality and the intertwinement between the normative and the descriptive. Here the Wittgensteinian notion of forms of life seems to go at the same pace as some pragmatist conceptual tools, putting the human nature of objectivity to the fore: both can be interpreted as proposing the concept of the background as a feasible alternative to the concept of ground. Yet, Wittgenstein tends to guard against the *theoretical* assumption of the concept of form of life, as well as of other concepts, keeping philosophical practice on a linguistic-grammatical terrain and therefore keeping it not only distinct but separate from scientific practice. As for the pragmatists, *pace* Wittgenstein, they too distinguish between philosophical and scientific activities. Nevertheless, the distinction they draw does not preclude dialogue; on the contrary, it sometimes favours it: the continuity between the philosophical and the scientific plane is more

Conclusion: 'I'll teach you differences' 269

an opportunity than a problem for them, in their embodiment of a kind of philosopher who is attentive and receptive to scientific praxes. Therefore, while on certain topics both Wittgenstein and the pragmatists tend to tone down, or perhaps even reject dichotomies, on the central issue of the relationship between science and philosophy the former feels the need to keep a neat demarcation, whereas the latter see the opportunity for an alliance, finding this general claim to be the natural outcome of the anti-dichotomist attitude often argued for in more specific domains. This continuity—which, let me repeat, is not indistinction—between science and philosophy is one of the chief features of the pragmatist *Weltanschauung*, and with regard to precisely this aspect, one can see the most significant difference from Wittgenstein.

However, while this may be the difference in what seems similar, some similarities in what seems different can also be identified. Indeed, although James usually pursues the continuity between science and philosophy, when philosophizing he often works on the same wavelength as Wittgenstein does. Not only the phenomenological richness of his descriptions but also the repeated appeal he makes to the ethical and existential dimension of philosophical activity are aspects which probably taught Wittgenstein a great deal. In this view, a philosopher is someone who addresses persons in their entirety, endeavouring to educate her own and their attention, and convert their way of seeing, while showing them the way out of the bottle of thought puzzles, to once again use Wittgenstein's metaphor (PI, §309).

Curiously, the obstinate behaviour of an insect (in this case a wasp) inside a bottle is used by Peirce to describe himself, with a mixture of pride and resignation.

> ...I am by nature most inaccurate,... quite exceptional for almost complete deficiency of imaginative power, and whatever I amount to is due to two things, first, a perseverance like that of a wasp in a bottle & 2nd to the happy accident that I early hit upon a METHOD of thinking, which any intelligent person could master, and which I am so far from having exhausted it that I leave it about where I found it,—a great reservoir from which ideas of a certain kind might be drawn for many generations....[3]

---

[3] From a letter written to Francis Russell in 1904, quoted in Brent (1998, pp. 323–324).

Without thereby suggesting that Wittgenstein appreciated James' attitude and opposed Peirce's view, what seems interesting to me in the 'inverse' coincidence of this image is that, what Wittgenstein considered a problem (maybe *the* problem), a pragmatist, on the other hand, could consider a vindication. The question remains open as to whether Peirce's wasp is able, differently from Wittgenstein's fly, thanks to its perseverance, to see the way out of the trap itself.

Finally, in the same quoted lines there is another fascinating metaphor, with which I would like to close this work. It is the image of the reservoir, evoking the idea of the philosopher as someone who, by offering his or her work as a tool, makes the resources found in the inquiry available to others. For certain aspects, the image again calls to mind Wittgenstein and his sensation of being a soil, rather than a seed[4]: of being able to help the ideas of others, rather than his own, grow by providing them with the right environment in which to evolve. In both cases, the accent is placed on the instrumental and useful nature, in the noblest sense, of a technique of thought. Indeed, to conclude, it is on methods and techniques that the Wittgensteinian and the pragmatist perspectives show not only their closeness but each one its fertility; the fertility of a soil or of a reservoir, which rather than offering solutions offers *itself* as a place in which to grow, recover and flourish.

---

[4] This image, from CV, p. 36, was the starting point of the present study (see the *Introduction*). See also Cavell (2006, p. 10).

Bibliography

L. Wittgenstein's Writings

BBB—*The Blue and Brown Books*. Ed. R. Rhees. Oxford: Blackwell, 1969.
BEE—*Wittgenstein's Nachlass. The Bergen Electronic Edition*. Oxford: Oxford University Press, 2000.
BT—*The Big Typescript: TS 213, German-English Scholars' Edition*. Ed. C.G. Luckhardt, M.A.E. Aue. Oxford: Wiley-Blackwell, 2005.
CE—Ursache und Wirkung: Intuitives Erfassen / Cause and Effect: Intuitive Awareness. In *Philosophical Occasions 1912–1951*. Ed. J. Klagge, A. Nordmann. Indianapolis, IN: Hackett, 1993.
CV—*Vermischte Bemerkungen / Culture and Value*. Ed. G.H. von Wright. Oxford: Blackwell, 1980.
LC—*Lectures and Conversations on Aesthetics, Psychology and Religious Belief*. Ed. C. Barrett. Oxford: Blackwell, 1966.
LCA—*Wittgenstein's Lectures. Cambridge, 1932–1935*. Ed. A. Ambrose. Oxford: Blackwell, 1982.
LCL—*Wittgenstein's Lectures. Cambridge, 1930–1932*. Ed. D. Lee. Oxford: Blackwell, 1980.
LCM—Wittgenstein's Lectures in 1930–1933, by G.E. Moore. In *Philosophical Occasions 1912–1951*. Ed. J. Klagge, A. Nordmann. Indianapolis, IN: Hackett, 1993.

LE—A Lecture on Ethics. In *Philosophical Occasions 1912–1951*. Ed. J. Klagge, A. Nordmann. Indianapolis, IN: Hackett, 1993.
LFM—*Wittgenstein's Lectures on the Foundations of Mathematics*. Ed. C. Diamond. Ithaca, NY: Cornell University Press, 1976.
LPP—*Wittgenstein's Lectures on Philosophical Psychology 1946–47*. Ed. P.T. Geach. Hemel Hempstead: Harvester Wheatsheaf, 1988.
LW—*Letzte Schriften über die Philosophie der Psychologie / Last Writings on the Philosophy of Psychology*. Ed. G.H. von Wright and H. Nyman, 2 voll. Oxford: Blackwell, 1982–1992.
MTD—Movements of Thought: Diaries 1930–1932, 1936–1937. In *Public and Private Occasions*. Ed. J.C. Klagge, A. Nordmann. Lanham: Rowman & Littlefield, 2003.
NB—*Tagebücher 1914–1916 / Notebooks 1914–1916*. Ed. G.H. von Wright, G.E.M. Anscombe. Oxford: Blackwell, 1979.
OC—*On Certainty*. Ed. G.E.M. Anscombe, G.H. von Wright. Oxford: Blackwell, 1974.
PE—Notes for Lectures on 'Private Experience' and 'Sense-Data'. In *Philosophical Occasions 1912–1951*. Ed. J. Klagge, A. Nordmann. Indianapolis, IN: Hackett, 1993.
PG—*Philosophical Grammar*. Ed. R. Rhees. Oxford: Blackwell, 1974.
PI—*Philosophische Untersuchungen I / Philosophical Investigations*. Ed. P.M.S. Hacker, J. Schulte. Oxford: Wiley-Blackwell, 2009.
PO—*Philosophical Occasions 1912–1951*. Ed. J. Klagge and A. Nordmann. Indianapolis, IN: Hackett, 1993.
PPF—*Philosophische Untersuchungen II / Philosophy of Psychology—A Fragment*. Ed. P.M.S. Hacker, J. Schulte. Oxford: Wiley-Blackwell, 2009.
PPO—*Public and Private Occasions*. Ed. J.C. Klagge, A. Nordmann. Lanham: Rowman & Littlefield, 2003.
PR—*Philosophische Bemerkungen / Philosophical Remarks*. Ed. R. Rhees. Frankfurt am Main: Suhrkamp; Oxford: Blackwell, 1964.
RC—*Bemerkungen über die Farben / Remarks on Colour*. Ed. G.E.M. Anscombe. Berkeley: University of California Press, 1977.
RF—Bemerkungen über Frazers *Golden Bough* / Remarks on Frazer's *Golden Bough*. In *Philosophical Occasions 1912–1951*. Ed. J. Klagge, A. Nordmann. Indianapolis, IN: Hackett, 1993.
RFM—*Remarks on the Foundations of Mathematics*. Ed. G.H. von Wright, G.E.M. Anscombe. Oxford: Blackwell, 1978.

RPP—*Bemerkungen über die Philosophie der Psychologie / Remarks on the Philosophy of Psychology.* Ed. G.E.M. Anscombe, G.H. von Wright, 2 voll. Oxford: Blackwell, 1980.
TLP—*Tractatus Logico-Philosophicus.* London: Kegan Paul, Trench, Trubner & Co.,1933.
WA—*Wiener Ausgabe: Band II—Philosophische Betrachtungen, Philosophische Bemerkungen.* Ed. M. Nedo, Vienna: Springer, 1994.
Z—*Zettel.* Ed. G.E.M. Anscombe, G.H. von Wright. Oxford: Blackwell, 1981.

C. S. Peirce's Writings

CLL—*Chance, Love and Logic.* London: Kegan Paul, Trench, Trubner & Co., 1923.
CP—*The Collected Papers of Charles Sanders Peirce*, voll. I–VI. Ed. P. Weiss, C. Hartshorne. Cambridge, MA: Harvard University Press, 1935; voll. VII–VIII. Ed. A.W. Burks. Cambridge, MA: Harvard University Press, 1958.
EP—*The Essential Peirce*, 2 voll. Ed. N. Houser, C. Kloesel, the Peirce Edition Project. Bloomington, IN: Indiana University Press, 1991–1998.
RLT—*Reasoning and the Logic of Things. The Cambridge Conference Lectures of 1898.* Ed. K.L. Ketner. Cambridge, MA: Harvard University Press, 1992.
SW—*The Philosophy of Peirce: Selected Writings.* New York: Harcourt, Brace & Co.; London: Routledge and Kegan Paul, 1940.
W—*Writings of Charles S. Peirce: A Chronological Edition*, voll. I–VI and VIII (writings from 1857 to 1892). Ed. the Peirce Edition Project. Bloomington, IN: Indiana University Press, 1982, 1984, 1986, 1989, 1993, 2000, 2010.

W. James' Writings

EPH—*Essays in Philosophy.* Cambridge, MA: Harvard University Press, 1978.
ERE—*Essays in Radical Empiricism.* Cambridge, MA: Harvard University Press, 1976.
MEN—*Manuscripts, Essays and Notes.* Cambridge, MA: Harvard University Press, 1988.
MT—*The Meaning of Truth.* Cambridge, MA: Harvard University Press, 1975.
P—*Pragmatism.* Cambridge, MA: Harvard University Press, 1975.

PBC—*Psychology. Briefer Course*. Cambridge, MA: Harvard University Press, 1984.
PP—*The Principles of Psychology*. Cambridge, MA: Harvard University Press, 2 voll., 1981.
PU—*A Pluralistic Universe*. New York: Longmans, Green & Co., 1909.
TT—*Talks to Teachers on Psychology and to Students on Some of Lifes Ideals*. New York: Henry Holt & Co., 1899.
VRE—*The Varieties of Religious Experience*. Cambridge, MA: Harvard University Press, 1985.
WB—*The Will to Believe and Other Essays in Popular Philosophy*. Cambridge, MA: Harvard University Press, 1979.

Secondary Literature and Other Writings

Acero, J. J. 2005. Mind, Intentionality and Language. The Impact of Russell's Pragmatism on Ramsey. In *Frank P. Ramsey. Critical Reassessments*, ed. M.J. Frápolli. London: Continuum.
Agam-Segal, R. 2015. Aspect-Perception as a Philosophical Method. *Nordic Wittgenstein Review* 4 (1): 93–121.
Ameriks, K.A. 2005. A Commonsense Kant? *Proceedings and Addresses of the American Philosophical Association* 79 (2): 19–45.
Andronico. M. 1998. *Antropologia e metodo morfologico. Studio su Wittgenstein*. Naples: La Città del Sole.
———. 2008. Relativismo o suspensión del juicio. A propósito de Wittgenstein, la ciencia y las formas de vida. In *Sentido y sinsentido. Wittgenstein y la crítica del lenguaje*, ed. C.J. Moya. Valencia: Colección Filosofías, Pre-textos.
Baghramian, M. 2004. *Relativism*. Abingdon: Routledge.
Bain, A. 1868. *Mental Science. A Compendium to Psychology and the History of Philosophy*. New York: Appleton & Co.
Bambrough, R. 1981. Peirce, Wittgenstein and Systematic Philosophy. In *Midwest Studies in Philosophy, Volume* VI, *The Foundations of Analytic Philosophy*, ed. P.A. French, T.E. Uehling Jr., and H.K. Wettstein. Minneapolis, MN: University of Minnesota Press.
Bax, C. 2011. *Subjectivity After Wittgenstein*. London: Continuum.
———. 2013. Reading *On Certainty* Through the Lens of Cavell: Scepticism, Dogmatism and the 'Groundlessness of our Believing'. *International Journal of Philosophical Studies* 21 (4): 515–533.

Bennett-Hunter, G. 2012. A Pragmatist Conception of Certainty: Wittgenstein and Santayana. *European Journal of Pragmatism and American Philosophy*, IV (2): 146–157.
Bergman, M. 2010. Serving Two Masters: Peirce on Pure Science, Useless Things, and Practical Applications. In *Ideas in Action: Proceedings of the Applying Peirce Conference*, ed. M. Bergman, S. Paavola, A.-V. Pietarinen and H. Rydenfelt. Helsinki: Nordic Pragmatism Network.
Bernstein, R. 1961. Wittgenstein's Three Languages. *The Review of Metaphysics*, XIV (2): 278–298.
———. 1983. *Beyond Objectivism and Relativism*. Philadelphia, PA: University of Pennsylvania Press.
———. 2010. *The Pragmatic Turn*. Cambridge, UK; Malden, MA: Polity Press.
Biancini, P. 2011. From *Umgebung* to Forms of Life: A Genealogical Reading. In *Forms of Life and Language Games*, ed. J. Padilla Galvez and M. Gaffal. Frankfurt: Ontos Verlag.
Biesenbach, H. 2014. *Anspielungen und Zitate im Werk Ludwig Wittgensteins*. Sofia, Bulgaria: St. Ohridski University Press.
Bilgrami, A. 2004. Scepticism and Pragmatism. In *Wittgenstein and Scepticism*, ed. D. McManus. Abingdon: Routledge.
Bogen, J. 1972. *Wittgenstein's Philosophy of Language: Some Aspects of its Development*. Abingdon: Routledge.
Boncompagni, A. 2012a. 'The Mother-Tongue of Thought': James and Wittgenstein on Common Sense. *Cognitio. Revista de Filosofia* 13 (1): 37–59.
———. 2012b. James' Stream of Thought in Wittgensteins Manuscripts 165 and 129. *European Journal of Pragmatism and American Philosophy* 4 (2): 36–53.
———. 2013. Enactivism and the 'Explanatory Trap'. A Wittgensteinian Perspective. *Methode—Analytic Perspectives* 2 (2): 27–49.
———. 2014. On Trying to Say What 'Goes Without Saying'. Wittgenstein on Certainty and Ineffability. *Journal of Theories and Research in Education / Ricerche di Pedagogia e Didattica* 9 (1): 51–68.
———. 2015. Elucidating Forms of Life. The Evolution of a Philosophical Tool. *Nordic Wittgenstein Review*, Special Issue 'Wittgenstein and Forms of Life', ed. D. Moyal-Sharrock and P. Donatelli: 155–175.
———. forthcoming*a*. Wittgenstein and Pragmatism: A Neglected Remark in Manuscript 107. In *Pragmatism and the European Traditions: Encounters with Analytic Philosophy and Phenomenology Before the Great Divide*, ed. M. Baghramian and S. Marchetti, Abingdon: Routledge.

———. forthcoming*b*. The 'Middle' Wittgenstein (and the 'Later' Ramsey) on the Pragmatist Conception of Truth. In *The Practical Turn: Pragmatism in Britain in the Long 20th Century*, ed. C. Misak and H. Price.
———. forthcoming*c*. James and Wittgenstein. In *The Oxford Handbook of William James*, ed. A. Klein. Oxford: Oxford University Press.
Bordogna, F. 2008. *William James at the Boundaries. Philosophy, Science, and the Geography of Knowledge*. Chicago and London: The University of Chicago Press.
Boutroux, E. 1916. *The Contingency of the Laws of Nature*. Chicago and London: Open Court.
———. 1911. *William James*. Paris: Libraire Armand Colin.
Bouveresse, J. 1987. *Le mythe de lintériorité. Expérience, signification et langage privé chez Wittgenstein*. Paris: Les Éditions de Minuit.
Bouwsma, O.K. 1986. *Wittgenstein: Conversations 1949–1951*. Indianapolis, IN: Hackett, 1986.
Brandom, R. 2002. Pragmatics and Pragmatisms. In *Hilary Putnam: Pragmatism and Realism*, ed. J. Conant and U.M. Żegleń. Abingdon: Routledge.
———. 2004. *Making It Explicit*. Cambridge, MA: Harvard University Press.
Breithaupt, F., Raatzsch, R., and Kremberg, B. eds. 2003. *Goethe and Wittgenstein. Seeing the Worlds Unity in Its Variety (Wittgenstein Studien 5)*. Frankfurt am Main: Peter Lang.
Brent, J. 1998. *Charles S. Peirce. A Life*. Bloomington, IN: Indiana University Press.
Brice, R. 2014. *Exploring Certainty. Wittgenstein and Wide Fields of Thought*. Lanham, MD: Lexington.
Britton, K. 1967. Portrait of a Philosopher. In *Wittgenstein: The Man and His Philosophy*, ed. K.T. Fann. New York: Dell.
Broyles, J.E. 1965. Charles S. Peirce and the Concept of Indubitable Belief. *Transactions of the Charles S. Peirce Society* 1 (2): 77–89.
Busch, W. 1974. *Hans Huckebein/Fipps der Affe/Plisch und Plum*. Zurich: Diogenes Verlag.
Calcaterra, R.M. 2003a. *Pragmatismo. I valori dellesperienza*. Rome: Carocci.
———. 2003b. Lo spazio normativo dei sentimenti nell'ottica di Peirce. In *Normatività fatti valori*, ed. R. Egidi, M. Dell'Utri and M. De Caro. Macerata: Quodlibet.
———. 2012. Truth in Progress: The Value of the Facts-and-Feelings Connection in William James. In *American and European Values:*

Contemporary Philosophical Perspectives, ed. M.C. Flamm, J. Lacks, and K.P. Skowronski. Newcastle-upon-Tyne: Cambridge Scholars Press.

———. 2014. Testimony and the Self. In *Charles Sanders Peirce in His Own Words. 100 Years of Semiotics, Communication and Cognition*, ed. T. Thellefsen and B. Sorensen. Berlin: De Gruyter.

———. 2015. Reality in Practice. *Esercizi Filosofici* 10: 136–153.

Cavell, S. 1976. Knowing and Acknowledging. In Cavell, S. *Must We Mean What We Say?* Cambridge: Cambridge University Press.

———. 1979. *The Claim of Reason*. Oxford: Oxford University Press.

———. 1989. *This New Yet Unapproachable America. Lectures After Emerson After Wittgenstein*. Albuquerque, NM: Living Batch Press.

———. 1992. *The Senses of Walden. An Expanded Edition*. Chicago, IL, and London: The University of Chicago Press.

———. 2005. *Philosophy the Day After Tomorrow*. Cambridge, MA, and London: Belknap Press.

———. 2006. The Wittgensteinian Event. In *Reading Cavell*, ed. A. Crary and S. Shieh. London and New York: Routledge.

Chauviré, C. 2003. *Le grand miroir. Essais sur Peirce et sur Wittgenstein*. Besançon Cedex: Presses Universitaires Franc-Comtoises.

———. 2012. Experience and Nature: Wittgenstein Reader of Dewey?. *European Journal of Pragmatism and American Philosophy* 4 (2): 81–87.

Christensen, A.M. 2011a. Wittgenstein and Ethics. In *The Oxford Handbook of Wittgenstein*, ed. O. Kuusela and M. McGinn. Oxford: Oxford University Press.

———. 2011b. 'What matters to us?' Wittgenstein's *Weltbild*, Rock and Sand, Men and Women. *Humana.Mente Journal of Philosophical Studies* 18: 141–162.

Citron, G. ed. 2015a. Wittgenstein's Philosophical Conversations with Rush Rhees (1939–1950): From the Notes of Rush Rhees. *Mind* 124 (493): 1–71.

———. ed. 2015b. A Discussion Between Wittgenstein and Moore on Certainty (1939): From the Notes of Norman Malcolm. *Mind* 124 (493): 72–84.

Colapietro, V. 1986. William James' Pragmatic Commitment to Absolute Truth. *The Southern Journal of Philosophy* 24 (2): 189–200.

———. 2011. Allowing our Practices to Speak for Themselves: Wittgenstein, Peirce, and Their Intersecting Lineages. In *New Perspectives on Pragmatism and Analytic Philosophy*, ed. R.M. Calcaterra. Amsterdam: Rodopi.

Coliva, A. 2010a. *Moore and Wittgenstein. Scepticism, Certainty and Common Sense*. Basingstoke: Palgrave Macmillan.
———. 2010b. Was Wittgenstein an Epistemic Relativist? *Philosophical Investigations* 33 (1): 1–23.
———. 2013. Hinges and Certainty. A *Précis* of *Moore and Wittgenstein. Scepticism, Certainty and Common Sense*. *Philosophia* 41 (1): 1–12.
———. 2015. *Extended Rationality. A Hinge Epistemology*. Basingstoke: Palgrave Macmillan.
Conant, J. 2011. Wittgenstein's Methods. In *The Oxford Handbook of Wittgenstein*, ed. O. Kuusela and M. McGinn. Oxford: Oxford University Press.
Conway, G. 1989. *Wittgenstein on Foundations*. Amherst, NY: Humanity Books.
Cook, J.W. 1980. Notes on Wittgenstein's *On Certainty*. *Philosophical Investigations* 3 (4): 15–37.
Cormier, H. 2000. *The Truth Is What Works: William James, Pragmatism, and the Seed of Death*. Lanham, MD: Rowman & Littlefield.
Crary, A. 2003. Wittgenstein's Pragmatic Strain. *Social Research* 70 (2): 369–392.
———. 2005. Wittgenstein and Ethics: A Discussion with Reference to *On Certainty*. In *Readings of Wittgenstein's* On Certainty, ed. D. Moyal-Sharrock and W.H. Brenner. Basingstoke: Palgrave Macmillan.
Crosby, D.A. and Viney, W. 1992. Toward a Psychology that is Radically Empirical: Recapturing the Vision of William James. In *Reinterpreting the Legacy of William James*, ed. M.E. Donnelly. Washington DC: American Psychological Association.
Descartes, R. 2001. *Discourse on Method, Optics, Geometry, and Meteorology*. Trans. Paul J. Olscamp. Indianapolis, IN, and Cambridge: Hackett.
Dewey, J. 1925. *Experience and Nature*. Chicago, IL: Open Court.
———. 1929. *The Quest for Certainty: A Study of the Relation of Knowledge and Action*. New York: Minton, Balch & Co.
———. 1948. *Reconstruction in Philosophy*. Boston: Beacon.
Diamond, C. 1991. Realism and the Realistic Spirit. In Diamond, C. *The Realistic Spirit*. Cambridge, MA: Mit Press.
Dias Fortes, A. 2015. 'Übersichtliche Darstellung' as Synoptic Presentation in *Philosophical Investigations* I, §122. In *Realism, Relativism, Constructivism. Contributions of the 38th International Wittgenstein Symposium (pre-proceedings)*, ed. C. Kanzian, J. Mitterer, and K. Neges. Kirchberg am Wechsel: Austrian Wittgenstein Society.

Donatelli, P. and Moyal-Sharrock, D. eds. 2015. Wittgenstein and Forms of Life. Special Issue of *The Nordic Wittgenstein Review*.
Dreyfus, H. ed. 1982. *Husserl, Intentionality and Cognitive Science*. Cambridge, MA: Mit Press.
———. 1992. *What Computers Still Can't Do: A Critique of Artificial Reason*. Cambridge, MA: Mit Press.
———. 2002. Intelligence without Representations. Merleau-Ponty's Critique of Mental Representation. *Phenomenology and the Cognitive Sciences* 1 (4): 367–383.
Durante, R. 2016. Peter Winch on the Concept of Persuasion. *Philosophical Investigations* 39 (2): 100–122.
Edie, J. 1987. *William James and Phenomenology*. Bloomington, IN: Indiana University Press.
Egidi, R. 1983. Intenzione e ipotesi in Wittgenstein. In *Wittgenstein. Momenti di una critica del sapere*, ed. A. Gargani, A.G. Conte, and R. Egidi. Naples: Guida Editori.
Emerson, R. W. 1862. Thoreau. *Atlantic Monthy* 10 (58): 239–249.
Emmett, K. 1990. Forms of life. *Philosophical Investigations* 13 (3): 213–231.
Engelmann. M.L. 2012. Wittgenstein's New Method and Russell's *The Analysis of Mind*. *Journal of Philosophical Research* 37: 283–311.
———. 2013a. *Wittgenstein's Philosophical Development*. Basingstoke: Palgrave Macmillan.
———. 2013b. Wittgenstein's 'Most Fruitful Ideas' and Sraffa. *Philosophical Investigations* 36 (2): 155–178.
Fabbrichesi, R. 2002. *Cosa significa dirsi pragmatisti. Peirce e Wittgenstein a confronto*. Milan: Cuem.
———. 2004. Peirce and Wittgenstein on Common Sense. *Cognitio. Revista de Filosofia* 5 (2): 180–193.
Fairbanks, M. 1966. Wittgenstein and James. *The New Scholasticism* 40 (3): 331–340.
Ferrari, M. 2015. William James navigava con Otto Neurath? *Rivista di Filosofia* 106 (2): 235–265.
Fine, A. 2007. Relativism, Pragmatism, and the Practice of Science. In *New Pragmatists*, ed. C. Misak. Oxford: Oxford University Press.
Fischer, H.R. 1987. *Sprache und Lebensform. Wittgenstein über Freud und die Geisteskrankheit*. Frankfurt am Main: Athenäum.

Flanagan, O. 1997. Consciousness as a Pragmatist Views It. In *The Cambridge Companion to William James*, ed. R. A. Putnam. Cambridge: Cambridge University Press.
Floyd, J. 2010. On Being Surprised. Wittgenstein on Aspect-Perception, Logic, and Mathematics. In *Seeing Wittgenstein Anew*, ed. W. Day and V.J. Krebs. Cambridge: Cambridge University Press.
Franken, F. 2015. Überreden und Überzeugen. Eine Verhältnisbestimmung aus der Perspektive des späten Wittgenstein. *Deutsche Zeitschrift für Philosophie* 63 (1): 58–86.
Franzese, S. 2008. *The Ethics of Energy. William James Moral Philosophy in Focus*. Frankfurt: Ontos Verlag.
Gallagher, S. 2014. Pragmatic Interventions into Enactive and Extended Conceptions of Cognition. *Philosophical Issues* 24 (1): 110–126.
Garver, N. 1994. *This Complicated Form of Life. Essays on Wittgenstein*. Chicago and La Salle, IL: Open Court.
Gava. G. 2014. *Peirce's Account of Purposiveness. A Kantian Perspective*. New York and London: Routledge.
Gellner, E. 1992. *Reason and Culture*. Oxford: Wiley-Blackwell.
Gennip, K. van 2008. *Wittgenstein's* On Certainty *in the Making: Studies Into Its Historical and Philosophical Background*, PhD Thesis. Groningen (Netherlands): University of Groningen.
———. 2011. Wittgenstein on Intuition, Rule-following, and Certainty: Exchanges with Brower and Russell. In *The Oxford Handbook of Wittgenstein*, ed. O. Kuusela, and M. McGinn. Oxford: Oxford University Press.
Gier, N. 1980. Wittgenstein and Forms of Life. *Philosophy of the Social Sciences* 10 (3): 241–258.
Gill, J. 1974. Saying and Showing: Radical Themes in Wittgenstein's *On Certainty*. *Religious Studies* 10 (3): 279–290.
Glock, H.J. 1996. *A Wittgenstein Dictionary*. Oxford: Blackwell.
———. 2005. Ramsey and Wittgenstein: Mutual Influences. In *Frank P. Ramsey. Critical Reassessments*, ed. M.J. Frápolli. London: Continuum.
Goldstein, L. 2004. Wittgenstein as Soil. In *Wittgenstein's Lasting Significance*, ed. M. Kölbel and B. Weiss. Abingdon: Routledge.
Goethe, J.W. 1840. *Theory of Colours*. London: J. Murray.
Gómez Alonso, M. 2012. Animal Logic and Transcendental Arguments: *On Certainty*'s two Levels of Justification. In *Doubtful Certainties. Language-Games, Forms of Life, Relativism*, ed. J. Padilla Gálvez and M. Gaffal. Frankfurt am Main: Ontos Verlag.

Goodman, R. 2002. *Wittgenstein and William James*. Cambridge: Cambridge University Press.
Gullvåg, I. 1981. Wittgenstein and Peirce. In *Wittgenstein. Aesthetics and Transcendental Philosophy*, ed. K.S. Johannessen and T. Nordenstam. Vienna: Hölder—Pichler—Tempsky.
Haack, R. 1982. Wittgenstein's Pragmatism. *American Philosophical Quarterly* 19 (2): 163–171.
Hacker, P.M.S. 1990. *Wittgenstein: Meaning and Mind. An Analytical Commentary on the PI, vol. 3*. Oxford: Blackwell.
———. 1996a. *Wittgenstein: Mind and Will. An Analytical Commentary on the PI, vol. 4*. Oxford: Blackwell.
———. 1996b. *Wittgenstein's Place in Twentieth Century Analytic Philosophy*. Oxford: Blackwell.
———. 2015. Forms of Life. *Nordic Wittgenstein Review*, Special Issue 'Wittgenstein and Forms of Life', ed. D. Moyal-Sharrock and P. Donatelli: 1–20.
Hamilton, A. 2014. *Routledge Philosophy Guidebook to Wittgenstein and* On Certainty. Abingdon: Routledge.
Harrison, B. 2012. *The Epistemology of Know-how*, PhD Thesis. University of Hertfordshire.
Hensley, J.M. 2012. Who's Calling Wittgenstein a Pragmatist? *European Journal of Pragmatism and American Philosophy* 4 (2): 27–35.
Hertzberg, L. 1980. Winch on Social Interpretation. *Philosophy of the Social Sciences* 10 (2): 151–171.
———. 2009. Peter Winch: Philosophy as the Art of Disagreement. In *Sense and Reality: Essays out of Swansea*, ed. J. Edelman. Frankfurt am Main: Ontos Verlag.
Hilmy, S.S. 1987. *The Later Wittgenstein*. Oxford: Blackwell.
Holt, D.C. 1989. The Defense of Common Sense in Reid and Moore. In *The Philosophy of Thomas Reid*, ed. M. Dolgarno and E. Matthews. Dordrecht: Kluwer.
Hookway, C. 2000. *Truth, Rationality and Pragmatism. Themes from Peirce*. Oxford: Oxford University Press.
———. 2005. Ramsey and Pragmatism. In *Frank P. Ramsey. Critical Reassessments*, ed. M.J. Frápolli. London: Continuum.
———. 2012. *The Pragmatic Maxim. Essays on Peirce and Pragmatism*. Oxford: Oxford University Press.

Howat, A. 2013. Regulative Assumptions, Hinge Propositions and the Peircean Conception of Truth. *Erkenntnis* 78 (2): 451–468.
Hutchinson, P. and Read, R. 2013. *Practicing* pragmatist-Wittgensteinianism. In *The Cambridge Companion to Pragmatism*, ed. A. Malachowski. Cambridge: Cambridge University Press.
Hutto, D.D. 2004. Two Wittgenstein too Many: Wittgenstein's Foundationalism. In *The Third Wittgenstein*, ed. D. Moyal-Sharrock. Aldershot: Ashgate.
Hutto, D.D., and Myin, E. 2013. *Radicalizing Enactivism. Basic Minds without Content*. Cambridge, MA and London: Mit Press.
Janik, A. and Toulmin, S. 1996. *Wittgenstein's Vienna*. Chicago, IL: Ivan R. Dee.
Johanson, A.E. 1994. Peirce and Wittgenstein's *On Certainty*. In *Living Doubt. Essays Concerning the Epistemology of Charles S. Peirce*, ed. G. Debrock and M. Hulswit. Dordrecht: Kluwer.
Jolley, K.D. 1994. Wittgenstein and Thoreau (and Cavell): the Ordinary *Weltanschauung*. *Reason Papers* 19: 3–12.
———. 1998. On Common Sense, Moore and Wittgenstein. *Ethnographic Studies* 3: 41–58.
Kilpinen, E. 2009. Pragmatism as a Philosophy of Action. In *Pragmatist Perspectives (Acta Philosophica Fennica vol. 86)*, ed. S. Pihlström and H. Rydenfelt. Helsinki: Societas Philosophica Fennica.
Kienzler, W. 2006. Wittgenstein and John Henry Newman on Certainty. *Grazer Philosophische Studien* 71: 117–138.
Klein, A. 2016. Was James Psychologistic? *Journal for the History of Analytic Philosophy* 4 (5): 1–21.
Koethe, J. 1996. *The Continuity of Wittgenstein's Thought*. Ithaca, NY: Cornell University Press.
Kober, M. 1996. Certainties of a World-Picture: the Epistemological Investigations of *On Certainty*. In *The Cambridge Companion to Wittgenstein*, ed. H. Sluga and D. Stern. Cambridge: Cambridge University Press.
———. 2005. 'In the Beginning was the Deed': Wittgenstein on Knowledge and Religion. In *Readings of Wittgenstein's On Certainty*, ed. D. Moyal-Sharrock and W.H. Brenner. Basingstoke: Palgrave Macmillan.
Koopman, C. 2014. Conduct Pragmatism: Pressing Beyond Experientialism and Lingualism. *European Journal of Pragmatism and American Philosophy* 4 (2): 145–174.
Kripke, S. 1982. *Wittgenstein on Rules and Private Language*. Oxford: Oxford University Press.

Kusch, M. 2013. Annalisa Coliva on Wittgenstein and Epistemic Relativism. *Philosophia* 41 (1): 37–49.

———. 2016. Wittgenstein's *On Certainty* and Relativism. In *Analytic and Continental Philosophy: Methods and Perspectives. Proceedings of the 37th Interrnational Wittgenstein Symposium*, ed. S. Rinofner-Kreidl and H.A. Wiltsche. Berlin: De Gruyter.

Laugier, S. 2013. *Why We Need Ordinary Language Philosophy*. Chicago, IL and London: The University of Chicago Press.

Law, J.D. 1988. Uncertain Grounds: Wittgenstein's *On Certainty* and the New Literary Pragmatism. *New Literary History* 19 (2): 319–336.

Lear, J. 1986. Transcendental Anthropology. In *Subject, Thought, and Context*, ed. P. Pettit and J. McDowell. Oxford: Clarendon Press.

Leavis, F.R. 1981. Memories of Wittgenstein. In *Ludwig Wittgenstein: Personal Recollections*, ed. R. Rhees. Oxford: Blackwell.

Leuba, J.H. 1896. A Study in the Psychology of Religious Phenomena. *American Journal of Psychology* 7 (3): 309–385.

Lovejoy, A. 1908. The Thirteen Pragmatisms. Part I: *The Journal of Philosophy, Psychology and Scientific Methods* 5 (1): 5–12; Part II: *The Journal of Philosophy, Psychology and Scientific Methods* 5 (2): 29–39.

Maddalena, G. 2010. La via pragmatista al senso comune. *Paradigmi. Rivista di critica filosofica* 28 (3): 57–71.

Madelrieux, S. 2012. Action as Philosophic Method. http://www.nordprag.org/papers/epc1/Madelrieux.pdf. Accessed 16 June 2016.

Madzia, R. 2013. Chicago Pragmatism and the Extended Mind Theory: Mead and Dewey on the Nature of Cognition. *European Journal of Pragmatism and American Philosophy* 5 (1): 193–211.

Majer, U. 1991. Ramsey's Theory of Truth and the Truth of Theories: A Synthesis of Pragmatism and Intuitionism in Ramsey's Last Philosophy. *Theoria* 57 (3): 162–195.

Malcolm, N. 1942. Moore on Ordinary Language. In *The Philosophy of G. E. Moore*, ed. P.A. Schilpp. Evanston, IL: Northwestern University Press.

———. 1949. Defending Common Sense. *Philosophical Review* 58 (3): 201–220.

———. 1952. Knowledge and Belief. *Mind* 61 (242): 87–92.

———. 1958. *Ludwig Wittgenstein. A Memoir*, Oxford: Oxford University Press.

Marchetti, S. 2015a. *Ethics and Philosophical Critique in William James*. Basingstoke: Palgrave Macmillan.

———. 2015b. Unfamiliar Habits: James and the Ethics and Politics of Self-Experimentation. *William James Studies* 11: 102–113.

Marconi, D. 1987. *L'eredità di Wittgenstein*. Bari: Laterza.

Marcuse, H. 1964. *One-Dimensional Man: Studies in the Ideology of Advanced Industrial Society*. Boston: Beacon Press.

Margolis, J. 2007. *Pragmatism without Foundations. Reconciling Realism and Relativism*. London and New York: Continuum.

———. 2012a. A Philosophical Bestiary. *European Journal of Pragmatism and American Philosophy* 4 (2): 128–145.

———. 2012b. Contesting John Searle's Social Ontology. In *Knowing without Thinking. Mind, Action, Cognition, and the Phenomenon of the Background*, ed. Z. Radman. Basingstoke: Palgrave Macmillan.

Marion, M. 1998. *Wittgenstein, Finitism, and the Foundations of Mathematics*. Oxford: Oxford University Press.

———. 2012. Wittgenstein, Ramsey and British Pragmatism. *European Journal of Pragmatism and American Philosophy* 4 (2): 54–80.

McDowell, J. 1998. Wittgenstein on Following a Rule. In McDowell, J. *Mind, Value and Reality*. Cambridge, MA: Harvard University Press.

McGinn, M. 1989. *Sense and Certainty*. Oxford: Blackwell.

———. 2001. Saying and Showing and the Continuity of Wittgenstein's Thought. *The Harvard Review of Philosophy* 9 (1): 24–36.

McGuinness, B. 2002. In the Shadow of Goethe: Wittgenstein's Intellectual Project. *European Review* 10 (4): 447–457.

———. 2006. Wittgenstein and Ramsey. In *Cambridge and Vienna: Frank P. Ramsey and the Vienna Circle*, ed. M.C. Galavotti. Dordrecht: Springer.

———. ed. 2012. *Wittgenstein in Cambridge. Letters and Documents 1911–1951*. Oxford: Wiley-Blackwell.

McGuinness, B., Asher, M.C., and Pfersmann, O. eds. 1996. *Wittgenstein—Familienbriefe*. Vienna: Hölder-Pichler-Tempsky.

Medina, J. 2004. The Meanings of Silence: Wittgensteinian Contextualism and Poliphony. *Inquiry* 47 (6): 562–579.

———. 2006. *Speaking from Elsewhere*. Albany, NY: State University of New York Press.

Menand, L. 2001. *The Metaphysical Club*. New York: Farrar, Strauss and Giroux.

Menary, R. 2003. Peirce and Wittgenstein on Doubt: A Comparison. In *Knowledge and Belief. Papers of the 26th International Wittgenstein Symposium*, ed. W. Löffler and P. Weingartner. Kirchberg am Wechsel: Austrian Wittgenstein Society.

Methven, S.J. 2015. *Frank Ramsey and the Realistic Spirit*. Basingstoke: Palgrave Macmillan.
Meyers, R. G. 1967. Peirce on Cartesian Doubt. *Transactions of the Charles S. Peirce Society* 3 (1): 13–23.
Misak, C. 2004. *Truth and the End of Inquiry. A Peircean Account of Truth*. Oxford: Oxford University Press.
———. ed. 2007. *New Pragmatists*. Oxford: Oxford University Press.
———. 2008. The Reception of Early American Pragmatism. In *The Oxford Handbook of American Philosophy*, ed. C. Misak. Oxford: Oxford University Press.
———. 2011. Presidential Address: American Pragmatism and Indispensability Arguments. *Transactions of the Charles S. Peirce Society* 47 (3): 261–273.
———. 2016. *Cambridge Pragmatism. From Peirce and James to Ramsey and Wittgenstein*. Oxford: Oxford University Press.
Monk, R. 1991. *Wittgenstein. The Duty of Genius*. London: Vintage.
Moore, G.E. 1959. *Philosophical Papers*. London: George Allen & Unwin.
———. 1970. William James' Pragmatism. In Moore, G.E. *Philosophical Studies*. London: Routledge.
———. 1993. Being Certain that One Is in Pain. In *G. E. Moore, Selected Writings*, ed. T. Baldwin. London; New York: Routledge.
Moser, A.A. 2012. Early Wittgenstein, Pragmatist. In *Ethics, Society, Politics. Papers of the 35th Wittgenstein Symposium (pre-proceedings)*, ed. M.G. Weiss and H. Greif. Kirchberg am Wechsel: Austrian Wittgenstein Society.
Mosser, K. 2009. Kant and Wittgenstein: Common Sense, Therapy, and the Critical Philosophy. *Philosophia* 37 (1): 1–20.
Moyal-Sharrock, D. 2000. Words as Deeds: Wittgenstein's 'Spontaneous Utterances' and the Dissolution of the Explanatory Gap. *Philosophical Psychology* 13 (3): 355–372.
———. 2003. Logic in Action: Wittgenstein's Logical Pragmatism and the Impotence of Scepticism. *Philosophical Investigations* 26 (2): 125–148.
———. ed. 2004. *The Third Wittgenstein*. Aldershot: Ashgate.
———. 2007. *Understanding Wittgenstein's* On Certainty. Basingstoke: Palgrave Macmillan.
———. 2013a. On Coliva's Judgmental Hinges. *Philosophia* 41 (1): 13–25.
———. 2013b. Realism, but not Empiricism: Wittgenstein *versus* Searle. In *A Wittgensteinian Perspective on the Use of Conceptual Analysis in Psychology*, ed. T.P. Racine and K.L. Slaney. Basingstoke: Palgrave Macmillan.

Moyal-Sharrock, D. and Brenner, W.H. eds. 2005. *Readings of Wittgenstein's On Certainty*. Basingstoke: Palgrave Macmillan.

Myers, G.E. 1986. *William James. His Life and Character*. New Haven, CT: Yale University Press.

Newman, J.H. 1979. *An Essay in Aid of a Grammar of Assent*. Notre Dame, IN: University of Notre Dame Press.

Norris, A. 2015. Doubt in Wittgenstein's 'Remarks on Frazer's *Golden Bough*'. *Wittgenstein Studien* 6 (1): 1–18.

Nubiola, J. 1996. Scholarship on the Relations between Ludwig Wittgenstein and Charles S. Peirce. In *Studies on the History of Logic. Proceedings of the III Symposium on the History of Logic*, ed. I. Angelelli and M. Cerezo. Berlin: De Gruyter.

———. 2000. Ludwig Wittgenstein and William James. *Streams of William James* 2 (3): 2–4.

Nyíri, J.C. 1982. Wittgenstein's Later Work in Relation to Conservatism. In *Wittgenstein and His Times*, ed. B. McGuinness. Oxford: Blackwell.

Ogden, C.K. and Richards, I.A. 1960. *The Meaning of Meaning*. London: Routledge & Kegan Paul.

Padilla Galvez, J. and Gaffal, M. eds. 2011. *Forms of Life and Language Games*. Frankfurt: Ontos Verlag.

Paul, M. 2012. *Frank Ramsey (1903–1930). A Sister's Memoir*. Huntingdon: Smith-Gordon.

Perissinotto, L. 1991. *Logica e immagine del mondo. Studio su* Über Gewissheit *di Ludwig Wittgenstein*. Milan: Guerini.

———. 2011. '... to begin at the beginning'. The Grammar of Doubt in Wittgenstein's *On Certainty*. In *Doubt, Ethics and Religion. Wittgenstein and the Counter-Enlightment*, ed. L. Perissinotto and V. Sanfélix Vidarte. Frankfurt: Ontos Verlag.

———. 2016a. How Long Has the Earth Existed? Persuasion and World-Picture in Wittgenstein's *On Certainty*. *Philosophical Investigations* 39 (2): 154–177.

———. 2016b. Concept-formation and Facts of Nature in Wittgenstein. *Paradigmi. Rivista di critica filosofica* 34 (3).

Perry, R. B. 1935. *The Thought and Character of William James*, 2 voll. Boston, MA: Little, Brown and Co.

———. 1938. *In the Spirit of William James*. New Haven, CT: Yale University Press.

Peterman, J.F. 1992. *Philosophy as Therapy: An Interpretation and Defence of Wittgenstein's Later Philosophy*. Albany, NY: State University of New York Press.

Picardi, E. 1987. Ramsey fra Wittgenstein e Russell. In *L'epistemologia di Cambridge 1850–1950*, ed. R. Simili. Bologna: Il Mulino.

Pich, R.H. 2012. A filosofia do senso comum de Thomas Reid e o 'Critical common-sensism' de C.S. Peirce. *Cognitio. Revista de Filosofia* 13 (2): 279–299.

Pichler, A. and Smith, D. 2013. A List of Correspondences between Wittgenstein's TS-310 and MS 115ii. In *Mind, Language and Action. Papers of the 36th International Wittgenstein Symposium (pre-proceedings)*, ed. A. Coliva, D. Moyal-Sharrock, and V.A. Munz. Kirchberg am Wechsel: Austrian Wittgenstein Society.

Pihlström, S. 2003. On the Concept of Philosophical Anthropology. *Journal of Philosophical Research* 28: 259–285.

———. 2012. A New Look at Wittgenstein and Pragmatism. *The European Journal of Pragmatism and American Philosophy* 4 (2): 9–26.

Pleasants, N. 2000. Winch and Wittgenstein on Understanding Ourselves Critically: Descriptive not Metaphysical. *Inquiry* 43 (3): 289–318.

Price, H. 2011. Ramsey on Saying and Whistling. A Discordant Note. In Price, H. *Naturalism Without Mirrors*. Oxford: Oxford University Press.

Pritchard, D. 2011. Wittgenstein on Scepticism. In *The Oxford Handbook of Wittgenstein*, ed. O. Kuusela and M. McGinn. Oxford: Oxford University Press.

———. 2015. Wittgenstein on Faith and Reason: The Influence of Newman. In *God, Truth and other Enigmas*, ed. M. Szatkowski. Berlin: De Gruyter.

———. 2016. *Epistemic Angst. Radical Skepticism* and *the Groundlessness of Our Believing*. Princeton, NJ: Princeton University Press.

Pryor, J. 2000. The Skeptic and the Dogmatist. *Noûs* 34 (4): 517–549.

Putnam, H. 1979. Analiticity and A Priority: Beyond Wittgenstein and Quine. In *Midway Studies in Philosophy. Vol. IV: Studies in Metaphysics*, ed. P. French, T. F. Uehling Jr. and H. K. Wettstein. Minneapolis: University of Minnesota.

———. 1991. Wittgenstein on Religious Belief. In *On Community*, ed. L. S. Rouner. Notre Dame, IN: University of Notre Dame Press.

———. 1992a. The Permanence of William James. *Bulletin of the American Academy of Arts and Sciences* 46 (3): 17–31.

———. 1992b. *Renewing Philosophy*. Cambridge, MA: Harvard University Press.

———. 1995. Was Wittgenstein a Pragmatist? In Putnam, H. *Pragmatism. An Open Question*. Oxford: Blackwell.

———. 1997. James' Theory of Truth. In *The Cambridge Companion to William James*, ed. H. Putnam and R.A. Putnam. Cambridge: Cambridge University Press.

———. 2000. Rethinking Mathematical Necessity. In *The New Wittgenstein*, ed. A. Crary and R. Read. London: Routledge.

———. 2001. Rules, Attunement, and 'Applying Words to the World'. The struggle to Understand Wittgenstein's Vision of Language. In *The Legacy of Wittgenstein: Pragmatism or Deconstruction*, ed. L. Nagl and C. Mouffe. Frankfurt am Main: Peter Lang.

———. 2006. Philosophy as the Education of the Grownups. Stanley Cavell and Skepticism. In *Reading Cavell*, ed. A. Crary and S. Shieh. London and New York: Routledge.

Putnam, H. and Putnam, A.R. 1992. William James' Ideas. In *Realism with a Human Face*, ed. J. Conant and H. Putnam. Cambridge, MA: Harvard University Press.

Radman, Z. ed. 2012. *Knowing Without Thinking. Mind, Action, Cognition and the Phenomenon of the Background*. Basingstoke: Palgrave Macmillan.

Ramsey, F.P. 1920–1930. *Frank P. Ramsey Papers 1920–1930*, ASP. 1983.1, Archives of Scientific Philosophy, Special Collections Department, University of Pittsburgh.

———. 1924. Review of C.K. Ogden and I.A. Richards' *The Meaning of Meaning*. *Mind* 33 (129): 108–109.

———. 1931. *The Foundations of Mathematics and Other Logical Essays*. Ed. R.B. Braithwaite. London: Routledge & Kegan Paul.

———. 1990. *Philosophical Papers*. Ed. D.H. Mellor. Cambridge: Cambridge University Press.

———. 1991a. *On Truth*. Ed. N. Rescher and U. Majer. Dordrecht: Kluwer.

———. 1991b. *Notes on Philosophy, Probability and Mathematics*. Ed. M.C. Galavotti. Naples: Bibliopolis.

Reid, T. 1863. *Works*. Ed. W. Hamilton. Edinburgh: Maclachlan and Stewart.

———. 1997. *An Inquiry Into the Human Mind on the Principles of Common Sense*. Ed. R. Brookes, University Park, PA: Pennsylvania State University Press.

---. 2002. *Essays on the Intellectual Powers of Man.* Ed. D. Brookes, University Park, PA: Pennsylvania State University Press.
Rhees, R. 1965. Some Developments in Wittgenstein's View of Ethics. *The Philosophical Review* 74 (1): 17–26.
---. ed. 1984. *Recollections of Wittgenstein.* Oxford: Oxford University Press.
---. 2002. Five Topics in Conversations with Wittgenstein (Numbers; Concept-Formation; Time-Reactions; Induction; Causality). Ed. D.Z. Phillips. *Philosophical Investigations* 25 (1): 1–19.
---. 2003. *Wittgenstein's* On Certainty. *There—Like Our Life.* Ed. D.Z. Phillips. Oxford: Blackwell.
Richardson, R.D. 2006. *William James in the Maelstrom of American Modernism: A Biography.* Boston and New York: Houghton Mifflin Company.
Rorty, R. 1961. Pragmatism, Categories and Language. *The Philosophical Review* 70 (2): 197–223.
---. 1979. *Philosophy* and *the Mirror of Nature.* Princeton, NJ: Princeton University Press.
---. 1989. *Contingency, Irony, and Solidarity.* Cambridge: Cambridge University Press.
Rosso, M. 1999. Introduzione. In Wittgenstein, L. *Osservazioni Filosofiche.* Torino: Einaudi.
Rudder Baker, L. 1984. On the Very Idea of a Form of Life. *Inquiry* 27 (1–4): 277–289.
Russell, B. 1910. *Philosophical Essays.* London: Longmans, Green & Co.
---. 1912. Review of 'William James' by Emile Boutroux. *The Cambridge Review* 34 (December 5): 176.
---. 1921. *The Analysis of Mind.* London: George Allen & Unwin.
---. 1926. Theory of Knowledge. *Encyclopedia Britannica.* 13th edition.
---. 1936. The Limits of Empiricism. *Proceedings of the Aristotelian Society, New Series* 36: 131–150.
---. 1946. Foreword to J. Feibleman, *An Introduction to Peirce's Philosophy Interpreted as a System.* New York: Harper.
---. 1984. *The Collected Papers. Vol. 7, Theory of Knowledge: The 1913 Manuscript.* London: George Allen and Unwin.
Rydenfelt, H. 2009. The Meaning of Pragmatism. James on the Practical Consequences of Belief. *Cognitio—Revista de Filosofia* 10 (1): 81–89.

Ryle, G. 1945. Knowing How and Knowing That: the Presidential Address. *Proceedings of the Aristotelian Society, New Series* 46: 1–16.
Sahlin, N.E. 1990. *The Philosophy of F.P. Ramsey* Cambridge: Cambridge University Press.
———. 1995. On the Philosophical Relations between Ramsey and Wittgenstein. In *The British Tradition in 20th Century Philosophy. Proceedings of the XVII Wittgenstein Symposium*, ed. J. Hintikka and K. Puhl. Vienna: Hölder–Pichler–Tempsky.
Sanfélix Vidarte, V. 2001. La Mirada distante: Wittgenstein y el pragmatismo. In *El retorno del pragmatismo*, ed. L. Arenas, J. Munoz, and A.J. Perona. Madrid: Trotta.
———. 2011. Wittgenstein and the Criticism of Technological and Scientific Civilization. In *Forms of Life and Language Games*, ed. J. Padilla Galvez and M. Gaffal. Frankfurt: Ontos Verlag.
Santayana, G. 1923. *Skepticism and Animal Faith: Introduction to a System of Philosophy*. New York: Scribners; London: Constable.
Scharfstein, B.A. 1980. *The Philosophers. Their Lives and the Nature of their Thought*. Oxford: Blackwell.
Scheman, N. 2011. *Shifting Ground. Knowledge and Reality, Transgression and Trustworthiness*. Oxford: Oxford University Press.
Schönbaumsfeld, G. 2016. 'Hinge Propositions' and the 'Logical' Exclusion of Doubt. *International Journal for the Study of Skepticism* 6 (2–3): 165–181.
Schulte, J. 1993. *Experience and Expression. Wittgenstein's Philosophy of Psychology*. Oxford: Oxford University Press.
———. 1999. Wittgenstein—auch ein Pragmatist? In *Philosophieren über Philosophie*, ed. R. Raatzsch. Leipzig: Leipziger Universitätsverlag.
———. 2005. Within a System. In *Readings of Wittgenstein's* On Certainty, ed. D. Moyal-Sharrock and W.H. Brenner. Basingstoke: Palgrave Macmillan.
Shieh, S. 2006. The Truth of Skepticism. In *Reading Cavell*, ed. A. Crary and S. Shieh. London and New York: Routledge.
Searle, J. 1979. *Expression and Meaning*. Cambridge: Cambridge University Press.
———. 1983. *Intentionality*. Cambridge: Cambridge University Press.
———. 1995. *The Construction of Social Reality*. London: Penguin.
———. 2010. *Making the Social World: The Structure of Human Civilization*. Oxford: Oxford University Press.

———. 2011. Wittgenstein and the Background. *American Philosophical Quarterly* 48 (2): 119–128.
Shusterman, R. 2008. *Body Consciousness. A Philosophy of Mindfulness and Somaesthetics*. New York: Cambridge University Press.
———. 2012a. The Body as Background. Pragmatism and Somaesthetics. In *Knowing Without Thinking. Mind, Action, Cognition, and the Phenomenon of the Background*, ed. Z. Radman. Basingstoke: Palgrave Macmillan.
———. 2012b. *Thinking Through the Body: Essays in Somaesthetics*. New York: Cambridge University Press.
Spengler, O. 1933. *The Decline of the West*. New York: Knopf.
Steiner, P. 2012. Une question du point de vu. James, Husserl, Wittgenstein et le sophisme du psychologue. *Revue Internationale de Philosophie* 1 (259): 251–281.
———. ed. 2013. Special issue of *Intellectica*, 2 (60), 'Pragmatism and Cognitive Science'.
Stern, D. 1995. *Wittgenstein on Mind and Language*. Oxford: Oxford University Press.
———. 1996. The Availability of Wittgenstein's Philosophy. In *The Cambridge Companion to Wittgenstein*, ed. H. Sluga and D. Stern. Cambridge: Cambridge University Press.
Strawson, P.F. 1985. *Skepticism and Naturalism. Some Varieties*. London: Routledge.
Stroll, A. 1994. *Moore and Wittgenstein on Certainty*. Oxford: Oxford University Press.
———. 2004. Wittgenstein's Foundational Metaphors. In *The Third Wittgenstein*, ed. D. Moyal-Sharrock. Aldershot: Ashgate.
Thayerm, H.S. 1981. *Meaning and Action. A Critical History of Pragmatism*. Indianapolis, IN, and Cambridge: Hackett.
Tiercelin, C. 1989. Reid and Peirce on Belief. In *The Philosophy of Thomas Reid*, ed. M. Dalgarno and E. Matthews. Dordrecht: Kluwer.
———. 1992. Vagueness and the Unity of Peirce's Realism. *Transactions of the Charles S. Peirce Society* 28 (1): 51–82.
———. 2010. Peirce et Wittgenstein face au défi sceptique. *Paradigmi. Rivista di critica filosofica* 28 (3): 13–28.
———. 2015. Chance, Love and Logic: Ramsey and Peirce on Norms, Rationality and the Conduct of Life. In *Against Boredom. 17 Essays*, ed. J. Persson, G. Hermenèr, and E. Sjöstrand. Stockholm: Fri Tanke.

———. 2016. In Defense of a Critical Commonsensist Conception of Knowledge. *International Journal for the Study of Skepticism* 6 (2–3): 182–202.

Tripodi, P. 2009. Wittgenstein e il naturalismo. *Etica e Politica / Ethics and Politics* 11 (2): 121–141.

———. 2013. Wittgenstein on the Gulf between Believers and Non-Believers. *Philosophia* 41 (1): 63–79.

Uebel, T. 2015. American Pragmatism and the Vienna Circle: The Early Years. *Journal for the History of Analytical Philosophy* 3 (3): 1–35.

Upper J. 1998. Wittgenstein and Peirce: Appendix. https://web.archive.org/web/20120921223450/http://www3.sympatico.ca/johnupper/mypapers/wp-apndx.htm. Accessed 24 February 2016.

Varela, F., Thompson, E., and Rosch, E. 1991. *The Embodied Mind. Cognitive Science and Human Experience*. Cambridge, MA: Mit Press.

Venturinha, N. 2010. The Ramsey Notes on Time and Mathematics. In *Wittgenstein After His Nachlass*, ed. N. Venturinha. Basingstoke: Palgrave Macmillan.

———. 2012. Sraffa's Notes on Wittgenstein's *Blue Book*. *Nordic Wittgenstein Review* 1 (1): 181–192.

von Wright, G.H. ed. 1972. *Problems in the Theory of Knowledge/Problèmes de La Théorie de La Connaissance*. Nijhoff, The Hague: Kluwer.

———. ed. 1974. *Wittgenstein's Letters to Russell, Keynes and Moore*. Oxford: Basil Blackwell.

———. 1982. *Wittgenstein*. Oxford: Blackwell.

———. 1993. The Wittgenstein Papers. In *Ludwig Wittgenstein. Philosophical Occasions 1912–1951*, ed. J. Klagge and A. Nordmann. Indianapolis, IN: Hackett.

Waismann, F. 1979. *Ludwig Wittgenstein and the Vienna Circle. Conversations Annotated by Friedrich Waismann*. Ed. B. McGuinness. Oxford: Blackwell.

Wellmer, A. 2004. The Debate About Truth: Pragmatism Without Regulative Ideas. In *The Pragmatic Turn in Philosophy: Contemporary Engagements between Analytic and Continental Thought*, ed. W. Egginton e M. Sandbothe. Albany, NY: State University of New York Press.

West, C. 1989. *The American Evasion of Philosophy. A Genealogy of Pragmatism*. Madison, WI: The University of Wisconsin Press.

Weyl, H. 1921. Über die neue Grundlagenkrise der Mathematik. *Mathematische Zeitschrift* 10 (1–2): 39–79.

Williams, M. 2003. Wittgenstein's Refutation of Idealism. In *Wittgenstein and Scepticism*, ed. D. McManus. Abingdon: Routledge.

———. 2005. Why Wittgenstein Isn't a Foundationalist. In *Readings of Wittgenstein's On Certainty*, ed. D. Moyal-Sharrock and W.H. Hunter. Basingstoke: Palgrave Macmillan.

Wilshire, B. 1968. *William James and Phenomenology: A Study of The Principles of Psychology*. Bloomington, IN: Indiana University Press.

Winch, P. 1964. Understanding a Primitive Society. *American Philosophical Quarterly* 1 (4): 307–324.

———. 1990. *The Idea of a Social Science and its Relation to Philosophy*. London: Routledge.

———. 1998. Judgement: Propositions and Practices. *Philosophical Investigations* 21 (3): 189–202.

Witherspoon, E. 2003. Conventions and Forms of Life. In *Socializing Metaphysics. The Nature of Social Reality*, ed. F. Scmitt. Lanham: Rowman & Littlefield.

Wolgast, E. 1987. Whether Certainty is a Form of Life. *The Philosophical Quarterly* 37 (147): 151–165.

Wolterstorff, N. 2000. Reid on Common Sense, with Wittgenstein's Assistance. *American Catholic Philosophical Quarterly* 74 (3): 491–517.

Wright, C. 2004a. Warrant for Nothing (and Foundations for Free)? *Aristotelian Society Supplement* 78 (1): 167–212.

———. 2004b. Wittgensteinian Certainties. In *Wittgenstein and Scepticism*, ed. D. McManus. Abingdon: Routledge.

Wrigley, M. 1995. Wittgenstein, Ramsey and the Infinite. In *The British Tradition in 20th Century Philosophy. Proceedings of the XVII Wittgenstein Symposium*, ed. J. Hintikka and K. Puhl. Vienna: Hölder–Pichler–Tempsky.

Wu, Y. 1994. Peirce's Arguments for His Pragmatic Maxim. In *Living Doubt. Essays Concerning the Epistemology of Charles S. Peirce*, ed. G. Debrock and M. Hulswit. Dordrecht: Kluwer.

Zerilli, L.M.G. 2001. Wittgenstein Between Pragmatism and Deconstruction. In *The Legacy of Wittgenstein: Pragmatism or Deconstruction*, ed. L. Nagl and C. Mouffe. Frankfurt am Main: Peter Lang.

Author Index

A
Acero, J.J., 30
Agam-Segal, R., 231
Ameriks, K.A., 113
Andronico, M., 166, 219
Aristotle, 232

B
Baghramian, M., 191
Bain, A., 142, 171
Bambrough, R., 6, 64, 121, 173, 206
Bax, C., 76, 199, 208, 212
Bennett-Hunter, G., 5
Bergman, M., 38, 233
Berkeley, G., 107
Bernstein, R., 6, 192, 207, 217
Biancini, P., 185

Biesenbach, H., 33
Bilgrami, A., 71–74
Bogen, J., 20
Boncompagni, A., 17, 32, 46, 99, 119, 126, 135, 156, 174, 189, 190, 212, 244, 246
Bordogna, F., 253
Boutroux, E., 245, 246, 248
Bouveresse, J., 48, 127, 185
Bouwsma, O.K., 4, 119
Brandom, R., 5, 84, 207
Breithaupt, F., 166
Brenner, W.H., 3, 60, 118
Brent, J., 269
Brice, R., 81, 84, 206
Britton, K., 5
Broyles, J.E., 64, 86, 88, 89, 91, 93, 135, 216
Busch, W., 22

Author Index

C
Calcaterra, R.M., 6, 85, 104, 123, 125, 148, 152, 203–205, 212
Cavell, S., 75, 76, 195, 199, 235, 270
Chauviré, C., 4, 157, 259
Christensen, A.M., 192, 193, 200, 206, 230
Citron, G., 61, 70, 173, 200, 225, 231, 232, 257, 259
Colapietro, V., 36, 175, 226
Coliva, A., 63, 65–67, 70, 82–85, 125, 171, 191, 192, 202–204, 207
Conant, J., 242
Conway, G., 125, 211
Cook, J.W., 77, 80
Cormier, H., 36
Crary, A., 206, 207
Crosby, D.A., 250

D
Darwin, C., 107
Democritus, 107
Descartes, R., 63, 64, 128, 143
Dewey, John, 4, 5, 37, 38, 123, 174, 213, 234, 246
Diamond, C., 257
Dias Fortes, A., 237, 238
Donatelli, P., 190
Dreyfus, H., 212
Durante, R., 193, 197

E
Edie, J., 251, 252
Egidi, R., 24, 164
Einstein, A., 43
Emerson, R.W., 234, 235
Emmett, K., 209
Engelmann, M.L., 18, 38, 49, 164

F
Fabbrichesi, R., 6, 20, 105, 122, 126, 127, 183, 204
Fairbanks, M., 120, 214
Ferrari, M., 39, 259
Fine, A., 192
Fischer, H.R., 182
Flanagan, O., 250
Floyd, J., 231
Franken, F., 197
Franzese, S., 169, 251
Frege, G., 122

G
Gadamer, H.G., 217
Gaffal, M., 185
Gallagher, S., 213
Garver, N., 182
Gava, G., 97, 102
Gellner, E., 196
Gennip, K. van, 60, 61
Gier, N., 182
Gill, J., 81, 156, 197, 203
Glock, H.J., 25–27, 130
Goethe, G.F., 61, 166, 172, 227, 238
Goldstein, L., 1
Gómez Alonso, M., 115, 125
Goodman, R., 6, 32, 85, 120, 122, 126, 136, 173, 212, 227, 230, 253, 255
Gullvåg, I., 4, 40

Author Index

Hacker, P.M.S., 6, 119, 185, 187
Hamilton, A., 65, 66, 69, 80, 126, 159, 191, 208, 211, 257
Harrison, B., 118
Hegel, G.W.F., 263
Heidegger, M., 212
Hensley, J.M., 259
Heraclitus, 245
Hertzberg, L., 192, 195, 226
Hilmy, S.S., 6, 228, 259
Holt, D.C., 100
Hookway, C., 35, 40, 94–98, 105, 136, 143, 145, 149, 150–152, 234
Howat, A., 86, 93–96, 98
Husserl, E., 212
Hutchinson, P., 255
Hutto, D.D., 61, 174

James, W., 2–11, 20, 27, 29–39, 42, 43, 49, 53, 78, 82, 85, 86, 93, 96–99, 113, 119–149, 151–153, 158, 160–162, 166–169, 171, 173–175, 177, 184, 185, 198, 205, 207, 212–218, 222, 224, 226–232, 234, 238, 241–253, 255, 258, 260–261, 263–270
Janik, A., 185
Jastrow, J., 6
Johanson, A.E., 86, 90–93, 205
Jolley, K.D., 114, 226, 236

Kant, I., 41, 96, 97, 108, 113, 169
Kienzler, W., 70, 129
Kierkegaard, S., 131
Kilpinen, E., 169, 175
Klein, A., 249, 259
Kober, M., 84, 130, 131
Koethe, J., 32
Koopman, C., 145, 168
Kripke, S., 76, 193
Kusch, M., 191, 192

Laugier, S., 257
Lavoisier, A.L., 69
Law, J.D., 196, 202
Lear, J., 118
Leavis, F.R., 25
Leuba, J.H., 130
Lovejoy, A., 151, 152

Mach, E., 167, 258
Maddalena, G., 113
Madelrieux, S., 227
Madzia, R., 213
Majer, U., 27
Malcolm, N., 70, 73, 80, 88, 89, 153
Marchetti, S., 36, 148, 169, 175, 229
Marconi, D., 191
Marcuse, H., 196
Margolis, J., 5, 192, 211
Marion, M., 18, 25, 27, 39
McDowell, J., 201, 204, 207
McGinn, M., 75, 81, 84, 133, 156

McGuinness, B., 25, 33, 38, 153, 166, 237
Mead, G.H., 5
Medina, J., 4, 208
Menand, L., 142, 246
Menary, R., 65, 67
Merleau-Ponty, M., 212
Methven, S.J., 31, 257
Meyers, R.G., 63
Misak, 5, 17, 25, 37, 39, 40, 43, 94–98, 143, 240
Monk, R., 4, 25, 33, 119, 153
Moore, G.E., 8, 16, 36, 37, 43, 70–74, 79, 80–83, 100, 113, 116, 118, 129, 154, 196, 253, 264
Moser, A.A., 6
Mosser, K., 113
Moyal-Sharrock, D., 3, 47, 60, 61, 80, 83–85, 118, 133, 156, 161, 171, 190, 211, 257
Myers, G.E., 249

N
Newman, J.H., 70, 130
Nubiola, J., 6, 37, 40
Nyíri, J.C., 196

O
Ogden, C.K., 25, 38–40, 164

P
Padilla Galvez, J., 185
Paul, M., 39, 253, 254

Peirce, C.S., 2–8, 10, 20, 29, 30, 32, 37–39, 42, 61, 64–69, 74–78, 81, 85–89, 90–99, 101–105, 108, 112, 113, 119, 121–124, 126–128, 134–136, 140–147, 149–153, 157, 158, 161, 162, 164–166, 168, 169, 171, 174–177, 183, 184, 187, 202, 204, 205, 207, 215–218, 224–227, 232–234, 242–244, 248, 251, 258, 261, 263–267, 269
Perissinotto, L., 50, 60, 61, 65, 67, 72, 73, 84, 128, 197, 231, 242, 255
Perry, R.B., 106, 243, 251, 252
Peterman, J.F., 238
Picardi, E., 30
Pich, R.H., 101
Pichler, A., 185
Pihlström, S., 85, 118, 173
Plato, 232
Pleasants, N., 192
Price, H., 5, 27
Pritchard, D., 70, 76, 82, 83, 88, 96, 129
Pryor, J., 71
Putnam, A.R., 36, 229
Putnam, H., 5, 6, 36, 76, 84, 131, 152, 175, 191, 192, 201, 202, 206, 229, 230

R
Radman, Z., 212
Ramsey, F.P., 5, 7, 20, 24–33, 36, 39, 40, 42–44, 46, 53, 54, 161,

Author Index

163, 164, 198, 224, 225, 246, 253, 255, 257, 264
Read, R., 255
Reid, T., 68, 99–101, 108
Rhees, R., 16, 33, 40–42, 61, 81, 84, 119, 163, 182, 200, 228, 231, 259, 264
Ribot, T., 252
Richards, I.A., 38–39, 164, 166
Richardson, R.D., 166
Rorty, R., 4, 5, 121, 125, 161, 162, 191, 192, 196, 201, 202, 207
Rosch, E., 212
Rosso, M., 20, 115
Royce, J., 215
Rudder Baker, L., 201, 202
Russell, B., 16, 25, 30, 31, 33, 36–39, 43, 54, 85, 164, 246, 253, 255, 264, 269
Rydenfelt, H., 152
Ryle, G., 85, 119

Sahlin, N.E., 25, 27
Santayana, G., 5
Scharfstein, B.A., 20
Scheman, N., 207, 208
Schiller, F.C.S., 5, 37, 106
Schönbaumsfeld, G., 83
Schulte, J., 6, 17, 47, 49, 79, 80, 159–161, 172, 240, 241, 260
Searle, J., 210–212
Shakespeare, W., 263
Shieh, S., 76
Shusterman, R., 173, 174, 213
Skinner, F., 185

Smith, D., 185
Spengler, O., 237–239
Sraffa, P., 49, 114
Steiner, P., 174, 213, 247
Stern, D., 17, 18, 61
Strawson, P.F., 200, 257
Stroll, A., 70, 81, 82, 92, 125, 211

Thayerm, H.S., 25
Thompson, E., 212
Thoreau, H.D., 234, 235
Tiercelin, C., 25, 65–67, 76, 87, 88, 92, 101, 105, 224
Toulmin, S., 185
Tripodi, P., 192, 257

Uebel, T., 39, 259
Upper, J., 20

Varela, F., 212
Venturinha, N., 25, 114
Viney, W., 250
von Wright, G.H., 23, 27, 37, 60, 80, 81

Waismann, F., 23, 230
Wellmer, A., 207
West, C., 235
Weyl, H., 27

Williams, M., 70, 82, 212
Wilshire, B., 251
Winch, P., 80, 82, 174, 192–195, 197
Witherspoon, E., 72, 187, 193, 219
Wolgast, E., 84
Wolterstorff, N., 100
Wright, Crispin, 71, 72, 76, 96

Wright, Chauncey, 142
Wrigley, M., 25
Wu, Y., 142, 151
Wundt, W., 167

Zerilli, L.M.G., 195, 196, 202

Subject Index

A

Action(s), 3, 9, 16, 20, 29–31, 36, 42, 45–47, 51, 62–63, 65, 82, 84, 86, 101, 103, 106, 111, 122, 125–128, 137, 139–142, 147, 149–154, 156, 158–159, 164–178, 181, 183, 185–186, 189, 195, 198, 201–202, 209–211, 214, 219, 230, 233, 266–267
  habit of, 63, 150, 151, 216
  involuntary vs. voluntary, 166–167, 173, 178
  James on, 166–169, 173, 175
  rule of, 101, 154, 158
  See also Behaviour
Activity(ies), 48, 74, 110, 131, 142, 184, 186
  philosophical, 10, 49, 114, 132, 166, 223, 228, 268, 269
  See also Practice(s); Praxis(es)

Advantage(s), 47, 52, 109, 248, 264, 265
Agreement(s)
  as consonance of voices, 62, 117
  in forms of life, 72, 185–187, 193, 195, 201, 206
  of ideas with reality, 29
Animal(s), 30, 31, 66, 85, 127, 166, 170, 171, 185, 187–189
Anthropology, anthropological approach, 41, 103, 185, 194, 247, 251
Anti-Cartesianism, anti-Cartesian, 8, 61, 98, 123, 265
Anti-foundationalism, anti-foundational, anti-fondationalist, 92, 93, 124, 181, 191, 211, 216–217
Anti-scepticism, anti-sceptical, 71, 74, 75, 82, 83
Anti-theoretical, 218, 222, 229, 260

Subject Index

Assumption(s), 8, 72, 77, 82, 85, 86, 93–98, 136, 210–211, 251, 266, 268
  regulative, 8, 85–86, 93–98, 266

B

Background, notion of, 9, 61–62, 64–65, 84, 89, 117, 126, 131, 141, 158, 174–178, 181–182, 185, 189, 199, 201, 205, 209–219, 247, 267–268
Banknotes, 109, 160
  See also Cash value; Credit system; Money
Bearing(s)
  practical, 9, 141, 143, 144, 224
  upon conduct, 146, 148–150, 152, 161
  See also Consequence(s); Effect(s)
Bed (of the river) *see* Riverbed
Bedrock, 125, 128, 217
Behaviour, behavioural, 9, 30, 31, 105, 140, 148, 151–153, 162, 165, 169, 171, 173, 175, 177, 188, 211, 216, 230, 268, 269
  See also Action(s)
Behaviourist, 31, 216
Belief(s)
  animal, 31
  common sense, Weltbild belief(s), 100–107, 109, 113, 119, 122, 123, 125, 128–131, 135–136, 161, 196, 212, 216–217
  as habit of action, 63, 142, 148–151, 173, 216
  indubitable, 68, 75, 86–88, 91, 93, 98, 119, 135
  (*see also* Indubitable(s))
  James' conception of, 109–113, 130, 250
  original, 74–75, 86–91, 96, 119
  religious, 29, 34, 111–112, 128–132, 192

C

Calculus, calculating, calculation, 45, 47–49, 67, 164, 185, 264
Cartesianism, Cartesian, 61–65, 89, 98, 123, 204, 217, 226, 265
  See also Descartes
Cash value, truth as, 35, 53, 160
  See also Money; Banknotes; Credit system
Causality, 26, 31, 157
Cause(s), 23, 30, 127, 161, 164, 165, 189, 254–256
  and effect(s), 30, 164, 165, 254, 255
Certainty(ies)
  animal, 85
  common sense, Weltbild certainty(ies), 8, 18, 64–66, 72–84, 87–88, 91–92, 98, 101–102, 104, 112, 115–126, 129–137, 154–158, 170, 188–189, 192, 199, 201–202, 208, 212, 217, 257, 266–268
  doubt and, 8, 16, 61, 62, 65, 70, 72, 77, 87, 91, 98, 101, 104, 141, 265, 267
  mathematical, 77, 79, 102–105, 157, 188, 189
  unshakable, 59–98

Subject Index 303

vs. knowledge, 18, 81, 126, 132, 136, 154–156, 170–171, 188, 266–268
  See also Hinge(s); Sureness
Child, children, 22, 47, 66, 69, 87, 170, 171, 194, 202, 222
Civilization(s), 238, 259
Common sense, 8–9, 16, 68, 70, 86–88, 98–102, 105–109, 112–119, 122–126, 128, 132–133, 135–137, 139, 155, 161, 178, 195, 208, 216, 266–267
  and Weltbild, 113, 116–137
Common-sensism (sensist), critical, 8, 68, 75, 86, 88, 100–101, 105, 119, 136–137, 140, 266
Community(ies), 62, 85, 87, 117, 123–124, 137, 155, 185, 191, 193–196, 201–204, 208, 229, 250, 260, 266
  of researchers, 36, 91, 123
Conduct, 28, 34, 126, 144–152, 155, 158, 161, 165, 199
Consciousness, 120, 123, 149, 151, 211
Consequence(s)
  behavioural, 9, 67, 153–159, 268
  practical, 37–39, 144, 145, 151, 153–159, 165, 177, 227, 241, 257
  See also Bearing(s); Effect(s)
Conservatism, conservative, 10, 71, 182, 190, 196, 197, 200, 218
Contextualism, contextualist, 4, 82, 147, 155, 159, 162, 165

Continuity, principle of, 111, 128, 132–133, 247, 267–269
Convention(s), conventional, 62, 72, 193
Conventionalism, conventionalist(s), 72, 185, 190, 193, 211
Conversion, converting, 76–77, 131, 196–199, 207, 231, 269
Correspondence, truth as, 29, 34–35, 43, 46
Correspondentist, 28, 46, 48
Credit system, 109, 160
  See also Banknotes; Cash value; Money
Culture(s), cultural, 1, 4, 15, 84–85, 90, 99, 117, 141, 174–175, 177, 182, 185–187, 191, 193, 196, 198–200, 207–208, 210, 212, 218–219, 238, 256, 258, 260

Data, datum, 21, 70, 154–155, 185, 214–215
  See also Given
Denkmittel, 108, 113, 126
Doubt(s), 62, 65, 77, 87, 91, 104, 265
  Cartesian, 62, 89
  and certainty, 8, 16, 61, 70, 72, 98, 101, 141, 267
  complete, radical, total, universal, 62–65
  genuine, true, 64, 66–68, 88, 91, 101
  on hinges, 8, 69, 72, 77–78, 80, 84, 87, 90, 95

Doubt(s) (cont.)
  methodical, 64
  paper, 64, 68, 88, 101
  philosophical, 62, 64, 265
Dream, dreaming, 63, 71, 72, 241
Dubitability, dubitable, 87, 90, 91, 93, 112, 119
Duck-rabbit, 6, 52

Effect(s)
  cause(s) and, 30, 164, 165, 254, 255
  perceptive, perceivable, 152, 153, 167, 224
  practical, 140, 143–144, 228
  See also Bearing(s); Consequence(s)
Effort, 135, 166–167, 173, 248
Empirical *vs.* grammatical, logical, 9, 11, 69, 74, 84, 93, 118, 127, 134–137, 154, 244, 245, 247, 249, 250, 254, 255, 261, 267
Empiricism, empiricist, 34, 130, 185, 243, 248–250, 253–257
  radical, 33, 35, 168, 243, 253
Enactivism, enactivist, 174, 212
Epistemic account (approach, attitude, perspective, reading, view), 72, 75–76, 82–83, 85, 126, 133, 136, 156, 171, 266
Epistemology, epistemological, 34, 72, 76, 78, 85, 88, 95, 105, 195, 202, 204, 206–208
Ethics, ethical, 90, 189, 195, 199, 200, 206, 207, 219, 221, 222, 228–234, 260, 261, 267, 269
  theories, 230–234, 261
Ethnology, ethnologist, ethnological, 199, 200
  See also Anthropology
Everyday, the, 132, 225, 227, 260
  activities, practices, 48, 74, 75, 131, 154
  beliefs, 129, 132, 147
  certainties, 79, 131–132, 154
  language, 23
  life, 19, 21, 157, 158, 242
  sentences, propositions, 17
  See also Ordinary
Evidence, empirical, 18, 44, 80, 104, 105
Evolution, evolutionary, evolutive, 87, 90, 106–107, 134, 135, 151, 169, 233, 248, 249
Evolutionism, evolutionistic, 100, 112, 113, 266
Expectation (s), 19–22, 24, 145, 146, 153, 165
Experience (s)
  flux of, 18, 162
  immediate, 19, 21
  religious, 33
Experiential, 23, 89, 91, 134, 135, 244, 246, 250, 255, 258, 268
  See also Empirical
Experiment, experimental, experimentation, 68, 69, 146, 150, 227, 251, 253
Externalism(ist), 6, 82, 105, 123, 148

F

Faith, 128–132, 142, 168
Fallibilism, fallibilist, 61, 70–75, 89, 93, 98, 102, 104, 112, 119, 132, 155, 156, 225
Fallible, 91, 105, 113, 133
Family resemblance(s), 6, 120–121, 238
Faust (Goethe's), 61, 166
Feeling(s)
  of believing, 110, 142
  of effort, 167
  of innervation, 167
  and meaning, 82, 224, 254
  of tending, tendency, 162, 213
  of understanding, 247
Flux, 120, 134, 174–175, 183–184, 244, 248, 267
  of experience, 18, 112, 162
  of life, 175, 184
  See also Stream
Form(s) of life, 9–10, 46, 51, 72, 76, 79, 108, 126, 127, 131, 141, 159, 165, 175, 182, 183, 190–197, 199–201, 204, 206, 208, 212, 218, 219, 229, 230, 260, 266–268
  See also Way(s) of life
Foundation(s), foundational, 9, 38, 61, 69, 79–81, 84, 91–93, 95, 97, 100, 105, 108, 117, 122, 124–126, 129, 137, 170, 181, 186, 200, 204, 211, 212, 215, 217, 226, 259, 268
  See also Ground(s)

Foundationalism, foundationalist, 81, 82, 92, 93, 124, 125, 181, 211, 216, 217
Fringe, 111, 113, 120, 161, 213, 214

G

Given, the, 183, 185, 188, 199, 204, 215
Good in/of pragmatism, 49, 51, 52, 184, 222–228
Grammar, 6, 45, 62, 65, 70, 73, 74, 117, 118, 130, 132, 160, 161, 165, 226, 236, 247, 250, 254, 256
Grammatical, 9, 11, 69, 72–74, 84, 93, 101, 117, 118, 127, 133–137, 154, 156, 158, 182, 189, 190, 225, 244, 246, 247, 249, 250, 254, 255, 261, 267, 268
  vs. empirical/experiential, 69, 74, 118, 127, 134, 154, 244, 250, 254, 255, 261, 267
Ground(s), 9, 18, 65, 71, 76, 79, 80, 81, 85, 88, 95, 115, 125, 127, 129, 130, 167, 170, 181–183, 197, 205, 207–209, 212, 214, 216, 251, 258, 268
  See also Foundation

H

Habit(s), 28, 30, 67, 85, 93–94, 101, 105, 111, 126–128, 141–142, 146–152, 158, 165, 169, 173–176, 178, 184, 199, 209, 211, 231, 246, 248, 267

306 Subject Index

Habit(s) (cont.)
  of action, 63, 150, 151, 216
  of conduct, 147, 152
Hinge(s), 8, 19, 69, 72, 74, 77–86, 90, 93–96, 98, 124, 131, 133, 154, 157, 202, 209, 225, 245, 257, 266
  and empirical propositions, 69, 84, 133, 245
  epistemology(ies), 85, 202
  and indubitables, 86–93
  propositions, 72, 77, 79, 80, 84–85, 95, 96, 98
  and regulative assumptions, 86, 93–98
  secondary literature on, 80–85, 98
Hortative, hortatory, 148, 200, 222, 260
Hypothesis(es), 17–19, 21–24, 27–29, 41–43, 46, 68, 91, 95, 97, 109, 122, 129, 132–136, 143, 146, 150, 154, 168, 247, 250, 264, 267
  vs. proposition(s), 17, 18, 21, 23, 24, 27, 41–42, 46, 68, 95, 154
Hypothetical(s), variable, 24, 26–28

I

Idleness, idle, 64, 65, 147, 226, 227
Immediate, the, 183, 184
Imponderable evidence, 188, 189
Indispensability, arguments of, 96, 97
Indubitability, 68, 72, 78, 86, 88, 89, 93, 119, 122, 135

Indubitable(s), 8, 61, 66, 68, 72, 74, 75, 84–98, 101, 105, 113, 119, 120, 135, 136, 266
  See also Belief(s), indubitable
Induction, 27, 40–42, 74, 90, 119, 234, 264
Infallibility, infallible, 61, 73, 74, 90, 91, 102, 103, 155
Inference(s), 30, 72, 75, 86, 93–94, 101, 122, 124, 126, 136, 215, 266
  acritical, 86, 93, 126
Inquiry, scientific, 67, 69, 135, 157, 204, 260
  block the way of, 215, 216
Instinct(s), instinctive, instinctiveness, 3, 19, 86–88, 90–91, 105–106, 126–128, 166, 171, 173, 188, 233, 234
Instrument(s), 21, 69, 76, 107–108, 140, 147, 181–182, 210, 223, 242, 256–258
  conceptual, 120, 126, 242, 266
  See also Tool(s)
Instrumental, 10, 22, 159, 160, 176, 200, 219, 223–224, 260, 264, 270
Instrumentalism, instrumentalist, 22, 36, 159
Introspection, introspective, 6, 102, 123, 124

J

Justification(s), justified, 34, 41, 45, 46, 71, 72, 85, 91, 95, 96, 102, 125, 127, 170, 182, 188, 198, 200, 202, 205, 211–212, 245

Subject Index

K
Know(ing)-how, 81, 84–85, 118, 171, 173–174, 177, 211, 266
vs. knowing-that, 171

L
Language game(s), linguistic games, 49–51, 62, 65, 81, 92, 125, 141, 161, 169, 170–172, 175, 176, 185, 186, 189, 194, 197, 200, 206, 209
Logic, 17, 20, 22, 23, 28, 40, 46, 69, 73, 77, 84, 87, 117, 127, 128, 136, 146, 156, 170, 171, 206, 245, 246, 248–250, 253–254
Logical
  pragmatism, 84, 133, 171
  vs. empirical / experiential, 9, 11, 69, 74, 84, 93, 118, 127, 134–137, 154, 244, 245, 247, 249, 250, 254–255, 261, 267

M
Mathematical
  certainty, 77, 79, 102–105, 157, 188, 189
  propositions, 50, 77, 78, 103, 104, 157
  truths, 48, 50
Mathematics, mathematicians, 25, 48–50, 67, 77, 103–105, 157, 188, 206, 249, 264
Maxim, pragmatic, 9, 33, 39, 60, 78, 86, 119, 137, 139–153, 155–156, 158–159, 161–162, 165, 177, 224, 241, 261, 268

Meaning as use, 46–48, 140, 159–162, 165, 177, 224, 264
Metaphysical Club, 142
Metaphysics, metaphysical, 35, 72, 76, 125, 128, 143, 147, 191, 212, 226–228, 242, 251–253, 258
Method(s)
  pragmatist, 9, 54, 55, 140, 147–148, 221, 224, 226–227, 253, 268–270
  of synoptic presentation, 10, 222, 236–244, 261
  and Weltanschauung, 221–260
Methodological, 1, 9, 10, 16, 53, 54, 133, 147, 154, 177, 190, 200, 218, 219, 221, 222, 224, 227–230, 242, 257, 265, 267, 268
Money, 160
  See also Banknotes; Cash value; Credit System
Morality, morals, moral, 6, 36, 38, 76, 84, 90, 101, 167, 200, 229, 232–234, 236
Mythology, 124, 134, 201, 244

N
Naturalism, naturalist, naturalistic, 118, 161, 189, 202, 218, 249, 250, 255–257
Naturalness, 115, 171, 195
Non-epistemic, 75, 81, 83, 118, 133, 266
Non-propositional(ity), 27, 81, 83, 84, 172

Normative, normativity, 20, 24, 84, 85, 171, 175–177, 202–206, 245, 268
Norm(s), 84, 171, 201
See also Rule(s)

O

Objectivity, 10, 93, 100, 125, 178, 182, 209, 218, 268
  human, 200–209
Ordinariness, the ordinary, 17, 19, 51, 62, 72, 157, 158, 197, 221, 224–226, 236, 257, 260
See also Everyday
Ordinary language, 17, 100, 116, 118, 235

P

Perception(s), perceptual, perceptive, 65, 71, 72, 85, 86, 89, 101, 105, 108, 111, 117, 147, 149–153, 158, 162, 164, 165, 167, 177, 213, 219, 268
Persuasion, 76–77, 131, 196–199, 207, 231, 232
Phenomenology, phenomenological, 17, 18, 49, 212, 223, 251, 269
Picture of the world, world picture, 8, 54, 69, 78, 100, 113, 116, 191, 197, 208
See also Weltbild
Platitude(s), 18, 80, 112, 115, 116, 154, 171, 225
See also Truism(s)
Posteriori, a, 134, 246

Practice(s), 3, 8, 9, 38, 43–44, 46, 48, 65, 67–69, 74–75, 81, 85, 90, 96, 103, 112, 117–118, 125–126, 128, 133, 135, 141, 156, 158–159, 165, 173, 175–177, 184, 193–195, 197, 199–204, 206–208, 210, 212, 215–216, 218–219, 228, 232–234, 240, 265–266, 268
  vs. theory, 38, 233, 234
See also Praxis
Pragmaticism, 146, 169, 234
Praxis (es), 3, 81, 118, 141, 172, 175–178, 199, 212, 218, 269
See also Practice
Prejudice(s), 63, 99, 106, 110, 178, 209, 217, 258
Presupposition(s), 82, 97, 127, 208, 261
Primitiveness, primitive, 87, 88, 101, 127, 170, 171, 173, 185, 189, 197, 201, 203, 230
Priori, a, 41, 108, 134, 216, 219, 246
Privacy, privateness, private, 6, 61, 76, 101, 124, 184, 229, 230
Probability, 24, 27, 30, 40, 42, 104, 119, 129, 264
Progress, 109, 161, 199, 259, 261
Proposition(s)
  empirical, 69, 84, 85, 118, 127, 133, 154, 190, 244, 245, 249
  hinge, 72, 77, 79, 80, 95–96, 98
  vs. hypothesis(es), 17, 18, 21, 23, 24, 27, 41, 42, 46, 68, 95, 154
  mathematical, 50, 77, 78, 103, 104, 157
  vs. sentence(s), 17, 18
Propositional reference, 29

Psychology
  James', 109–112, 166–167, 227, 246, 247, 251, 255
  philosophical (Wittgenstein's lectures on), 4, 49, 51, 222, 223, 247
Purpose(s), 30, 37, 44, 50–51, 97, 106, 108, 160, 164, 223, 228, 252, 256, 265
  of descriptions, 51, 221–223, 260, 265
  of sentences, 21, 22
Puzzles, 114, 216, 226, 269

Rationality, 83, 85, 100, 125, 130, 136, 169, 171, 181, 182, 196, 198, 200, 202–207, 214–215, 218, 252, 268
Realism, realist, 46, 76, 87, 101, 122, 128, 152, 254, 255, 257
Realistic spirit, 257
Reasonableness, reasonable, 44, 62, 65, 125, 155, 205, 218, 231
Regulative assumption(s), *see* Assumption(s)
Relativism, relativist(s), relativistic, 10, 92–93, 182, 190–200, 211, 218, 268
Religion, 34, 49, 90, 106, 111, 112, 120, 128–132, 137, 168, 230, 234
  and common sense, 112, 128–132, 137
River, 10, 11, 125, 134, 175, 176, 244–248

Riverbed, 10, 11, 79, 93, 134, 244–248
Rule(s)
  of action, 101, 158
  following, 45, 169, 175–176, 187, 202, 222, 248
  See also Norm(s)

Saying / showing distinction, 26, 81, 84, 156
Scaffolding, 79, 122, 134
Scepticism, sceptic, sceptical, 9, 61, 63, 66, 70–73, 75, 76, 87, 98, 100, 112, 113, 125, 126, 128, 133, 156
  truth of, 76
Science and philosophy, 11, 68, 93, 99, 100, 109, 125, 132, 133, 136, 137, 250–261, 267, 269
Seeing-as, aspect seeing, 6, 52, 53, 127, 231
Semiotics, semiosis, semiotic, 6, 39, 124, 126, 146, 162, 215, 266
Sensation(s), 33–34, 110–111, 124, 145, 151, 162–165, 172–174, 184
Sense-data, 154–155
Service, 49–50, 160, 224, 264
Stream of thought, 10–11, 111, 120, 123, 134, 162, 167, 213, 241, 244, 246–248, 250
  See also Flux
Sureness, 19, 78, 117, 131, 133, 155, 170–171, 201, 205, 266, 268
  See also Certainty(ies)

Synopticality, 236–237, 241–242
Synoptic presentation, 10, 222, 236–244, 261

T

Third Wittgenstein, 3, 60, 75, 157, 171
Tool(s)
  conceptual, 8, 62, 218, 242, 268
  methodological, 9, 190, 229
  See also Instrument(s)
Tractatus, tractarian, 5, 18, 22, 24–28, 30, 39, 156
Transcendentalism, transcendental, transcendentalist, 41, 96–97, 102, 113, 118, 190, 192, 207, 211, 230, 234–236, 260
Tribes, 184, 186–187, 191
Truism(s), 79
  See also Platitude(s)
Trust, 65–67, 105, 168, 207
Truth(s)
  and consequences, 5, 141, 151–153
  Jamesian conception of, 16, 20, 29, 34–39, 42, 46, 53, 54, 60, 109, 112, 152, 160, 168, 229, 264
  Peirce on, 29, 32, 42–43, 86, 91, 94–95, 97, 101, 128, 149, 152
  Pragmatist conception of, 7, 16, 20, 24, 29, 31–32, 34, 37, 39, 42–44, 46, 51, 54
  Ramsey on, 26, 28, 29, 32, 46, 54, 264
  theory(ies) of, 28, 29, 36, 43, 44, 51
  and usefulness, 19–20, 34, 35, 37, 39, 42, 46, 48, 50–51, 264
  Wittgenstein on, 7, 16, 19, 20, 28, 32, 38, 42–44, 46, 48, 50, 51, 53, 54, 91, 153–155 190, 259, 264

U

Uncertainty(ies), 62, 115, 148, 188, 189
Ungroundedness, ungrounded, 83, 125, 127, 128, 191, 197, 212
Use, meaning as, *see* Meaning and use
Usefulness, useful, 19–20, 28–39, 42, 46–51, 107–108, 112, 159–161, 257, 258, 264–265, 267, 270
  and truth, *see* Truth
  See also Utility
Utility, 105, 160, 233, 242
  See also Usefulness

V

Vagueness, vague, 87, 88, 96, 101, 111, 113, 119–122, 135, 136, 161, 162, 165, 213, 214, 266
Verification(s), 17–20, 23, 24, 35, 36, 44, 109, 136, 151
Verificationism, verificationist, 19, 149, 150, 152
Volition *see* Will

W

Warrant, warranted, 72, 82, 97
Way(s) of life, of living, 47, 88, 99, 101, 182, 186–189, 194, 197, 218, 225, 228
  See also Form(s) of life
Weltanschaulich(e,r), 10, 240, 241, 243
Weltanschauung, 3, 7, 10, 15, 54, 55, 116, 140, 155, 158, 221–222, 236–243, 250, 253, 261, 265, 268–269
  method and, 221–261
  pragmatism and, 242–244
  Synoptic presentation and, 222, 236–244
  See also World view
Weltbild(er), 76, 80, 84, 91, 100, 104, 113, 116–118, 122, 124, 126–137
  certainty(ies) (*see* Certainty(ies))
  and common sense (*see* Common sense)
  See also Picture of the world; World-picture
Will, 9, 66, 67, 110–111, 166–168, 178
World-picture, *see* Picture of the world
World view, 227, 236, 239–244, 258, 261, 268
  See also Weltanschauung